BEATING
THE
NBA

TALES FROM
A
FRUGAL FAN

MOTEZ BISHARA

LEEDS TRINITY UNIVERSITY

ISBN:1-4792-6418-0
ISBN-13: 978-1-4792-6418-6
Library of Congress Control Number: 2012916792
CreateSpace Independent Publishing Platform
North Charleston, SC

To Dad, for starting me off with the sports section of the New York Times every Sunday.

And to Mo, for turning me on to the NBA in seventh grade. I miss you big guy.

CONTENTS

PART EIGHT

PART NINE

PART TEN

OVERTIME

PROLOGUE

I think it was Kurt Vonnegut who, in one of his classic novels back in the early 1960s, first coined the phrase "You get what you pay for." I love the quote. It's a punchy line, a saying that I borrow from time to time to sound clever when I'm discussing anything money-related.

The problem, of course, is that it's a big fat lie.

Instead of getting what we pay for, most of us grossly overpay for things all the time.

Whether it's everyday charges like $4.50 ATM fees and $4.90 venti caramel macchiatos, or travel expenses like $8 hotel bottled water and $20 valet parking, or fleeting fashion trends like $35 baseball caps and $320 ripped jeans…the list of rip-offs is long. Heck, Adam Sandler movies alone have wasted over $2 billion globally. If only Vonnegut were around to spend $12 on *Jack and Jill* he'd be singing a different tune.

But what people consistently overpay for is live entertainment: tickets to concerts, the theater, the opera, and especially sports. Game after game, year after year, Americans shell out more and more to watch professional athletes compete. At last count the figure stood at over $25.5 billion, or $82 a year for every man, woman, and child in the country. It's a remarkable number. So remarkable, in fact, that we're reaching a tipping point—and here's where it gets interesting.

Enter Leonard and Yvonne Gionet of Portland, Oregon. The Gionets developed a successful real estate business and by the late 1980s decided to splurge on premium seats to the Trailblazers, just as they were making consecutive runs to the NBA Finals. Their season tickets started at a reasonable price, $200 a pop for floor seats in the very front row behind the basket. But when the Blazers moved to their new arena in 1995, their prices doubled even though they moved back a row. Not only that, but the team asked for a six-year commitment to secure the seats. Being hardcore Portland fans, the Gionets agreed to pay over $30,000 a year to lock up their new second-row seats.

And that's when the problems started. "When we had front-row seats we had Clyde 'The Glide' Drexler and Terry Porter; it was their best team ever," says Leonard. "And then we got something called the Jail-blazers."

The so-called Jail-blazers were a bunch of underperforming athletes on the court, and minor felons off it, routinely getting arrested for speeding, drunk driving, drugs, and spousal abuse. "They were so bad, and they were so stupid," Yvonne recalls. "Just to show you how stupid they were, this one guy, the little guy [Damon Stoudemire], he went through the metal detector at the airport with marijuana wrapped in aluminum foil."[1]

Oh dear. The Blazers slid from perennial title contenders in the 1990s to losers of sixty-one out of eighty-two games in 2006.

"We couldn't give away our tickets," Yvonne recalls. "People would be like, 'Oh no, we're busy.' For a while they'd beg you for these tickets because they were great, but then when even our son didn't want to go anymore…"

It's a sad situation. Not to mention, a terrible waste of money. If you can't give away your $800 pair of floor seats, then they're not worth $800 anymore. They're pretty worthless in fact.

How did the Gionets get into this mess? It's simple: They agreed on a fixed price for the tickets years before knowing what their actual value would be at the time of delivery. And that's how the vast majority

---

1   It was a full ounce, according to *Bleacher Report*.

of sports tickets are sold. In this case the transaction benefited the team, and it screwed its biggest paying fans.

And this is where I come in. I like buying tickets off the disgruntled, uninterested, or otherwise engaged. It presents golden opportunities; I've been to countless games where my seats were subsidized by the likes of the Gionets, who got stuck with forty-one pairs of tickets they no longer used.

Of course, not every team is mired in quicksand like the Trailblazers of the 2000s, but deals can still be had at just about every arena in the NBA on the right night.

Just follow me.

BROOKLYN, NEW YORK: DECEMBER 4, 2012

```
THUNDER 117
NETS 111
ATTENDANCE: 17,732 (sellout)
```

It's 5:00 p.m., and the tipoff over on Atlantic Avenue is only two and a half hours away.

Ever since the Barclays Center opened with a Jay-Z concert in September, I've been desperate to watch the Nets play in Brooklyn. In fact, I've really been waiting twenty years for the Nets to be relevant, and this season marks their transition into the national spotlight.

In the past few years, the Nets moved from the swamps and ghettos of New Jersey to the rebirth of cool in New York City. Brooklyn is undeniably one of the hippest patches on Earth now, and having an NBA team grace the borough solidifies its status in the cultural zeitgeist.

My issue, though, is that along with their entrance into the world of cool, Nets' ticket prices have more than doubled since last year. And because I've only just realized that this game against the slammin'

jammin' Oklahoma City Thunder is on tonight, I've dropped everything in a mad scramble to get in without paying a fortune.

So I go into my online attack mode. I bombard ads on Craigslist, and
I go through StubHub and eBay with a fine-toothed comb. I'm look-
ing for prices outside of the price-gouging line of fire that marks New
York as its bulls-eye.

I start by working two leads on Craigslist. The first from a guy who's
supposedly in Midtown Manhattan with a pair of seats in the lower
bowl for $200 each. I offer $300 for the pair, telling him I'm near
Grand Central Station until 5:00 p.m., and I wait to hear back.

In the meantime, I run a search with a ticket aggregator that finds
all the listings floating around online before ranking their values. It's
like having an all-points bulletin out on the best deal in the house. So
I repeatedly check out the deals rising to the top of the ratings system
and bide my time, hoping prices keep dropping while wary of other
eager buyers on the sidelines.

If this behavior pattern sounds familiar, it's because it is a lot like
stock trading. You see, for years I've been professionally managing
a stock fund, patiently buying shares of companies like McDonald's,
Disney, and Nike when they trickle down to valuations that I think are
reasonable. For sixteen years I've been investing in American companies while based in London, never losing sight of the Yankees, Giants,
or Nets across the pond.

In England, I've adopted slick-passing Arsenal as my home soccer
team. I bided my time for ten years on the waiting list before secur-
ing front-row season tickets, somehow priced as the cheapest seats in
the house. Even when the Gunners disappoint, I reason that it's a deal
worth hanging on to. I may even be a tad spoiled by my seats, which
offer me global face time at nearly every game as I wave my red scarf
behind Mikel Arteta's corner kicks.

So it stands to reason that once I'm back in the United States and
craving some hoops action, I turn into the guy looking for the best
ticket deal I can get my hands on. That usually involves playing a

game of chance up until an hour before tipoff, hoping for a steal. Oddly, finding value on a ticket purchase poses a greater challenge than it does when buying a stock. That's because tickets have a buying window that shuts. At some point the game starts, and time is up.

So, like Larry Bird anticipating an errant Isiah Thomas pass, or Warren Buffet buying a chunk of Goldman Sachs, I know when it's time to act.[2]

Up until that trigger point, there's a feeling-out process with my potential transactee. Today, I'm haggling with Anthony Roth, who says there's "an issue" with me being in Midtown—despite advertising his ticket location as "Midtown." We then trade text messages, and he tells me he's located up on 125th and Park Avenue.

"That's in Harlem; your ad said Midtown," I reply, smelling something fishy. Everyone knows the internet is a cesspool of scams, and classified marketplaces like Craigslist accept no liability.

Anthony assures me his tickets are legit, and that he normally works in Midtown. I ask him to call me with a meeting point, but he never does. It's just as well; I didn't have a good feeling about him. You have to trust your instincts when you're potentially exchanging hundreds of dollars with people you've never met before.

The other listing was also in Midtown, but he was taking too long to get back to me (no doubt involved in his own game of cat and mouse). In the meantime, I had one eye scrolling through e-tickets on StubHub until I found my Larry Bird moment, swooping in for the steal.

I nabbed two tickets in the fifth-row corner, which were going for nearly $800 on Ticketmaster. Instead I paid $445 for the pair of borderline "floor seats," with access to the Calvin Klein lounge for free food and soft drinks thrown in. Glancing at the printout, I noticed that

---

2   I know I just compared myself favorably to both the greatest shooter and the greatest stock picker in modern times. I just wanted to make sure you were paying attention. It's my book; no one else was going to do it. Rest assured everything else in this work is nonfiction.

my price was only a marginal increase on the $205 each that Nets season ticketholder Angel C paid for her (or his?) seats.[3]

With the barcodes in hand, my fellow New Yorker Ahmed and I hopped on the 4 train to the Barclays Center. The billion-dollar facility is a marvel; the lighting is just dim enough, the seats just steely enough, the screens sharp and huge enough, and the aisles wide enough to call it the most gleaming entry into NBA homes. Call it Jay-Z's ultimate MTV Crib, with more B-boy-inspired characters in the crowd than all the other NBA arenas combined.

We scarf up some shrimp and noodles in the lounge before gliding around the Nets' slick herringbone-patterned floor in time for intros. The game is a slugfest from the outset. Dueling Team USA Olympians Deron Williams and Russell Westbrook trade baskets at each end of the court. Scoring champ Kevin Durant nearly breaks his neck skying over headbanded parolee Andray Blatche for the missed dunk of the year. Kris Humphries has bulked up into a six-foot-nine Goliath, but his jump shot's turned sloppier than Scott Disick at an open bar.

By the fourth quarter, the Nets have cut their sixteen-point deficit to just three, behind Gerald Wallace's three consecutive three-pointers. As he sinks each one, his braids swing like a wind chime in a hurricane. Brooklyn's going wild.

Ultimately, though, all the elongated "Brook-lyn" chants are wasted. The Nets can't quite get the job done, losing on a hairline goaltending call on Humphries. But there's an undeniable flame lit under the Barclays Center. The energy fuelled by that kind of intensity is infectious, which helps explain why I go through what I do to get the deals that I do.

Sadly, for a great swath of NBA fans, experiencing that energy in person is nothing more than a pipedream. But I can say firsthand that it should be far from a pipedream. It's true that for years fans have been shut out of games by teams or gouged by ticket brokers. We either had

3   Subsequently, I've noticed that Angel C sells his or her seats to every Nets home game, from anywhere between $320 to $550.

to splash out a fortune, or get on a multiyear waiting list for a season ticket and wait for the dubious right to pay for an entire season in advance.

Today, if you play your cards right, you could be watching LeBron James and the Heat play for as little as $15. And that's in the playoffs.

I'm here to tell you how to play your cards right. I've done all the hard work, gone to all the far-flung arenas, taken all the commuter flights, and spent an ungodly amount of time trolling the internet and streets of the United States. All in the name of providing my fellow sports fans with something they've been deprived of since the beginning of time: access to an equal playing field.

Join me on this wild ride across the continent; I promise to impart all the knowledge I've accumulated, and share all the laughs (as well as the funny-to-everyone-but-me missteps) along the way.

Back in the Barclays Center, during the game's waning moments, a fitting Jay-Hova lyric bounces over the loudspeakers: *I'm on to the next one.*

PAID: $222.48

SINGLE-GAME FACE VALUE: $392.55
DISCOUNT ON SINGLE-GAME PRICE: 43%

SEASON-TICKET FACE VALUE: $205
PREMIUM TO SEASON TICKETHOLDER PRICE: 8.5%

PART ONE

REWINDING THE TAPE

```
LOS ANGELES: JANUARY 7, 2005
LAKERS 111
ROCKETS 104
ATTENDANCE: 18,997 (sellout)
```

Southern California in January is not a bad place to be. Not only is the sun out, but today the Houston Rockets are in town. They boast two bona fide superstars, Yao Ming, their seven-foot, six-inch Chinese center, and Tracy McGrady, a shooting guard with a lazy eye and a killer throw down.

The Lakers, on the other hand, are going through a transitional season. Shaquille O'Neal and coach Phil Jackson departed after 2004's calamitous meltdown in the finals against the Detroit Pistons. The current roster features Kobe Bryant, their mercurial star who's still embroiled in a sexual assault civil suit, Lamar Odom, a shy forward from New York who has yet to be exposed to reality TV, along with a battery of role players.

I'm in LA unexpectedly on business for a few days, so I'm catching the game on a whim. I have no tickets, of course.

I never have tickets.

Instead, I'm going to roll up to the arena and try my luck. I park my beat-up rental on an unlit street under the 110 freeway, a few blocks from the Staples Center. I'm going with the age-old routine of showing up close to tipoff so that scalpers get a bit desperate and prices drop like a stone. I also ignore sellers hustling too far from the arena. They want to get to you first, before you reach the pack and find out what everyone else is charging.

With that in mind, I find four to five guys who give me the "What you need?" routine camped out on the corner of Chick Hearn Court and South Figueroa Street, just spitting distance from the Staples Center.

When you're alone, it's a lot easier to haggle for a good deal. Singles are notoriously impossible to get rid of for street sellers, as most fans (aside from me) like to share their game experiences with friends.

So I always knock 'em down. And like going to an auction, I have a price limit in mind (in this case it's $80). I'm also sure to have some cash stuffed in my front pocket so that I don't take out my wallet in front of the pack. My routine is to roll up a few twenties in one, and a spare $10 or $20 in the other for backup.

The guys show me a collection of tickets in different sections, but I'm dismissive. I can usually tell without looking at an arena map if a location is decent or not by the section number. Anything in the one hundreds is lower level, and anything in the three or four hundreds is in the nosebleeds. Only nosebleeds were on offer. So one of them runs off for five minutes, yells and gesticulates to guys on another corner, and returns with "something real good" for me.

I don't understand how in every city, all the scalpers know who among them is holding exactly what tickets. But they do, and there's always some kind of covert commission system in operation too. They fluidly lend each other tickets, sell them, and split the profits between each other, with the larger share going to the guy who had the ticket first.

In the seconds between getting my hand on the ticket and the launch of the quick-fire bargaining session, it's crucial to spot the ticket's face value. But this time I'm having some trouble. That's because, as the guy points out to me, there is no face value printed on the ticket. Instead, the stub is marked, "Price: $VIP."

He claims it's in a special section where you can order beer and food and whatnot from the comfort of your seat, and that they normally go for hundreds of dollars. I offer $50, and we eventually settle on $80.

To be sure, this seat in section PR3, row 11 is indeed great, on the first tier up, facing one of the free-throw lines. I even have access to the club restaurant and bar at halftime. Why people go to a basketball game to eat at a restaurant is beyond me, but as far as absurdities go in La La Land, this one doesn't move the needle.

Back to the game. I'm feeling pretty good about myself as my Bass Ale arrives, even after overhearing some goon next to me call his wife. "Honey, I'm staring at Jack Nicholson right now. Yeah, he's right here, in the same place as me, only about five hundred feet away. He's wearing his glasses. Yeah, I swear!" (How fucking annoying are those guys?)

Toward the end of the first quarter, a Lakers fan in his forties takes the empty seat next to mine. The first thing he says is, "So how much did you pay?"

I'm shifty, and I'm proud. So I nonchalantly tell him about my $80 deal. "Yeah, I got mine for $40," he said, throwing my $80 deal right back in my face. "These guys get desperate once the game starts. In LA, people are so fickle they often don't show up for games, so ticket agencies push their excess stock on those poor dudes on the street to move them."

He's shiftier. He's better at this than I am. He keeps going, telling me he's the head nurse at a nearby hospital, and he often pops in after a shift to unwind, always on a whim and always knocking down the price from scalpers. Incredibly, he says that when the Lakers played at the Great Western Forum in their heyday, he would show up in his nurse skivvies, park his car at the staff entrance, and sit on the floor, watching the games from the baseline. His audacity is unreal.

"One time Kareem Abdul-Jabbar banged his head really hard on the floor," he tells me. "And he wasn't moving. The whole place was staring at me. My heart was pumping, but as I got up the team doctors rushed to his side and motioned that they had a handle on it. I was so relieved."

I'm dumbfounded. Could there be a story like this in every arena? Furthermore, what about this pricing disparity? Is the difference between what teams charge their loyal fans and what someone with a bit of street smarts can walk away with that wide?

Yes, it is.

Since that night in 2005, the online exchange StubHub has completely shaken up the ticket aftermarket. All of a sudden, buyers are at a huge advantage. Instead of relying on shady deals, which may be illegal or simply a scam (I've been offered laughably bad fake tickets before), I can scan an entire area at my fingertips and gauge prices anywhere from several months to just a few minutes before tipoff.

In a surprisingly rapid move, all thirty NBA teams embraced the secondary market—the vast, open marketplace operated mostly on line—by signing deals with StubHub permitting ticket resale. The logic, it would seem, was to ensure some percentage of a kickback in the transaction. The deal ushered a seismic shift away from the virtual monopoly that had a chokehold on tickets sold in the United States for the previous eighty years.

Ticketmaster, the industry's eight-hundred-pound gorilla acting as the premium seller (and breadwinner) for twenty-four NBA teams, now has a competitor in StubHub that delivers a better buyer's experience. That's an issue for the league.

Acknowledging that for seven years customers had been comparing the secondary-market ticketing experience with theirs and usually opting for the former, Ticketmaster finally fought back. In August 2012 it inked a deal with the NBA to allow fans to post their own tickets for sale alongside the teams' inventory to try to regain business from StubHub and its peers. For Ticketmaster, the move embraced a staggering level of transparency, given its reluctance to evolve in the past. Technology and the market's thirst for an open playing field visibly forced its hand.

The playing field will only truly be open, however, if fans are given the freedom to list their tickets for sale alongside Ticketmaster's at any price, no matter how low. Once season-tickets lose their floor prices in the primary market, things could turn ugly.

Why would Charlotte season ticketholders, for instance, relist their seats through the team at a mandated minimum price when the Bobcats are twenty games out of first place in January? Understandably, team executives are resisting a total free-market system, but that's ultimately where they are headed. The NBA head office seems to concur. "We at the league believe that there should be no price floors so that the market can dictate what the right price is," Chris Granger, its head of marketing and business operations, told ESPN at the time Ticketmaster's deal was announced.

That's good news for the fan with the flexibility to wait until a few hours before the game, when purchasing in the aftermarket can be a no-brainer. The same applies for fans on the fence about paying for all forty-five home games (including preseason) just to get reasonable deals for the marquee matchups.

Ticket prices will ultimately succumb to the whims of the supply-and-demand curve. An online marketplace like StubHub is the great equalizer for fans. If we can skirt Ticketmaster's 76 percent premium for single-game seats, and instead pay nearly what the season ticketholder does to sit in the fifth row and watch one of the hottest team in the NBA (the Thunder) play in the hottest market (New York)—and often pay a fraction of subscribers' costs for less glamorous matchups—then the question must be asked if the major sports leagues have gotten their pricing all wrong.

There's been no impact on sales thus far, so it's unlikely that both high season-ticket prices and much higher single-game prices will wane anytime soon. But the long-term sustainability of the current pricing model is questionable.

The NBA is on course to rake in $5 billion for the 2012–2013 season, a bump of 20 percent since its most recent comparable, the non-strike-shortened NBA season of 2010–2011. The bulk of the revenues come from red-hot TV licensing deals, followed by advertising and merchandising.[4] But a full $1 billion will come directly from gate receipts. And three-quarters of that $1 billion relies on season-ticket sales, which recently renewed at a record 88 percent clip.

Based on my experiences, I can't understand why 88 percent of season ticketholders think renewing is a good idea. NBA tickets are priced with the assumption that the home team will be competitive enough to garner fan support throughout the season, even though over a quarter of the league's teams are perpetually in the doldrums.

In markets like New York, Los Angeles, and Chicago, demand is high enough and the market liquid enough that paying for forty-five games in advance is probably not a losing proposition. That's true for now, but even their fans will have a price point at which renewals will drop off if the teams get too greedy. The question is when.

The Knicks sell out nearly every night, but with a $980 million upgrade to Madison Square Garden in process, ticket prices have been aggressively on the rise, nearly tripling for some. Is their model sustainable? Or will the growing ticket aftermarket fight the good battle for fans and level off the league's pricing power?

There is only one way to find out.

---

4   The Lakers alone will reap $3.6 billion over the next twenty years thanks to a new agreement with Time Warner Cable, according to the *LA Times*. The deal nearly sparked a riot in LA as tough rebroadcast negotiations led to a blackout of seven Lakers games for over a million DirecTV subscribers in November 2012.

During the winters of 2011 and 2012, I circled the United States in an effort to buy tickets to games in as many NBA cities as I possibly could. The catch is I showed up to each city ticketless and used every available means to get the best deals possible, with an eye on getting the biggest discounts on offer under face value.

I haggled with street hustlers, weaved through seedy parking lots, bargained with stubborn season ticketholders, played the online auction market, and crossed a minefield of internet conmen along the way.

To be sure, tackling this schedule while based out of England was a major challenge. Once the first road trip began and I couldn't remember what city I was in, it was clear that I signed up for more than I bargained for. The litany of flights (ten of them transatlantic), bug-infested motels, rental cars, and Amtrak trains were brutal, but the results were eye opening.

That's because, as I've long suspected, the method used to price most tickets is inherently flawed. Allow me to explain why.

STOCKS VERSUS TICKETS

On the afternoon of April 12, 2010, the price of Best Buy Co. closed at $45.23 on the New York Stock Exchange. The electronic-gadget retailer had just surprised the Street with an upbeat earnings announcement; a Super Bowl promotion on heavily discounted flat-panel TVs contributed to a sales uptick of 7.4 percent compared to the previous year's quarter. The former Wall Street darling continued to quell fears of a collapse in TV sales and competition from online retailers, with its stock gaining 10 percent for the year.

April 12, 2010, was also the day that the Detroit Pistons put tickets for their next season up for sale. Reflecting economic times that had befallen the city most affected by the declining auto industry (Detroit's median household income for the year was only $25,787, about half the national average), the Pistons lowered their season-ticket prices at the cavernous Palace at Auburn Hills by an average of 10 percent to $42.76.

Though they executed the biggest chop of prices in the league going into the 2010–2011 season, the Pistons would still be positioned in the middle tier of NBA pricing, at sixteenth out of thirty teams. A game in

Detroit remained a more expensive ticket than those in more prosperous locations, like Utah, Charlotte, the Bay Area, and Philadelphia, all of which hosted teams that also lowered prices.

Utah and Charlotte were, incidentally, coming off playoff runs, whereas Detroit, employing its third coach in three years, was closing in on one of the sorriest records in the league. Even worse, they had no discernible stars and were next to last in scoring. They would finish the 2010 season a respectable eighth in attendance, but that was based on loyal season ticketholders renewing in the summer of 2009 in good faith that improvements would be made. The real test of faith was whether a 10 percent markdown would be enough to keep those same season ticketholders coming back in the summer of 2010.

Fast-forward one year. On April 12, 2011, Best Buy's stock closed at $30.51, down 33 percent in twelve months. Lingering unemployment and high gas prices had Americans spending less on discretionary items, and the few times they did spend they were looking for the best deals possible. Because those deals were nearly always at Amazon or Wal-Mart, Best Buy was forced to discount accordingly. Its business model, which relied on premium customer service in exchange for higher prices, was getting killed by discounting.

Even worse, Best Buy spent money on closing nine unprofitable stores in China. It had been a challenging year, but CEO Brian Dunn was working on a plan to reorganize stores and turn his ship around.

Meanwhile, back on the hardwood, the Detroit Pistons had another miserable season. They did improve marginally from their 2010 campaign, winning three more games, but this time fans stayed away in droves.

Who could blame them? The Pistons were a dysfunctional outfit, with players openly bickering with their coach during timeouts. Morale hit a low in February 2011, when five Pistons skipped a morning shoot-around to protest a teammate's benching. That night their coach, John Kuester, got ejected from a game for arguing with an official, only to elicit cackles of laughter on the bench from the same five players.

Unsurprisingly, the Pistons would drop from eighth to eighteenth in ticket sales, with average attendance falling from 85 to 75 percent of capacity. Season ticketholders became weary of committing hundreds of dollars early to watch a rebuilding team develop when they had other options—namely, to wait and see, and perhaps buy tickets on the open market when they felt like it (which was a lot less often than in recent times).

The problem for the Pistons front office was that although it dropped its average ticket price 10 percent before the season, it was not enticing enough to bring spectator demand back to the early 2000s, when the team was a championship contender.

While on any given day you can buy a share of Best Buy for the price determined by the open market down to the penny, calling up the Pistons' box office in March of 2011 would get you a quoted price that was deemed reasonable eleven months earlier, when the promise of starting fresh the next season was a selling point. Naturally, that archaic pricing model makes absolutely no sense to the fans, and it is rapidly catching up to sports franchises as well. More on that in a bit.

Let's look at Best Buy's shares exactly a year later, on April 12, 2012. Ticker BBY would close at $21.96. This was a 28 percent decline in twelve months after another string of disastrous results. Best Buy was fast becoming nothing more than a showroom for Amazon, and there was very little its management could do about it.

In fact, the practice of examining big-ticket electronic purchases at Best Buy before buying them cheaper at Amazon became so common that Amazon built a smartphone app to do exactly that. It would read a barcode from a product, say, a Samsung fifty-six-inch plasma, and spit out the Amazon price alongside a "One Click" purchase option. Moreover, Best Buy was stuck with long-term leases on giant retail spaces that used to stack aisles of CDs, DVDs, and TVs, all of which migrated to digital distribution or online purchases.

Surrendering to the inevitable, the retailer announced it was shutting fifty stores and firing four hundred employees. As though that wasn't enough, Brian Dunn was forced to resign following the outing of his affair with a subordinate. Perhaps more shocking was the dismissal of Richard Schulze, the company's founder and chairman of the board, for knowing about the affair. Best Buy was a rudderless ship going down, and its stock price's decline reflected that.

Meanwhile, the Pistons were still in what bad teams like to call a "rebuilding phase." For the third straight season the Pistons would finish with a winning percentage in the three hundreds. They would sell only 65 percent of the Palace's seats during the strike-shortened 2011 campaign, finishing a dismal twenty-eighth out of thirty in league attendance.

In three years the Pistons went from eighth to twenty-eighth in attendance, though the product on the court remained virtually unchanged. There's a simple reason why: The Pistons' arena holds too many seats, and their tickets are priced too high.

Everything has a price; the Pistons just weren't thinking outside the box to determine the point where supply (the highest in the league at 22,076 seats a night) would match demand (one of the lowest in the league), or the equilibrium price, for all you economists out there.

Going forward, Pistons' season-ticket prices for 2012–2013 were not even reduced. Instead, their press release cheerily announced that "there would be no increase" before listing a battery of merchandising discounts and promotions (including a golf day with current and former Pistons), none of which did much for demand. By the end of the 2012–2013 season, the Pistons' league-worst 67 percent home capacity fill was a gaping 12 percent lower than the Cavaliers'; this, despite giving away hundreds of tickets every night to the military and community workers.

Because I've spent years investing in stocks—and even longer honing my skills as a colossal sports geek—I am convinced that in today's world, there's no room for inefficient pricing of any sporting event.

Tickets to just about every live event are commodities, in that they are usually available in the thousands and replaceable by either the same show on another day, or a variety of other options available on that night.

In the same way that the internet once crippled Best Buy's business of selling overpriced CDs and hi-fi to the masses, it's now opening up the playing field for the discerning sports fan.

Those high up in sports management are finally picking up on this concept. Like Best Buy's executives, along with those at Tower Records, Borders, and Circuit City who were unprepared for Amazon's online discount model, it's taken a while for Ticketmaster and its major clients to react to their secondary-market competitors.

But they're finally starting to get it. "It seems really archaic to set prices at the start of the season," said the chief investment officer of the San Francisco Giants baseball team, Bill Schlough, to the *Wall Street Journal*. "You have no idea how the team is going to do."[i]

Based so close to Silicon Valley, it's no surprise that the Giants were the first professional sports team in the United States to try to correct the obvious hole in their legacy pricing model. In addition, baseball teams see a more extreme case of ticket mispricing than their counterparts in the NFL, NBA, and NHL because each team plays eighty-one home games in stadiums that mostly seat north of forty thousand.

To set their prices dynamically, the Giants consider the pitching matchup along with the action of the online ticket market for every game. Like an antiquated version of the stock market, Giants' ticket prices shift multiple times each day, with more fluctuation as it gets closer to game time (in the case of Best Buy stock, game time's equivalent is a monthly comparable store figure, a quarterly earnings report, a change in management, or any other announcement of relevance). The Giants have enjoyed wild success with this tactic, selling out an eye-opening 140 straight games, according to Schlough, serving notice to other pro sports teams.

At present, nearly half the NBA, including the Hawks, Rockets, Timberwolves, Cavaliers, and Jazz, use some form of dynamic pricing. According to Qcue, an Austin-based software company that handles ticketing for over forty pro and college organizations, teams see a revenue jump of 10 to 30 percent once their dynamic pricing model is put to use, so the trend is set to rise.

"In the next two to three years you'll see it in every team across major sports leagues in the US," says Barry Kahn, Qcue's founder and CEO. The company's website header says it all: "50% of tickets are never sold, while 10% of tickets are resold for twice face value. It's time to price better."

Even the beleaguered Pistons have figured this one out. Owner Tom Gores, a private equity mogul who bought the team in June 2011, put a curb on handing out freebies eighteen months later and is tinkering with dynamic pricing. It hasn't worked as of yet, mainly because Gores decided on this after the Pistons' prices were set for the 2012-2013 season, and pricing far enough down to trigger demand mid-season would have only served to annoy their fans who paid more in advance.

Unlike the airline and hotel business, where dynamic pricing has been in place for decades and the practice of paying vastly different prices for the same product is accepted, sports tickets have a natural floor price. There's an implied—if not specified—promise by teams not to undercut their season ticketholders by subsequently selling at prices below their cost when the market sours.

By now, those teams not joining the trend of dynamic pricing are at the very least using tiered pricing on season tickets, giving them flexibility to charge less for lower-demand matchups. In addition, the same teams are tinkering with the price printed on each season ticket to differentiate the premium events from the softer matchups. The move is a subtle way of telling the season ticketholders that at times their seats are worth far below their average cost per game.

Then there are owners like the Dallas Mavericks' Mark Cuban who think dynamic pricing is a bad idea altogether, opting to market "cheap and easy entertainment" through a "standard price that everyone understands." As recent NBA champs, the Mavs enjoy wild popularity in one of America's richest cities, yet they rank ninth in pricing at under $50 a ticket. There's little debate that Cuban is leaving good money on the table to appease his fans, something most owners—no matter their net worth—are unwilling to do.

In reality, even "dynamic pricing" is not actually dynamic. Tickets sold by teams don't actually behave like stocks. A sports ticket is prone to an upward adjustment when demand is there (unless they're sold by Mark Cuban), but, as mentioned, its fall is limited to the comparable season ticketholder's cost. Its price on the primary market won't plummet like the stock of Best Buy when demand drops.

But it will on the secondary market. For us fans that's the beauty of having access to every other market at our fingertips.

Having intensely followed the online ticket market for two years, I strongly suspect that a few sports teams hide behind StubHub to dump their excess stock anonymously on the cheap, but unless the New Jersey Nets were pricing their seats at a penny they weren't going to fall to the accurate level of demand. In the strike-shortened 2011–2012 season, at least forty listings to Nets home games played in Newark were available for one cent.

So dynamic pricing or no dynamic pricing, deals can still be had for the Nets, Wizards, Bobcats, and just about any team in the NBA on the right day…if you know how to work the system.

How? Let's start with the basics. Laws concerning the resale of tickets are unclear, to say the least, mainly because there is no related federal law. It all comes down to individual states, cities, and municipalities on whether ticket resale for profit is legal and how close to the venue the transaction can take place.

According to StubHub's president, Chris Tsakalakis, however, one thing is clear: It is perfectly legal to sell a ticket at or below face value in all fifty states. In addition, he claims that in forty-four states it's currently legal to sell above face value. But finding out which six states have not adopted the above-face-value law is worthy of an episode of *Unsolved Mysteries*.

In reality, it makes no difference because rules are enforced sporadically. I've seen policemen and scalpers act differently at the same venue on different days. "Technically they are on the books on some states, but basically they don't exist," Kahn affirms.

Not surprisingly, loopholes are also rampant. eBay, which bought StubHub in 2007, only considers ticket laws enforceable when selling to someone in the same state as the event. Otherwise there is no limit (which explains why the ticket agents serving New York are run out of New Jersey). In California, scalping is only considered scalping if it's done at the venue and above face value. What constitutes "at the venue" is a grey area. Is a block from the Staples Center still the venue, or is that far enough to be out of the reach of the long arm of the law?

Then there are those selling tickets who are not scalpers, just fans with spares. Unless teams go the way of airlines and check IDs at the door for every paper ticket issued (or go entirely paperless), there will always be fans selling spares close to game time.

If the NBA and the other sports leagues really want to cripple the aftermarket, they could adopt the same system in place for most of the soccer clubs in the United Kingdom. My season tickets to Arsenal FC are in the form of encoded membership cards. Every turnstile at the Emirates Stadium in North London has an electronic reader that fans swipe their cards on.

At Highbury, Arsenal's legendary stadium demolished before the card-reading technology was put in place in 2006, scalpers ran rampant before games. Now I rarely see scalpers patrol Emirates Stadium because there are virtually no paper tickets available. To sell their seats, season ticketholders must have faith that buyers will return their membership cards, eliminating anonymous transactions on the web or at stadiums.[5]

Would the NBA or NFL ever adopt the card system? "No," says the owner of a prominent ticket agency in New York. "They both need us." In other words, season-ticket sales would nosedive without an easy outlet to get rid of dates that are of no use to the subscriber. Committing to forty-one home games is unrealistic for most people, making a secondary market crucial.

"They'll often sell us their full season tickets and buy back only the games that they need," says the executive who asked not to be identified because it could damage her relationship with other ticket agencies. "It's a trust thing; it's the same as how you trust your stockbrokers."

And what happens when there's an excess of tickets? "When we're stuck with our seats at the end of the day we can put all our stuff on StubHub," she says, which explains the flood of spare seats I notice online. "It's like the stock market; we constantly have to see what's out there, and we drop and raise prices all day long."

In other words, the aftermarket provided by ticket agents, internet auction sites, and scalpers is really the dynamic one, nearly as efficient as the pre-digital stock market. On the other hand, the market provided by Ticketmaster so far has been static, and therefore it is subject to wide pricing inefficiency.

As a fan looking for a good deal, this presents opportunities. No agency wants to get stuck with tickets it can't monetize, even at a fraction of cost. So what happens if agencies can't get rid of their excess inventory on the web?

"Sometimes you get stuck," the agent tells me. "And if you do, then you send [a scalper] outside. They call every day to see if there's

---

5 I sell my spare Arsenal tickets to a very sketchy ticket agent in East London, and boy, what a chore that can be. He once gave me the run-around on £450 ($720) he owed me by faking a WC Fields accent and pretending he was out of town. After two months of phone harassment he finally paid up.

anything that we need to get rid of. We give them whatever we have, and they try to sell and move and shake people around looking for tickets; whatever they make, they keep some of it, and they give the rest of it to us."

Wow, so a lot of those guys on the street are legit?

"Yeah they work for us."

It would appear that no matter how far the world of ticketing has come, agents and fans with spares will always fall back on the same rule of thumb: If you can't push it online, then take it to the streets.

HOW THIS ALL GOT STARTED

Being a stub hoarder often leads to reverse price shock.

BOSTON: DECEMBER 9, 1988
CELTICS 121
SIXERS 107
ATTENDANCE: 14,890 (sellout)
FACE VALUE: $17
PAID: $40
PREMIUM: 235%

BOSTON: DECEMBER 16, 1988
CELTICS 110
LAKERS 96
ATTENDANCE: 14,890 (sellout)
FACE VALUE: $12
PAID: $45
PREMIUM: 375%

```
BOSTON: MARCH 26, 1993
CELTICS 106
MAVERICKS 97
ATTENDANCE: 14,890 (sellout)
FACE VALUE: $45
PAID: $40
DISCOUNT: 11%
```

Boston Decembers are bitter cold. That kind of *Oh my God, why do I live in this place, my face is about to freeze over* kind of cold. This was my first winter in Boston, having arrived as a freshman at BU just three months earlier. That morning, two guys in my dorm asked if I wanted to join them to watch the Celtics play the 76ers.

"You guys got tickets?" I asked, rather naively. This was the heyday of the Boston Celtics, and although Larry Bird was out for the season with bone spurs in his heels, the team still boasted future Hall of Famers Kevin McHale, Robert Parish, and Dennis Johnson, and tickets for the casual fan were nearly impossible to come by. The old rickety Boston Garden with its famous parquet floor, classical organ, and lack of air-con was still selling out every night.

"Nah, we're just gonna hit up some scalpers," replied Nao, a Japanese sophomore by way of Seattle. "Mike Ma's from Philly, and he really wants to see Charles Barkley. He says we'll get ticks from one of the guys selling on the street."

"Sure, I'm in," I replied.

And just like that, the first of many a ticket-scalping adventure was underway.

The guys and I hopped on the T to North Station, which back then was connected to "Da Gaaden." In no time we were flanked by three guys sporting hoodies and fanning tickets in our faces.

It would be my introduction to the world of scalpers.

Thinking he found a good seat, Mike Ma plucked a single for himself at $60. Nao and I settled for a pair at $40 each. In truth, all the seats were pretty crappy in the upper-deck corners. The game itself was noteworthy in that Danny Ainge, a pouty guard who always looked on the verge of bursting into tears, scored a career-high forty-five points. Taking over from Bird, he shot twenty for twenty-nine from the field to give the C's the win. "Sir Charles" Barkley—in full 260-pound beast mode—had thirty-five points, thirteen rebounds, and five assists in a losing effort.

Afterward, I could tell Mike was miffed that his seats were virtually identical to ours, though he paid $20 more and sat through the game alone. Clearly, there was a method to getting the best value for money on the black market.

The ticketing fever in me heated up. All of a sudden just getting into the Garden wasn't enough; I wanted more bang for my buck the next time around. Only a week later, I had my chance: The Los Angeles Lakers, the Celtics' arch nemesis over the past decade, were coming to town. Every Lakers game at the Garden was huge, but this was even more hyped as it was Kareem Abdul-Jabbar's last game ever in Boston.

Kareem, the NBA's all-time leading scorer (and whiner), was on a retirement farewell tour of NBA cities. This consisted of a pregame appreciation ceremony where the home crowd would be pressured into cheering for the same player they booed over the past nineteen seasons.

This time I took on the task of finding a ticket alone. I found a guy selling a single for $45, which seemed reasonable given the magnitude of the occasion. Once I got to my seat, though, I realized I'd been scammed. The old Garden probably did have a few ghosts protecting the Celtics, but it also had loads of obstruction-view seats where you could only see half the court. The rest of the view was blocked by a post or ceiling.

Unaware of this charming quirk (though the ticket was stamped "obstruction view" in red ink, right by the $12 ticket price), I was taken off guard when I squeezed into my seat behind one of the baskets, only to realize that the upper deck was blocking half my view. It's a bizarre situation when you're listening to 14,879 other fans cheer for something that you're guessing must be good.

Nevertheless, I watched Kareem receive a bunch of jazz CDs as a gesture of goodwill from Red Auerbach and then score ten points in a losing effort.

The seeds were sewn that night. I'd go on to buy seats off of scalpers to a few more games at the Garden over the years. The best ones arrived on a whim against a terrible Dallas Mavericks team on March 26, 1993. They had just signed Jimmy Jackson, a rookie out of Ohio State who would become known for having a spat with his future teammate Jason Kidd over the R&B singer Toni Braxton.

My buddy Hazim and I showed up just after the tipoff and were accosted by someone wearing a green hoodie yelling, "These are right by Johnny Most!" referring to the legendary Celtics announcer who had passed away only two months earlier. This time I stared at the $45 face value, and knowing the game was already ten minutes old and there were scant people outside, I mustered up the balls to offer just $40.

"Done. Thanks for doing business," he said as we swapped cash for tickets in one smooth motion. Before I knew it, Hazim and I were sitting pretty by the ghost of Johnny Most in the first balcony. So long, obstruction view.[6]

The amount I saved by not buying from the Celtics' ticket booth was miniscule (though all Celtics games were sold out anyway), but it represented a breakthrough. Two valuable lessons learned. One: Haggling is (usually) a lot easier minutes after the game starts. Two: Great seats for games against awful teams can often be had for pennies on the dollar.

---

6 When we got to our seats the guy who had originally sold them was sitting there. He'd been fooled into swapping his two seats for just one farther back, and he admitted this to us before sheepishly moving. The con job worked to our benefit. The scalper trade is a zero-sum game. Your benefit is always to someone else's detriment.

Of course, not all my ticket-seeking forays went quite as smoothly over the years. There was the time my buddy Mo and I nearly froze to death outside the Carrier Dome at Syracuse University. The Orangemen boasted a powerhouse college hoops program with Derrick Coleman and Billy Owens, and Notre Dame were in town. We went fishing for scalpers near the school's gigantic Carrier Dome. February in Syracuse is not a time to be wandering around anywhere, much less a sold-out arena in search of someone who may have tickets. Parking was scarce (because…wait a minute, it was a sold-out game), and so it was a good ten-minute walk to the dome.

I am not exaggerating when I say the next twenty and a half minutes were the coldest I have been in my entire life. The half minute between walks was spent looking around to see no one but shivering security guards near the door. It was clear we had a snowball's chance in hell of getting any tickets—or surviving in the outdoors for very much longer. We made a dash back to Mo's Acura and watched in the student rec center as Syracuse lost by a point. Lesson three: Weather matters.

It must be said that the few times I did legitimately pay for seats, I felt completely ripped off. In November 1993, I convinced two friends to join me at an LA Clippers home game against the New Jersey Nets, and when the middle-tier $45 seats were available at the booth of the old LA Sports Arena (a venue Springsteen would call, "the dump that jumps"), I insisted we nab them. Coming from New York, any available seat below the upper bowl was a big catch in my mind, so it surprised me to see swaths of empty seats around us. I soon realized why.

Not only were the Clippers a miserable franchise, but only the night before we partied alongside the starters from both teams at the Roxbury Club until 2:00 a.m. Needless to say, their play was listless, and it was hard not to think that for our collective investment in this game (which we could barely afford) we could have "larged it" back at the Roxbury. Thankfully the onerous concept of bottle service and "making it rain" hadn't kicked in yet, so larging it for us back then consisted of a $20 cover charge and a few Chivas and Cokes.

Still, NBA games are the best events to attend on a regular basis and on short notice. They last only about two hours and twenty minutes. Arenas tend to be easily accessible to city dwellers, and because of their urban proximity, they lend themselves to ticket scalpers patrolling the nearby streets.

NFL games, on the other hand, take a good three and a half hours, and stadiums tend to be on the outskirts of cities, thereby writing off an entire Sunday (tailgating is another story). Baseball games can be even longer…and duller.

Then there are rock concerts, which can have you waiting all night for the next Axel Rose to show up, after he tanks himself silly in the dressing room. But on any given day in an NBA season a fan can decide minutes before (or after) tipoff to show up and try his or her luck at finding a pretty good seat. Better still, these tickets can consistently be had below the league-sanctioned inflated prices via the open market.

I know that's true. Now it's time to go out on the road and prove it.

PART TWO

PRE-TRIP JITTERS: FIVE THINGS THAT CONCERN ME BEFORE I HIT THE ROAD

Okay, I've got about twenty-one hours before embarking on that Virgin Atlantic flight to Miami. It's just dawned on me that I'm really doing this. First leg: ten cities in just under three weeks. Holy crap.

Here are a few issues that I suddenly can't stop thinking about.

1—Will It Be a Pain in the Ass Getting into All Those Games?

I'm telling myself I'm good at this. For years I've been wrangling my way into games at a discount and have very rarely been foiled. But there are times—rare occasions—when demand just completely outstrips supply. And then I'll be struggling.

Will that happen on this trip? Almost certainly, and I can point to a few games where it'll be likely. The key is how I'm going to respond. This will likely require my full arsenal of tactics to get in while not paying through the nose.

Here are the upcoming games that have me worried:

January 31, 2011—Cleveland at Miami

The anti-LeBrons versus the LeBrons. The jilted lovers versus the new brides. The attraction to attend this game with its back story is obvious, but then again the Cavs are so horrible, losing eighteen in a row (yeah, really, eighteen. The record is twenty-three, in case you're wondering[7]) that the game itself will provide no drama at all. So, *in theory*, I should be able to buy a decent ticket at a fraction of face value.

February 3—Miami at Orlando

Big interstate rivalry between two teams that "just plain don't like each other." Orlando is a small city with only one pro sports team, so this is all anyone's going to be talking about that day. Could be a major bump in the road for me, especially if both LeBron and D-Wade are healthy.

February 5—LA Lakers at New Orleans and

February 7—LA Lakers at Memphis

Anytime the Lakers are in town it's a big-ticket event. Combine that with the fact that they are the current two-time defending champs and that the two host cities are small-market towns, and you've got a big supply/demand shift. Again, big challenge.

2—How Much Is This Trip Going to Cost?

This is definitely a case of putting the cart before the horse. In other words, I was so overtaken by the concept that I never thought much about costs. But now I am.

---

7   They eventually set an NBA record with twenty-six loses in a row, so I witnessed part of history. The 2011–2012 Bobcats came close, stopping just shy at twenty-three loses, though they did set the record for worst losing percentage in history at .106. I witnessed two of those as well. This is the downside to being hell-bent on watching as many home teams as you can in a limited amount of time. You're bound to watch some truly awful teams somewhere along the line.

Suffice to say I'm working on a budget, so staying at the Four Seasons is not in the cards.[8] Instead, I'm mostly staying at a bunch of Days Inns. Hey, can't beat that free wi-fi and breakfast.

As far as my ticket budget goes, ironically I've managed to scoop $1,000 for my pair of Arsenal seats to the three matches I'm going to miss (the huge Arsenal–Barcelona Champions League matchup being one of them). If I chop that up, I've got an average of $100 per game to play with.

Granted, that is still less than most arenas charge for a bottom-tier seat, but that is my challenge. Jeepers, for $100, a paying fan should be able to watch a game from a clear vantage point. I'm not saying I expect to be brushing up against Kim Kardashian, but I shouldn't be sitting behind the cast of *The Jersey Shore* either.

3—Will Ten Domestic Flights Spell Doom?

More to the point, will they get me where I need to be on time? I'm arriving in certain cities with a few hours to spare until game time. If a flight is delayed three hours, it could destroy my schedule.

Traveling solo and on a tight agenda, driving from city to city was never in the cards. So I'm relying on Delta, AA, and Continental to get me where I need to be in a reasonable amount of time. I'm not even going to talk about airport security and TSA. Let's see how that goes.

There's also the small matter of weather; I need to be ready for both Miami heat (literally) and Salt Lake City snow. It slipped my mind that I was visiting Denver and Utah in February. I thought this was going to be a leisurely jaunt through the South. I check the forecast in SLC—freezing with sleet showers. Now I have no idea how to pack.

4—Can I Stay Reasonably Healthy Relying on Arena Food?

No, of course I can't. But I'm sure I'll be having a beer or two at every game. And then what do you do in a new city where you don't

---

8   Except in Toronto. Ok, sue me. I needed a decent night's sleep.

know anyone? You hit a bar, of course. You have dinner and start talking sports with the people to your left and right. It's a recipe for coronary failure.

So I'm planning to take my running shoes and yoga mat and see if I can keep somewhat active. Did I mention I was going to New Orleans and Memphis? Have you seen what people eat there? On the one hand, I can't wait to sink my teeth into my first po'boy. On the other hand, all those dialysis centers in the South are there for a reason.

5—Will Spending Great Swaths of Time Alone Drive Me Nuts?

We're not talking James Franco in *127 Hours*, but I'll be singing to myself for a fair amount of time. So to stay engaged, I'm going to be doing a lot of tweeting and blogging from the road.[9]

---

9   Check @thefrugalfan, and catch the images that coincide with each game on www.thefrugalfan.com.

MIAMI: JANUARY 31, 2011

HEAT 117
CAVALIERS 90
ATTENDANCE: 19,600 (officially a sellout,
not accounting for hundreds of no-shows).

I am in South Beach. Exactly 6,416 miles away, one of the biggest
global news events since 9/11 is unfolding, but you wouldn't know it
if you were somehow condemned to reading *The Miami Herald.*

While the entire world was fixated on Cairo's Tahrir Square, where a million Egyptians have gathered in peaceful protest to oust their dictator of thirty years, the paper devoted barely a page to the events over the weekend. South Beach seems way more preoccupied with tans, chest waxing, and liposuction than anything going on in the Middle East.

I can't stress how ridiculous it feels kicking off a countrywide barnstorming tour of NBA cities from one of the most stylish and superficial places on Earth during the defining moment of my lifetime as a pro-democracy Arab. But this journey is what I signed up for, and Miami is one piece of a much larger puzzle I'm putting together.

My task for the weekend was to get a good ticket to last night's Heat-Cavs game without paying through the nose. A much bigger task was to turn off NPR and grab a piña-fucking-colada, which eventually helped matters.

The backdrop of the Arab Spring had been well-documented. A guy in Tunis peddling flowers from a cart to make a buck was slapped around and told to get off the street. In frustration he lit himself on fire. In a matter of days their crooked premier was on a flight out of town with whatever he could grab from the petty cash safe. The spectacular turnaround sparked nearly every country in the Middle East.

The backdrop of the upcoming Heat-Cavs game had some drama in it too. The Cavs entered the game on a twenty-game losing streak, on pace to be one of the worst teams in NBA history. This was complicated by the Heat's best player, LeBron James, wearing a Cavs uniform until last summer, before he famously "took his talents to South Beach." It's a messy story. Like bumping into an ex-girlfriend at a mall after she gains twenty pounds and you've just been promoted. And if her mom called you a quitter when the relationship ended, like the Cavs' owner said about James, the awkwardness would be compounded.[10]

---

10   Cavs owner Dan Gilbert issued a statement calling LeBron's decision a "cowardly betrayal," then told the AP that James "quit" in the 2010 season-ending series against Boston in a way that was "unlike anything in the history of sports for a superstar."

But back to the tickets. Scouring for seats on the web gave me a headache. There was a ton of inventory out there, and season ticketholders along with ticket brokers naturally hold out for a premium until the last minute. But with the Miami sun beaming, I was walking along the beach during that last-minute stretch rather than searching Craigslist, StubHub, and Twitter for the best deals. I gave it a half-hearted try over my cell, but my gut feeling was to just show up at the arena and try my luck haggling on the street corner.

I had plans to go with a friend who was only able to arrive at 8:00 p.m., thirty minutes after tipoff. This suited me fine, as Miami is notorious for its fans showing up late, allowing more time to bargain with latecomers or scalpers looking to dump their stock.

But while riding to the AA Arena in a cab, Alex called to say she had to cancel (something about volunteering for the Red Cross, bless her). So now I was looking for a single ticket, which is often beneficial (singles go for a discount as they are harder for scalpers to dump), though it can be a negative if you're faced with someone who only wants to sell pairs.

Fortunately, my cabbie was a big NBA fan and overheard my predicament. He dropped me off at the one spot where scalpers congregate, since, according to him, security is tight, and they're not allowed to sell too close to the arena. He was right. I walked around a full city block and saw no one. Then I found a toothless guy who said he had seats in the center of the lower section for $150 each. I offered $50, and he wasn't having it. He crossed the street and said he'd be back, but it wasn't looking very promising.

I was looking pretty scruffy myself, sporting three-day stubble, a black leather jacket, and a beanie hat, so loitering around a street corner actually made people mistake me for a scalper.[11] A guy in a Dwyane Wade jersey holding paper tickets flashed me a look. "You got any spares?" I asked. "I'm not a scalper, just looking to get in."

11   This is always a good thing. Fans will come up to you unsolicited, allowing you to nab tickets at scalper prices, and other scalpers will be a tiny bit more inclined to treat you with respect.

He was only willing to sell both of his seats (lower section, corner) so he moved on and approached the toothless guy. But a female police officer lost it on him, saying, "You're not fucking selling tickets right in front of me, are you? Don't make me arrest you. Get out of my face!"

The guy was completely frazzled, a total deer in the headlights. He made a beeline to the arena, and I followed him, offering $30 for a seat. "Ok, fine, I'll walk you in, just pay me inside," he said nervously. Looking back, I could have offered him $5, and he would have taken it. But assuming face value was a lot higher, I thought $30 was reasonable. The price on the ticket said $40, which is the deal season ticketholders get. It's a sizeable difference from what people who only buy tickets once in a while via Ticketmaster pay, which is $88, including the $13 fee.

Considering he said he normally gets $100 for them online, I think I came out comfortably ahead of the pack.

Inside, I grabbed an "imported beer" for $10 (ha) and made my way to section 115. Watching a basketball game from a corner is not a terrible experience, but it's not great either. Still, I couldn't complain, considering I was in the lower tier, and the cab driver told me he gladly pays $20 to sit in the nosebleeds. And as a bonus, the Cavs actually put up a fight, closing the Heat's lead to only three points at the start of the third quarter. But everyone in the world knew that they had no chance.

In a sport like soccer, anything can happen on a given day. A superpower like Real Madrid can lose to a team in a weaker division because goals are often flukes and outmatched teams can choose to solely focus on defense.[12] But in basketball, where there's a shot clock and possession is regulated between sides, there is no way to mask a

---

12   On October 26, 2009, soccer powerhouse Real Madrid lost 4–0 to Alcorcón, a third-division team in the Spanish league. Madrid, soccer's version of the New York Yankees, fielded a team worth a combined $200 million in transfer fees, while Alcorcón's budget was stretched at $1.6 million. This is the equivalent of the Miami Heat losing to Tennessee-Chattanooga in the NCAA's.

huge deficiency in talent and size. The Cavs were overpowered from the first minute, and it showed.

By the beginning of the fourth quarter, the Heat were up twenty, LeBron was rested, and it was my cue to exit.

Next stop, Atlanta.

A note about Heat fans: They take a lot of flak for not being die-hards, but they cheered loudly, even when the baskets were meaning-less. Yes, they showed up very late, but for most of the night the arena was pretty packed for a game that had little suspense.

FACE VALUE: $40[13]
PAID: $30
DISCOUNT: 25%

---

13   To avoid confusion and to stay consistent, my definition of face value for this book consists of only what was printed on the ticket. The concept of face value is changing rapidly in today's market. A ticket purchased in the aftermarket most often originates from a season ticketholder, and therefore it has a season-ticketholder price on it (which often comes at a steep discount to what casual fans pay off Ticketmaster). In the case of tickets I bought with no visible prices on them, I did my best to find out what they were worth through the official sales channels online.

ATLANTA: FEBRUARY 2, 2011

```
HAWKS 100
RAPTORS 87
ATTENDANCE: 14,025
(a laughably distorted figure)
CAPACITY: 18,729
```

What a difference a day makes. With low expectations coming into Atlanta, I found out via a desperate Facebook post that my cousin's roommate at USC is a budding correspondent at CNN. The gracious Nick Valencia picked me up from the Lenox Square mall in Buckhead and gave me a tour of the CNN Center. After spending three days among the *Jersey Shore* wannabes in Miami, my faith in the universe is restored. Staffers were consumed by the startling news unfolding in Tahrir Square—that Mubarak's henchmen launched a violent attack on the peaceful protesters—and it felt right to be following it among them.

Not only was Atlanta a more conscious city, but it was also freezing, a shock to the system after the Miami sun. A cold front swirling around the East nearly grounded the Toronto Raptors and threatened to postpone the game. Thankfully, that was not the case, and I proceeded with game two of my odyssey. I'm glad I did. The experience was fun, but pretty strange. I've never been somewhere quite as barren as Phillips Arena. My conservative estimate is that it was 70 percent empty. The official attendance of 14,025 out of a capacity of 18,729 is completely farcical.[14] It had to be four thousand, max.

Although the arena was built in 1999, it felt new and sleek. The steel-grey seats have a cool look to them (which helps when there's no one to cover them), as does the design that stacks all the luxury boxes on one side of the arena. This brings the people on the second and third tiers closer to the action than in other venues.[15] There's also a carnival-like feel to the common areas, along with a Mexican restaurant/sports bar. The bar was full, while the seats showcasing a live game, steps

---

14   Attendance statistics are a joke throughout sports. I don't know why they bother spewing out these lies when it's plain to the naked eye that you could drive a Smart Car around some of the rows. Arsenal Football Club in the UK bases its attendance on sold seats, not actual attendance figures (their president admitted this in a shareholders meeting). But at least there's some kind of base for Arsenal's lies. The Hawks must have some multiplier lie coefficient in place. Actual attendance to the power of pi^{10} might work.

15   In the UK this stadium effect of having a continuous tier on one end is known as a Kop, after some ancient war that was fought in South Africa on a hill called a Kop. I remember reading this on Wikipedia. The most famous Kop is at Anfield, Liverpool FC's stadium.

away, were empty. It made no sense. Maybe it was the plethora of beers on offer ($5.50 for Abita Ale, a good value).

But let's pause and go back to the ticket search process at the Days Inn. Having a strong inkling that attendance would be sparse, I turned to StubHub for a good deal. There were loads of seats on offer for $1, some for even less. My predicament though, as a solo attendee, was finding a single ticket for sale (on StubHub, buying in pairs is often the only option). Otherwise, I'd be paying the onerous StubHub transactions fees twice ($5 for the transaction and $5 to print out the ticket). I settled on a seat in the second-tier center for $4 plus the fees.[16]

Ironically, I had to go to a FedEx copy office so that I could print out the ticket, and the rip-off charges for going online set me back $5.50. But I asked the guys in the office if they go to Hawks games, and the response was that they couldn't afford them. Then I showed them my screen. They were startled. One guy thanked me profusely and said he'd finally be taking his kids.

By the time I left the CNN Center and turned the corner to the arena (the two are adjoined), the scalpers were out in full force. I spoke to one who had a stack of paper tickets. He flaunted a third-tier seat with a face value of $35 and said he'd give it to me for $20. Then I told him I had bought mine online for $14 in the second tier. He actually asked if we could switch. I felt bad for the scalpers. There was no market

---

16   StubHub fees of 15 percent to the seller and 10 percent to the buyer, plus a shipping fee, are a bone of contention for both buyers and sellers. "That is absolutely ridiculous," Barry Kahn, the CEO of ticketing software company Qcue, told me. "The fees on the secondary market of 25 percent are unsustainable. That's an absurd percentage."

Service charges on tickets "are relics to the industry," he explained. "They're relics of old rev-share laws related to music, where artists got paid on gross ticket sales. So if you could pull out expenses like the cost of the ticketing provider [and mask them as fees], that didn't get to the artist, and therefore the ticketing system could kick money back to the venue. So there's a lot going on here because of the way this industry has worked, and it hasn't always been above the books."

for their tickets to this low-profile game, and the likes of StubHub are drying up their business.[17]

The game turned into a fun two hours. The Hawks have a ton of swagger, and the PA guy was very upbeat. They played energetic music during the warm-ups and timeouts (Metallica, Kanye, etc.), and had a lot of promotional stuff in between. At one point they parachuted a bunch of stuffed-animal hawks into the crowd.

I took the liberty of moving up seven rows, just behind the press, to get a better view. It made a big difference; I had a great vantage point. The two season ticketholders behind me, in their sixties, told me Hawks games are priced in tiers. This game's ticket was only $16, though the Ticketmaster price was $51 plus $7.85 in fees for the single-game purchaser. It's insane. No one in their right mind would pay $59 for a mediocre seat in an empty arena, but to get a cheaper deal from the Hawks you have to pony up for forty-one home games. Still, they assured me the game last week against the Knicks was a sell-out (shows how far the Knicks have come). I guess it's worth it to some to get the entire package for the few big games, but I can't see the logic in it.[18]

---

17 This is what I thought at the time. Subsequently, I've come to realize it's just that no one wants to go to Hawks games.

18 Nathan Hubbard, the head of ticketing at Live Nation and Ticketmaster, agrees: "The season ticket is under attack," he said on an October 20, 2011, B.S. Report podcast with Bill Simmons. "For a fan, the secondary market has created great transparency around what the actual value for each individual game is. It's a scary proposition for the teams."

He expanded on this by comparing buying a season ticket with paying full price for rock albums twenty years ago (and we know what happened to the music business). "People felt like they were getting, in some cases, bundled stuff that they didn't want. Give the secondary marketplace credit. They've created a fluid market that actually values—debundles, decouples—those things and gives fans the personalized experience that they want."

If by "personalized experience" Hubbard means fans want to stop getting ripped off, then he's onto something.

Still, there's some merit to the theory that whatever you save on the ticket, you spend inside anyway. I had (gulp) three beers (average of $7) plus popcorn ($4), and I ordered a burrito that looked delicious but smelled awful. I couldn't even get close to my hands once they'd touched it. That was a waste of $8. But I even bought a Hawks thermal t-shirt on the way out. It was the 40 percent discount ($16) that nabbed me.[19] I think more prudent spending will be in order at my next stop.

On to Orlando, where the Magic play the Heat. Huge game. Tickets are going for $450 and up in the lower tier. My skills will be stretched to the limit.

```
FACE VALUE: $16
PAID: $14
DISCOUNT: 8.75%
```

19   It's legitimately worth the Hawks considering giving tickets away for a dollar or two to get people through the door. The cost of operating the arena would remain exactly the same, and their concession sales would go through the roof. Their only problem would be pissing off the few season ticketholders they have left. At some point the Hawks and a half dozen other NBA teams may have to bite the bullet on this.

ORLANDO: FEBRUARY 3, 2011

Open the door and let us in! We have tickets.

```
HEAT 104
MAGIC 100
ATTENDANCE: 18,945 (sellout)
```

"You want free? Go to Egypt, them is free!"

That was the reaction I got from an Orlando scalper after I told him I didn't want to pay too much for a good seat. I was practically laughed off the sidewalk, guffaws, knee slapping, and all.

I knew LeBron was a big-ticket attraction, but just how big became plainly evident when I arrived at the Amway Center a full two hours before tipoff to find a line of a thousand people waiting for the doors to open. There was a DJ outside pumping hip-hop ("Straight from London, ya ya, alright geezer"), loads of food and promotional stalls, as well as a giant inflatable Mickey Mouse. There were also a dozen satellite vans parked outside with newscasters practicing their lines on the pavement.

Talk about intimidating.

I'd flown in for less than twenty-four hours just to see this game; I had no ticket and was working on a budget. Pregame figures online were $450 and up in the lower-tier center sections. Even the guy who checked me in at the Days Inn thought I was a little nuts.

So I cautiously made the rounds, sort of befriending a few of the characters working the street corner just to get a feel of what this would take. Their strategy is to ask how much I'd be willing to spend, and mine is to stay coy and throw down outlandishly low numbers ($30? $50?). I was quoted $250 for something in the lower-section corner and $125 in the upper (nosebleed) corner. Forget it, I thought, I can do better than that. I told them I'd grab dinner and be back later, closer to tipoff at 8:00 p.m.

I was very pleasantly surprised with downtown Orlando. It's impressive, with rows of bustling cool bars sporting live bands, giant screens, and all kinds of food. There was a lot to choose from. I parked myself at a trendy tapas bar and ended up chatting with the guy next to me. He was a young businessman who does a lot of work in India and only has time to see a few games a season. He had plunked down $380 for a fourth-row seat in the center, buying off Ticketmaster Exchange.

I wolfed down my tapas and headed back to the arena with fifteen minutes to go till tipoff. Butterflies in my stomach. A guy tried to sell me his upper-tier ticket (face value of $120—really? To sit up there?) for $100. I offered $20, and he got offended. Whatever, to me they were worth $20 and no more.

I moved back to the corner where I'd made myself a familiar face. A fat guy who looked like he could be the brother of departed SNL regular Chris Farley recognized me and waved a ticket. "I got something for you! A single in the bottom section, man. Just what you wanted." He showed me the seating chart, and indeed, it was a great seat. Eleventh row just off the center. Furthermore, the face value said $0.00 on it, meaning it was a VIP ticket that was comped, either by one of the teams or the league.

Now came the bargaining.

Me: How much?

Him: $150.

Me: $80.

Him: $120.

Me: $80. I got cash right here.

Him: $120. I paid a lot for this.

Me: How much did you pay? I have $80, and that's my budget.

Him: Ok, just give me $100.

Me: $85. I can't go over $85.

Him (sensing other guys swarming around me, perhaps ready to make other offers): Ok, fine, $85.

A quick exchange, and I was in! I felt a rush knowing I'd bagged a good seat for a freakishly cheap price, relatively speaking. Once I settled in, two tall black guys who looked like they jumped out of a J-Crew ad walked over to my seat. Before even sitting down, one asked what I'd paid for my ticket.

I thought that was kind of weird and direct, so I asked why he wanted to know.

"Cos that's my ticket you bought," he said.

He explained that his girlfriend didn't feel like coming, so he sold his spare for $50. He'd gotten the tix comped by his cousin, who plays for the Magic.

"Oh, who's your cousin?" I asked.

"Jason Richardson," he deadpanned.

Ha! For $85 I was sitting in one of the Magic's best player's seats. A two-time Slam Dunk champion, no less! Fantastic.

Just to feel even smugger, I asked around to find out what face value was. The Indian guy sitting next to me with his daughter was a season ticketholder. His ticket said $265 (God, I'm nosey).

I almost forgot there was a big game to watch. And boy, did it live up to its hype. This was the most exciting basketball game I'd seen live in years. The place was packed to the rafters (the anti-Atlanta), and Magic fans are noisy.

LeBron, however, put on a clinic, as they say. In the first quarter alone he had twenty-three points. He simply could not miss, and the Magic had no answer for him. From the outset he played point guard. He is simply too big and too muscular for anyone to guard at the perimeter, allowing him to rain in jump shots at will.

I asked J-Rich's cuz why they didn't double him. It seemed obvious they should. "They can't. Too good a passer." And with that, LeBron whizzed a no-look assist to an open Chris Bosh.

He finished with a jaw-dropping line of fifty-one points, eleven rebounds, and eight assists. He played forty-three minutes and was seventeen of twenty-five from the field. I've seen some elite players live, including Jordan, Bird, and Kobe, and LeBron is right up there with them It was an awesome display. He was toying with the Magic in the same way you pull yarn away from a kitten.

Yet somehow the Magic clawed back to within three points with twenty seconds to go. It added to the electric atmosphere, even though they couldn't pull off the victory.

There's a tall spire connected to Amway Arena that lights up in blue when the Magic win. My cabbie told me that he can tell what color it is without looking because of the jovial vibe on the streets.

Alas, the spire shined red last night.

Next stop, New Orleans.

FACE VALUE: $265
PAID: $85
DISCOUNT: 68%

NEW ORLEANS: FEBRUARY 5, 2011

UNIVERSITY OF ALABAMA BIRMINGHAM 47
TULANE 39
ATTENDANCE: 2,131
CAPACITY: 3,600

LAKERS 101
HORNETS 95
ATTENDANCE: 18,426 (sellout)

This is the stop of the tour's leg that I'd been anticipating the most. New Orleans was my home for two years as a Tulane MBA student. I found it slow, odd, and provincial at first, but I grew to love the town and its quirkiness. It holds a special place for me, so the events surrounding Hurricane Katrina weighed heavily. This is my first visit back, and after a tedious day of transit through the Atlanta airport, I began a very cold Saturday by touring my old campus and checking out the Green Wave basketball team.

It's slightly disheartening that college attendance figures are thoroughly pumped up, just like in the pros. The reported mark for yesterday's Tulane-University of Alabama Birmingham game was 2,131. I can say with confidence that there were at most nine hundred people in Fogelman Arena, which is surely one of the coolest college basketball venues in America. The 3,600-capacity gym—for that is really what it is—was built in 1933 and refurbished in 1989, but it maintains a very basic high school-like feel to it. Benches with no backrests and dollar beers for students (no joke), along with mixed drinks if you feel like it. Can any other college basketball arena boast that?

Too bad the product on the hardwood couldn't match the atmosphere. Tulane was dire, scoring only twelve points in the first half and shooting 27 percent overall. Five minutes into the second half, I took a walk to visit some of my old haunts.

The basketball team's demise, however, is the antithesis of what the rest of the university has achieved. I can't say enough good things about Tulane. The university bounced back like a champ after Katrina, and it now boasts one of the toughest programs in the United States, accepting only 26 percent of applicants. My anemic GPA would not get me very far in the application process now, so I'm glad I studied there back in the 1990s. The campus is gorgeous, reflecting one of the most scenic cities anywhere, and its student life is enviable.

That said, New Orleans is still in rough shape. By recent count, the city's population stands at only 344,000, a third less than the figure in 2000 and dwindling every year. Small wonder—after Katrina more than a few big companies moved their headquarters elsewhere, while crime remains rampant, and the murder rate is still the highest in the United States.

Back in the day, everyone I knew—including me—had a run-in that involved either a mugging, a fight, jail, hospitalization, or all of the above. Most of my friends carried guns for protection. I remember a professor starting a lecture by saying, "Excuse me if I'm a little off today. I got carjacked on the way here." The rule of thumb was not to stop at a stop sign because you'd be a sitting duck. It was like Johannesburg, only this was a city somehow festering within the world's biggest economy.

Sadly, Katrina seems to have pressed the hyperspace button on New Orleans's demise. If not for the Saints and their incredible Super Bowl run in 2010, there would be little to celebrate. The Hornets are a winning team and exciting to watch, but as my friend Kim explained, the city just cannot support two pro teams, and the Saints are number one here.[20]

The chances that the team stays in town after next season are iffy. Its economics are so bad that the NBA had to step in and buy the franchise from Hornets owner George Shinn, who was bleeding money.[21] But last night was different. It's always different when the Lake Show is in town. New Orleans Arena (note that there is no sponsor) boasted its biggest night of attendance since Katrina, with a sell-out crowd of 18,426.

This, of course, made my life a little bit harder. Walking on the way via Poydras Street, I stopped a scalper who told me he had nothing. Not a good sign. Closer to the arena, I spoke to two other guys—still nothing. Gulp. Finally, just outside the doors of the arena, I saw a scalper buying two tickets off a season ticketholder. In a case like this, you may be tempted to meddle in the transaction, offering the ticketholder more than the low price you know the scalper is offering.

20   In April 2012 the Hornets were purchased by Tom Benson, a local car dealer who's owned the Saints since 1985. I am super happy for New Orleans. Benson is a committed owner who easily could have moved the Saints to San Antonio after Katrina crippled the city's economy but didn't. Not only are they staying in New Orleans, but Benson chose to shed the Hornets name for Louisiana's state bird, the Pelicans, as of the 2013–2014 season.

21   The NBA is heavily reliant on corporate sponsorship from each team's local Fortune 500 companies. Everything from sales of luxury suites to the sponsorships of lounge areas and an arena's naming rights all come down to the biggest companies in each city. New Orleans had only two Fortune 500 companies before Katrina and just one after (power company Entergy).

Don't even think about it.

You'd be messing with a guy's lunch money, and this is his turf. At best, you're asking for a major shakedown. At worst…well, you don't need me to explain. This is New Orleans, after all.

The scalper is there to provide a service. Be friendly, tell him what you need and what you're willing to pay, and he will try to help you. These were two tickets in the lower tier, just on the side and in the tenth row (really the seventh since they count the first three on the floor). Excellent seats by any measure.

After much bargaining, which involved me walking away several times and crossing paths with this guy on another street, we agreed on $220 for the pair. As I was with Kim, I didn't have the luxury of bargaining hard for a single, which is always more difficult for the scalper to get rid of. This was literally the only available pair of seats in the lower tier (I asked every single scalper). Yet somehow, for a game that commanded the biggest crowd in years, I managed to bag us fantastic tickets at a 25 percent discount off the box office face value ($146).[22] How? It was a combination of luck, patience, and persistence.

There's also some etiquette involved. There's a fine line between driving a hard bargain and insulting a guy. You don't want to be seen as annoying; otherwise, you will get blackballed, and no scalper will deal with you.[23]

Much like in Orlando, there was a festive buzz on the streets. New Orleans loves its Hornets, and it loves music, so there was a local 1980s cover band outside the gate along with a beer stand (drinking outside is tolerated in the Crescent City as long as you do it out of a cup). The arena itself is generic, but the food stands were unlike those

---

22   This was the only ticket I'd come across that had two face values on it, one that said "Gate $146" and the other "Season $101," marking the sharp price increase for single-game, or '"gate," buyers.

23   This has happened to me before, leaving me begging for a spare to a De La Soul concert in London.

I'd seen at any other NBA game (alligator po'boy, anyone?). Kim and I hit the Abita beer stand (a local microbrew), and ordered two ambers for $8.50 apiece. They came in half-pint glasses, which was a joke of a rip-off but didn't stop me from ordering two more.

The game itself was intense. Kobe and the Lakers played in tandem, constantly moving as dictated by the triangle offense. They also played jarring defense, led by loose cannon Ron Artest and overly tattooed small forward Matt Barnes. There are reports that Artest is losing it, but he looked sharp, making jumpers and being a menace to the Hornets.

Kobe, though effective (thirty-two points), did not look like himself. I caught him limping a few times, and I think his knee was really acting up on him. He's been a below-the-rim player this season, a sign that all the wear and tear of fourteen years in the league is slowing him down.[24] Yet he's still Kobe, and his battery of shake-and-bake moves still leaves defenders quaking. He's also deadly from long range. Because of Trevor Ariza's injury, Hornets rookie Quincy Pondexter was forced to guard Kobe for most of the night. He was quoted in the *Times Picayune* the next day as saying he considered it "really an honor." Enough said.

There was a lead change in the last three minutes, but the Hornets could not keep up. Their injuries left them just a little bit outmatched. But the playoffs may provide a different story, and three

---

24   Indeed, Kobe would travel to Dusseldorf, Germany, in the summer of 2011 to undergo a controversial procedure that involves withdrawing blood from a patient, incubating it for twenty-four hours, then injecting it into the patient's knee as an anti-inflammatory and healing agent. After recovery, Bryant finished the 2011–2012 season second in scoring with 27.9 points per game, and eleventh in minutes played. I think there's something to that procedure.

Update: In the final week of the 2012-2013 NBA season, Kobe tore his left Achilles tendon while resting barely two minutes a night at the end of a frantic playoff push. In his seventeenth season he logged the second most minutes in the league. Even a miracle worker in Germany can't cure an achy knee that's been pushed that hard.

more home games against the Lakers would be a nice boon to the city's pocketbook.[25]

After the game, Kim and I took in a fantastic meal at NOLA's in the French Quarter. The waiter told us that Chris Paul normally comes in after a win, and that he waited on him, along with LeBron, D-Wade, and Chris Bosh when Miami was in town.

Paul played the good host and picked up the tab. For now he seems content with being in New Orleans, which is fantastic news for the city. It needs a good guy like Paul and deserves to keep the Hornets in town.[26]

Next stop, Memphis, for another chance to see the Lakers and another big audience, no doubt.

PAID: $110

SINGLE-GAME FACE VALUE: $146
DISCOUNT TO SINGLE-GAME PRICE: 25%

SEASON-TICKET FACE VALUE: $101
PREMIUM TO SEASON-TICKET PRICE: 9%

---

25   This ended up happening in the first round, with the Hornets playing three home games, eventually succumbing to the Lakers 4–2.

26   While under the ownership of the NBA, Paul was traded to the Clippers for a bunch of draft picks and stiffs, leaving the team without a single marketable player and no shot at the playoffs.

MEMPHIS: FEBRUARY 7, 2011

LAKERS 93
GRIZZLIES 84
ATTENDANCE: 18,119 (sellout)

Maybe it was because of the subfreezing temperatures, but Memphis was distinctly lacking something. People maybe? Open stores? Cars? Everything seemed to be shut or in slow motion. I went looking for a winter coat, as I've been woefully unprepared for this cold front. I asked the concierge, shopkeepers, a bus driver, and a taxi driver where I could find a coat. I'd settle for anything—a flea market, Salvation Army, or outdoor store. I was finally dropped off at what was supposedly the nicest mall in town. There were only two stores open: a Victoria's Secret and a discount women's clothing store. Every other storefront was empty.

Instead, I ended up having to pile on the layers to protect me from the snow. So rather than pursuing a fruitless shopping expedition, I retreated back to my hotel to search for a ticket to the game. Surprisingly, there were a few on StubHub going for less than face value. One I had my eye on was priced at $89 in the center of the club tier, above the luxury boxes (it had a face value of $129).

Combing through Craigslist, though, I spotted an unbelievable deal: one floor seat with a face value of $200 going for $130. I immediately phoned the guy up, but he had just sold it. Dang! I couldn't believe it. He promised to make some calls and try to find me another spare, but I was out of luck. I've become pretty spoiled with my seats as of late, so anything short of the first ten rows feels a little too far from the action. As such, I bagged on the idea of buying the StubHub seat and decided to hit the streets before the game. Besides, hitting the streets makes for a better story.

A cab driver told me that scalpers were scarce because of a police crackdown on them, but I ignored his advice. Braving twenty-five-degree weather, I took the ten-minute walk from my hotel to the FedEx Forum (with a pit stop to warm up over a beer at the Flying Saucer). The cabbie was way off (like he was with the coat store). There was a thriving secondary ticket market just outside the gates. I'm pretty sure the exact same club seat I saw on StubHub was going for $150. There was not much else worth considering, so I decided to wait it out at another bar that had windows facing the arena. It was bitterly cold, after all.

I watched as scalpers traded tickets to and fro while I downed local ale (it had the word "snake" in it). With fifteen minutes to go until tipoff, I got restless and joined the fray. Thankfully, I quickly found a guy who had a single in the middle section of the lower tier. It was twenty rows back, but it offered a quality view. I held my ground at $80, and he capitulated. Face value says $107, so I was still riding that 25 percent discount mark. Honestly, I had no patience to stick it out in that weather, or else I may have done even better. Oh, the guy also gave me his business card (gotta love it). His name: Robert LeCruise Johnson; I'm not making this up. And his company's name? Cruise Enterprises, naturally.

Nevertheless, I got in with plenty of time to watch warm-ups and the line-up announcements. Those are always fun in the NBA, and the Grizzlies are the first team I've seen with actual fireworks and flares after each player is announced. Metallica must be making a fortune off the NBA. I've heard "Enter Sandman" in at least three arenas so far, and I've only just started.

Halfway through the first quarter, Snoop Dogg made a grand entrance with four burly bodyguards. He had a floor seat behind the basket and beside the Lakers' bench.

The game presented some intriguing matchups: the giant Catalan Gasol brothers going at one another, Ron Artest harassing Memphis' smooth jump shooter Rudy Gay, and Gay himself covering Kobe Bryant. The Grizz kept it close until midway through the fourth quarter when the Lakers pulled away. At one point Artest got poked in the eye by Marc Gasol and unleashed a burst of melodrama. He ran all the way down the court whining like a four-year-old. When the Lakers' trainer came to assist him, he angrily pushed him off. Artest is a clown, but he is the swing factor for the Lakers. When he has his head in the game, they are very tough to beat. In the last two games, he's been effective offensively and intimidating on defense, stealing the ball four times last night.[27]

Zach Randolph had a terrible game for the Grizz, going only two for fourteen from the field with four turnovers. Zach was the source of much amusement a few years ago when he was spotted at a Portland strip club while on bereavement leave from the Trailblazers.[28] Hey, why not get a lap dance while grieving? And for good measure he left without paying his tab. Class act.

A note about the arena: It's got the coolest luxury boxes I've seen. They're close to the action, spacious, and with wide-open panes for

---

27 Artest, who changed his name to Metta World Peace after the season, had a dreadful 2011 playoff series against Dallas, leading to the Lakers getting swept.

28 Randolph was a charter member of the Jail-Blazers.

viewing. They were more like terraces than boxes. But the fan base at the game was a good 40 percent Lakers. A lot of purple and gold was sprinkled into the crowd, something I did not see in New Orleans. Why are the Hornets a threat to move when the Grizzlies are not?[29]

After the game I hit Beale Street. It is by far the coolest thing about Memphis, other than Graceland. Although it was a Monday night, the street was bustling, with blues blasting out of every venue. I had a fantastic meal at the Tap Room and chatted with a couple of guys at the bar who, like me, were in transit. One was busy sampling my plate of southern catfish. The other, who was driving through town on his way back from watching the Super Bowl in Dallas, insisted on showing me bikini pictures of his pregnant Eastern European girlfriend while a band cranked up the blues.

The one fairly lucid guy at the bar was the bartender, who revealed that he was once thrown into the back of a police car for engaging with scalpers. He had given the seller cash but didn't yet receive the ticket. Sadly, he lost out on both. Buyer beware, because those discounts do come at a risk.

Next stop, Oklahoma City.

FACE: $107
PAID: $80
DISCOUNT: 25%

---

[29] A contractual obligation among the city, arena, and the Grizzlies binds the team in place until at least 2021, according to Memphis news source commercialappeal.com. Cementing the team further is Robert Pera's takeover in October 2012. The thirty-four-year-old wireless equipment billionaire spread shares among Tennessee personalities Justin Timberlake, Peyton Manning, and Penny Hardaway to get the deal done. Partial- and full-season ticket sales, starting at just $5 a game, rose 30 and 20 percent, respectively (sportsbusinessdaily.com), while the team's been a top playoff contender for the third season running. Meanwhile, as mentioned, the Hornets were rescued by Tom Benson and will become the Pelicans.

OKLAHOMA CITY: FEBRUARY 8, 2011

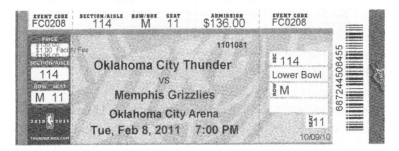

```
GRIZZLIES 105
THUNDER 101
ATTENDANCE: 17,868
CAPACITY: 18,203
```

I'm writing this from a booth at the Crabtown restaurant here in Bricktown, OKC (the fried okra is out of this world). The temperature outside is twelve. That's F and not C. A severe snowstorm hit town last night, and I'm still hoping my flight to Denver (via Dallas) gets me out of here this evening.

But OKC is not the worst place in the world to get stuck. In fact, I've found it very charming. For starters, the people are super friendly, and you get a feel of prosperity and old country style here. As soon as the plane touched down at Will Rogers Airport, I marveled at the cool infrastructure. Sanded brick and high ceilings, along with a retro spaciousness you don't get in other domestic airports.

"Oklahomans are some of the most altruistic people you'll ever meet," says Joe, my partner in crime for the night. Joe and I met two blocks from the Oklahoma City Arena (since named Chesapeake Energy Arena) while we were haggling with a scalper at the same time. I was angling for a ticket in the lower tier, just off the center. I offered $40, and he wanted $100. Joe stepped in, and I was worried we'd get into a bidding war, but instead we formed a team and haggled the guy down to $100 for the pair.[30] Not bad considering the face said $136 each.

"We could have gotten them for $20 each had we waited it out," Joe tells me. But in that sort of weather we'd be waging a war of attrition, and I wasn't prepared to catch hypothermia over $30.[31] Besides, we still came out 63 percent ahead.

The Thunder is a big-ticket team boasting Kevin Durant, the NBA's current scoring leader. Oklahomans don't seem to mind spending on the Thunder, with the reported attendance only 150 off of capacity in the midst of a severe weather alert. Joe tells me he's attended five games so far this season and always waits until the last minute to haggle on the streets. "That's just my style," he says.

Joe looked like your average churchgoing white guy from the Bible Belt who sang in choir, captained the high-school basketball team and settled into a life with a wife and three kids. He stopped to get a beer on the way in.

Before the national anthem, a preacher walked onto the court and gave a brief sermon, asking the Lord to protect the players as well as "our brothers and sisters in Egypt." I thought it was a nice touch.

---

30   I'm a fan of pairing up with other randoms looking for a single ticket. It gives you buying power and also some insight into the local culture. I just didn't realize how much insight until later that evening.

31   It was so cold I physically could not make the ten-minute walk from the hotel to the arena in one shot. I had to stop at Rooster's Chicken & Beer to knock one down halfway and get the blood flowing again.

A prayer was also delivered pregame in New Orleans. It was the first time I had seen such a thing, but it's common practice in the South apparently. Somehow I don't see that happening before a Knicks game.

But we had a real game on our hands, the most competitive I've seen thus far on the trip. The Grizzlies, the same team I'd watched the Lakers walk over the day before, played hard from the outset, though they were down by ten at the half.

Joe got up to hit the Jack Daniels-sponsored bar on the concourse at halftime and didn't come back until the end of the third quarter (not coincidentally, that's when last call is at NBA games). He was raving about two women he'd met at the bar and offering to take me along to meet them at the bar of the neighboring Marriott Hotel after the game.

Back on the court, Tony Allen and Zach "Bereavement Leave" Randolph picked up the slack for the absence of injured leading scorer Rudy Gay. Randolph had a monster of a game. He came up with thirty-one points, fourteen rebounds, and four assists in forty-seven minutes, while making one big bucket after another. Allen, meanwhile, played stellar defense on Durant while scoring twenty-seven points himself. Durant still got his thirty-one points (rather quietly), but Allen's five steals show just how aggressively he played.

With a few seconds to go in regulation, James Harden had a chance to break the tie, but the would-be fifth member of the Black Eyed Peas came up just short. We were going into overtime. Durant slipped with a chance to tie the game in the final seconds, and the Grizzlies pulled out a gritty win.

After the game, Joe and I hit the town. This was after I swore to myself I'd have a quiet night. I was hitting a wall on my sixth stop in nine days, yet with the allure of Oklahoma City and a frosty walk, I found the will to power on. We started at the aforementioned Marriott bar, where a lot was going on except for the appearance of the two women Joe met at the game.

After I scarfed down a grilled salmon dinner, and Joe knocked back a few G+Ts, we powered on to OKC's nicest steakhouse, Mickey Mantle's.[32]

At one point in Mickey's bar (he was an Oklahoma native), a girl next to me proclaimed she dated three members of the Thunder, but that they're "all just little boys." Naturally I asked which ones.

"Westbrook, Green, and Durant," she blurted out.

"Wow, are you a Thunder groupie?" Seemed like an obvious question.

"No, they just all liked me, but we're friends now," she smiled, knowingly pointing upstairs where a few of the players were apparently having dinner.

Meanwhile, Joe was getting more sloshed. At one point he came back in from smoking a cigarette in the cold, grabbed his glass of red wine in his right hand, wrapped his left arm around me, and yelled, "This is my buddy Motez!" across the wood-paneled bar. It was a classic fork-in-the road moment; the choices were to swallow hard and commit to the evening, or cut and run.

And with that, Mantle's closed, and we all moved up to the Sky Bar. Yes, there is a Sky Bar in Oklahoma City. Not the Sky Bar on Sunset in LA or even the Sky Bar of Beirut. But there's a Sky Bar in OKC, and it was going off that night. The hip-hop could be heard blasting down the sidewalk—not bad for a snowy Tuesday.

Once inside the Sky Bar, things took a turn for the worse. Joe approached three very attractive Oklahoma girls and started making small talk, from what I could see.

Suddenly, one of them came up to me and lost it, asking, "Is this guy with you? He just asked us if we were strippers! I'm going to have him

---

32   On the way out of the Marriot I found a $10 and a $20 bill rolled up on the floor of the lobby. What do you do in those situations? There's always a worry someone's got an invisible string attached to it, ready to make an ass out of you. There wasn't. I did a quick look around, stuffed them in my pocket, and powered on.

thrown out. I'm a respectable business-owning woman; he can't talk to me that way!"

Oh shit. I could feel her wrath on me and wanted no part of it. I ended up defusing the situation by telling her I was doing this tour and writing a book. "Oh yeah? Well, put down that Oklahoma City sucks," said the best looking of the three. She reminded me of Tyra Collette from *Friday Night Lights*, only with two-toned hair. In fact, all three of them were sporting the blonde hair on the top with darker, longer hair on the bottom. It must have been a local thing.

It was all looking pretty rosy, and I was enjoying the banter...until I misunderstood Tyra's suggestion that "go get your friend" meant that everything was cool with Joe now. So I motioned for him to join us. Yeah, dumb, I know.

As soon as Joe came within two feet of them, it all started again.

After the melee of bouncers and promises to behave, I left Joe standing on his own on the dance floor, smoking a cigarette in his windbreaker, staring into the abyss. I have no idea where Joe is now, but I have to thank him for showing me a cool time that night, and leaving me with a great impression of OKC.

I have to dash so that I can finally buy a coat before I hit Denver and Utah. A cab's taking me to a Western store on the way to the airport. I cannot wait.[33]

FACE: $136
PAID: $50
DISCOUNT: 63%

---

33 The Western stores sucked. I went to two, in fact. They were huge, but the only coats they had were Carhartts for manual laborers. I powered on regardless.

DENVER: FEBRUARY 11, 2011

NUGGETS 121
MAVERICKS 120
ATTENDANCE: 16,273
CAPACITY: 19,155

My Denver stop coincided with the stepping down of Hosni Mubarak in Egypt. The transfer of power took more twists and turns in the final twenty-four hours than anyone could have foreseen.

Congratulations go out to the Egyptian people, especially their youth for making this happen. Can't say enough about how terrific they have been throughout, especially maintaining composure when Mubarak unleashed his thugs on them a few days into the demonstrations. They had the resolve to persevere until justice was served. I assumed they would eventually tire, but they proved me and most of the world wrong. Indeed, today I am proud to be an Arab.

On to Denver, where I watched these events unfold in the home of my close friend Wahab and his gracious family. Wahab and I, along with his brother and cousin, watched a game last night that had nearly as many plot twists as the Egyptian revolution. Forgive the comparison for a second, and I'll talk you through this. First there was a great surge by the underdogs (the Denver Nuggets, who went up by eighteen), but then they lost their momentum and blew their lead to the incumbents (the Dallas Mavs). For a while it was touch and go. There were lead changes back and forth, and with precious little time remaining it looked like the upstarts would lose, only to pull out an unbelievable victory in the dying seconds. The crowd in the Pepsi Center erupted, like a mini-Tahrir Square.

There, I did it.

The one major subplot leading up to this game was all about where Carmelo Anthony would be traded to. In fact, I worried over the past two weeks that Carmelo would be gone by now, and I'd be seeing a much lesser version of the Nuggets. But Denver's star was still sporting light blue.[34] Every day brings a new rumor to the table. First it was the Nets, then the Knicks, and then the Lakers. The crowd seemed conflicted on whether to cheer him (he had forty-two points after all, including five three-pointers), or mock his refusal to sign the three-year $65 million contract that Denver had put on the table.

Anthony will likely end up with the Knicks, but whether that takes place this month or at the end of the season is unclear.[35] Though he dominated for much of the game (he makes scoring look easy, averaging thirty-eight points in his last five games), Melo fouled out with the Nuggets down by a point and nineteen seconds to go. Step up Arron

---

34   This would be his last home game in a Denver uniform.

35   He did indeed end up with the Knicks, who mortgaged their future on him. The debate on whether he's made the Knicks better or worse was one of biggest sagas of the 2011–2012 season. He would finish the 2012–2013 season as the NBA scoring leader and an MVP candidate, leading the Knicks to second place in the Eastern Conference.

Afflalo. The former UCLA guard had a standout fourth quarter, hitting every shot in sight and finishing with twenty-four. When Chauncey Billups was double-teamed, Afflalo was ready and launched a jumper from nineteen feet. Nothing but net. Pandemonium in the Pepsi Can.

This was the first game I'd seen in a while that finished with a walk-off jump shot. It's an awesome experience. Denver fans are known for their passion; although the Nuggets have never had a whiff of the NBA Finals, they are a well-supported franchise. Even their mascot Rocky is adored, while he high-fives his way around the court during breaks. He swished a backward shot from half court for good measure.

Procuring the tickets was a very smooth affair. Plaudits go out to Wahab for scrolling through Craigslist and bargaining a season ticketholder down to $200 for his four seats plus a VIP parking pass. Face value said $115 (for season ticketholders, not a la carte fans), saving us 56 percent, excluding the parking. In total, Matt, the affable season ticketholder, subsidized our night by $260. I heard more than one fan say it was the best game of the season, so a big thanks goes out to Matt. By my estimate, he's plunking down a shade under $19k for his four season tickets. The more high rollers willing to pay for half of my night out the better, although like I've said, I think this season-ticket model is on delicate legs.

Outside Pepsi Arena, the street trade was thriving. At least half a dozen scalpers held up laminated signs that read, "I need tickets." That's also the legally kosher code for "I'm selling tickets."

Testing the market, we found a guy selling seats in our row (eighteen rows up, dead center) for $75 each, leaving us feeling like we'd come out ahead.

Denver has an appealing downtown scene, with numerous high-end sports bar and grills. We parked ourselves at Earls on the Sixteenth Street Mall, which had great sushi rolls and Fat Tire Ale, a local brew. Inside the arena, Dale's Pale Ale provided a very hoppy local flavor. Both get my seal of approval.

Salt Lake City is next, and right now it's warmer than Denver, so that's something. Fingers crossed...

```
FACE: $115
PAID: $50
DISCOUNT: 57%
```

SALT LAKE CITY: FEBRUARY 13, 2011

SUNS 95
JAZZ 83
ATTENDANCE: 19,911 (sellout)

I'm about to write one painful chapter.

Maybe I've been getting too confident, borderline cocky. Well, the Salt Lake City scalpers were not having any of my swagger.

I should have suspected when I saw almost no tickets available online for last night's game. There were only three listings on StubHub, which is unheard of. It's normally in the dozens. Two in the lower level were going for $180 each, but that was it. Craigslist wasn't offering much quality either.

The dryness of the online market may have had something to do with a shocking news announcement the day before. Jerry Sloan, the longest-tenured coach in the NBA, had suddenly resigned from the Jazz. After twenty-three successful years of serving a loyal fan base, the news in Utah must have been hard to take. Perhaps the buzz created more demand. Or maybe the Mormon community really loves the Jazz, and going to a game on a Friday night is the thing to do.

The street trade was in full force, just like everywhere else. Only this time, there was a distinct feeling of collusion in the air. All the scalpers seemed to work in tandem, understanding what pricing was for each section and not budging under the agreed floor. It was like American Airlines and Delta in the 1990s. In all my years, I'd never really seen activity like this.

I can understand why this works here and not in most other cities. For starters, the Jazz *are* hugely popular. Most games in the colossal twenty-thousand-seat arena are sellouts, leaving the aftermarket as the only option for casual fans or out-of-towners. And—just like Memphis, Orlando, and Oklahoma City—the NBA represents the only professional sports outlet in town. Unlike the other cities, however, the Jazz have been entrenched in Utah since moving from New Orleans in 1979, and were once half owned by Adnan Khashoggi.[36]

At any rate, I showed up at Energy Solutions Arena fifteen minutes before tipoff, taking the free tram through a charming but freezing Salt Lake City (apologies for going on about the cold; I'm off to Phoenix next). I piled on five full layers but still felt underdressed compared to the scalpers in their skiwear.

As usual, I asked around for a ticket in the lower tier's center, but there were none available. Scalpers were also not willing to split up any pairs, so I was stuck with what little inventory was left. I offered $20 for a corner seat ten rows up, but was refused. Another corner eighteen rows up was offered for the face value of $80, but I was not interested, preferring to wait it out for a good spare ticket to show up.

I went from one street corner to another asking around, but scalpers were either holding groups of tickets or upper-bowl seats for $30.

---

36   In July 1984, Khashoggi paid $8 million for a 50 percent interest in the team ("A Saudi Digs the Jazz in Utah" (*Time*, July 9, 1984)).

A season ticketholder offered me his $35 upper seat for $10, but I was still hoping to stick it out. He ended up selling it to a scalper.[37]

Twenty minutes rolled by. The game had already started, and I was still out there (a first on this trip). But instead of the market drying up, a lot more people without tickets were showing up, and they were willing to spend. I was stumped and getting very cold. Again, I bounced around all the scalpers. The guy with the corner seat for $80 was not willing to part with it for anything less (I offered $40 but would have gone up). "The game started already," I pleaded.

"Oh, I'll get rid of it; people keep coming 'till halftime," he countered.

I couldn't believe it. My pride was getting in the way, but shivering after thirty-five minutes in the cold, I was happy to take a cheap seat in the upper deck. A guy who looked like a taller Scott Caan offered me an upper-bowl second-row ticket for $30 (face $35). I offered $20. He switched that ticket for another upper on the thirteenth row (seven rows down from the absolute worst seat in the house), offering it for $20. Desperate to be relieved of this mess of a situation and get some warmth, I grabbed it out of his hand, passed him the cash, and dashed in. When I got close to the turnstile I looked at the ticket and felt my stomach turn.

The face value said $17.

It was a strange sensation—one of crushed pride, anger, bitterness, and regret. Regret for breaking my cardinal rule and not reading the face value before making the swap. Yes, I paid a grand total of $3 over face, and with ticket-agent fees it was probably a breakeven, but that's not how I roll.[38] The Salt Lake City street crew foiled me, and I have to come clean.

---

37   I totally should have taken it.

38   On the Jazz ticketing website, for a $17 ticket they charge a facility fee of $2, a convenience fee of $4.75, and finally an order-processing fee of $5.

My cab driver confirmed their cartel tactics. "I've seen guys actually eat the ticket and refuse to sell instead of going under their price," he explained. A big Lakers fan, he tried to roll in late to get a deal when they were in town but got nowhere. "I just couldn't afford it, and they weren't willing to budge."

The game itself provided an intriguing matchup. Steve Nash, the Canadian point guard and former two-time MVP going up against Deron Williams, the Jazz guard accused of plotting against aforementioned coach Jerry Sloan.[39] The Suns also boasted two aging players who were once marquee names, Vince Carter (still my all-time favorite dunker) and Grant Hill (an injury-prone former All-Star who made $93 million over seven seasons in Orlando while playing in just two hundred games).

But once I sat down, I lost my appetite for the game. I hadn't been in a seat that awful in many years. The arena is huge and old (built in 1991, it doesn't even provide escalators to go up to those nosebleeds), and my seat was placed right in the middle of a pack of Junior Jazz. I don't know whether those seven-year-old kids were part of a youth basketball team, but they sure liked to kick the back of my seat and yell at each other. Maybe they were a youth soccer team. But really, who could blame them for taking out their aggression on the seats? From that spot, we were watching ten ants running around, so following the game was not much of an option.

The Jazz do have the most kid-friendly arena I've seen thus far. I saw more children under twelve last night than I have at any NBA game. I also saw more white people than I had at any NBA game.

Being in Utah, it really shouldn't have been that surprising. I saw two African Americans walking around the concessions area (three if

39   The Jazz organization's revenge on Williams was to trade him to the lowly Nets for Devin Harris. Williams sulked his way through a season and a half in New Jersey before re-signing with the Nets to spearhead their new campaign in Brooklyn. He's since indicated Dwight Howard duped him into thinking he would be joining him, but that didn't materialize. That old saying about karma and bitches…

you include a promotional appearance by Karl Malone, the legendary Utah forward who Kobe Bryant once accused of hitting on his wife), and two of the scalpers appeared Latino. But that was it. I didn't feel awkward, but living in London and being a frequenter of New York, LA, and other melting pots, I wasn't used to the homogeny.

By the end of the third quarter, the game was still close, but it was running late (10:00 p.m.), and I was hungry. That was enough of an excuse to bail and head to a sports bar for dinner. My view became a lot better, obviously, and the Suns closed out a win—a tiny moral victory for me.

One more point: All I'd heard about Utah was that arcane rules on drinking still exist. From what I got out of the cabbie, you can drink normally in restaurants and bars, but grocery stores only offer low-alcohol-content beers (3.25 percent), and wine or liquor must be purchased from official state alcohol shops.

As a visitor, though, you don't feel the effect. There are two big microbreweries outside my hotel, and even the arena offered pale ale along with the normal slew of domestic beers. Good thing, because I needed a drink after that experience.

On to Phoenix.

FACE: $17
PAID: $20
PREMIUM: 17%

PHOENIX: FEBRUARY 16, 2011

```
KINGS 113
SUNS 108
ATTENDANCE: 17,798
CAPACITY: 18,422
```

Nothing beats racing down an American highway in a muscle car belting out classic rock. That's one of my great indulgences in life. So when the opportunity of two spare days in Arizona presented itself, I jumped at the chance to rent a Mustang, connect my "cruising music" iPod, and put the pedal to the metal.

My destination: Sedona, home of the red rocks. The drive down Highway 17 is mind-blowing. Two hours (well, one and a half if you're going as fast as I was) of some of the most scenic road views you'll ever see. I've always been more of an ocean person when it comes to long drives. Cruising up the coast (like Highway 1) offers a can't-lose escape from reality, but driving through the Arizona desert, with all its peaks and intense colors, is something else entirely. I get the whole spiritual retreat to the sands now.

The crowning jewel of the journey was spotting the Chapel of the Holy Cross on a cliff rising in between the red rocks. Just as the sun was setting, I hiked up to the top of the hill. I could hear singing and realized a service was in progress. What luck. I took it all in while in the midst of the awesome sandstone. Glorious stuff.

Oh, and if you ever do make it to Sedona, have dinner at the Barking Frog and try the local Arizona Stronghold wine. Yes, I was skeptical too, but it went down very nicely.

Rewinding the tape, I started out this Phoenix leg frantically searching for tickets to the game Sunday night. Unlike Utah, there were some options in the online secondary market. Although StubHub wasn't offering much, Craigslist showed a few season ticketholders dumping their tickets at the last minute.

I found a guy selling two front-row seats in the center. Or so I thought. I quickly bargained him down to $220 for the pair, but when it came time to exchange, he said he only accepted PayPal and to send the money to ezticketz@yahoo.com. Hmm...my filter on Craigslist specified ticketholders only, not agents, so the dodgy Yahoo account rang alarms. (What's with the overuse of Zs? Was he a former member of NWA?) I asked to speak to the guy before making the deal, just to gauge how shifty he was. His reply: "Won't have my phone till 5:00 p.m."

Needless to say, I told him to forget it. He actually had the guts to ask me to just send him half the money first. Ha. Be very wary of people wanting to email you their e-tickets in exchange for a PayPal transaction. Face to face is always the way to go.

Undaunted, I continued combing the classifieds and found a guy selling four tickets on the eighteenth row, center. "$100 tickets, make me an offer" read the ad. After a brief phone exchange (funny, he had his on him), we settled on $150 for two tickets and a parking pass thrown in (worth $10). All in all, a savings of 32 percent, including both $4.75 service fees.

When we met at the Mexican place where I ate lunch, he confessed that the tickets were freebies from work. Never underestimate people's greed to cash in on free stuff; it just presents more opportunity for bargains.

And guess what? It was *Star Wars* night at the US Airways Center! I never figured out why it was *Star Wars* night, but it was definitely a popular theme. Fans dressed up as their favorite characters, Darth Vader conducted quizzes and gave out prizes, and even the Suns' mascot, the Gorilla, got in on the act. Perhaps the most famous mascot in American sports, he was sporting an Obi Wan Kenobi costume while dunking off a trampoline. A guy in a gorilla suit wearing a *Star Wars* costume. Yup, I'm not making this up.

The game was tight; lead changes went back and forth, but the Suns just don't play much defense. And without Amar'e Stoudemire, they don't rebound anymore either.[40] It seemed like Sacramento, the worst team in the Western Conference, was able to dominate on the offensive boards. Marcin Gortat and Channing Fry looked good offensively, but they're lacking in defensive prowess, despite the fact that Gortat is nicknamed the Polish Hammer and is one of the scariest-looking players in the league.

Meanwhile, Vince Carter was benched for the entire fourth quarter again. Good thing he's only making $17.5 million this season. You read that correctly, $17.5 million, and he only played fifteen minutes. According to my calculator, that's $216,000 per game or $14,400 per

---

40   Amar'e, the Sun's dynamic All-Star, had been let go by owner Robert Sarver in a salary-cap dump during the off-season. The Knicks picked him up, and he averaged twenty-five points, eight rebounds, and two blocks per game in 2010–2011 while shooting 50 percent from the field and 80 percent from the free-throw line.

In other news, the active Facebook group "Robert Sarver, Stop Destroying the Phoenix Suns" has 738 likes.

minute Sunday night. Hey, it was God's day of rest after all, so a little extra pay was in order.

By the beginning of the fourth quarter Steve Nash was given a four-minute breather, and that was enough for the Kings, who never relinquished their lead. At thirty-seven, Nash needs periodic rest during games, or else his production declines rapidly.[41] The Suns have no adequate replacement, and that's going to be a problem for them as the season drags on. They're battling for the final playoff spot in the West, but I doubt they'll get there.[42]

Nash, incidentally, just left his Paraguayan wife, announcing his decision on the day after she gave birth to his son. Nice. Before that, Nash would have been a lock for an all-goody-two-shoes team in the NBA. Who knows what went on, but really, the day after she gives birth? They also have a pair of twins. I can see the *US Weekly* spread: "NBA Stars, They Can Be Sleazebags Just Like Us!"

As far as arenas go, the Suns' is very sleek, not quite like Atlanta's, but the purple chairs and festive common areas gave it an uplifting vibe. Full bars were plentiful as well, with Grey Goose mixes going for $7.50 and domestic beers at $9.

On to Houston.

```
FACE: $104.75
PAID: $75
DISCOUNT: 28%
```

---

41   After turning thirty-eight, Nash joined the Lakers in the fall of 2012 looking like an even bigger defensive liability.

42   They didn't.

HOUSTON: FEBRUARY 19, 2011

```
SIXERS 114
ROCKETS 105
ATTENDANCE: 14,476
CAPACITY: 18,043
```

I made a friend last night. His name is Richard. Richard is the resident fixer to the scalpers around the Toyota Center, a sort of middleman who procures what you're after and takes a slice of the pie. I met Richard while wandering around fifteen minutes before game time, looking for the street trade.

To paint the scene accurately, I have to begin with the decibel-busting squawking around the arena. Once I opened the cab door, I heard a deafening sound, which I assumed was artificial noise pumped onto the sidewalks as a gimmick. I looked up and saw dozens—check that—hundreds of flying creatures swarming from tree to tree, gawking in crazed, high pitches. I guessed that they were bats by the pace at which they were gliding and their pitch-black glare, but I soon discovered they were actually birds. What type of birds I'm not sure of, but they were black, loud, and angry. Kind of like Public Enemy in its heyday.[43]

Thus began the Hitchcockian setting for my evening. Walking across the street from the angry bird-fest, I found Richard, who naturally asked me if I was selling any tickets. That's always how it starts since scalpers are not supposed to solicit anything. So by way of asking, it's an implicit sign that they are also selling. And my standard answer by now is, "No, I'm looking myself."

And then it's a "let the games begin" moment. Questions are asked. Phone calls are made. Sidewalks are crossed, all in search of the perfect seat, or at least one that's close enough to what I'm after. During the proceedings, I had time to chitchat with Richard, who in all fairness looked two degrees removed from being a crackhead. If it weren't for the fact that he had a functioning cell phone, I would have suspected as much. But for better or for worse, it became apparent that Richard would be the guy who would get me my ticket for that night's game. He called all his buddies, asking if they had any lower-tier seats.[44] One said yes, and we went to the designated meeting point, but he wasn't there. So we walked to the other side of the block, where he paraded me around to other scalpers like JonBenét Ramsey's mom did before the kid was found dead in the basement, yelling, "He's looking for a lower! You got any?"[45]

In the meantime, I asked Richard whether the cops give him any hassle. He said they often fine him, but that it was part of the job.

---

43 A local told me they call those birds Grackles, saying that along with being annoying and loud, they crap everywhere for good measure.

44 It seemed clear that Richard approached me "dryly," meaning he was looking for a buyer without holding any stock, simply to get a cut. The practice is well-documented in an April 7, 1997, *Sports Illustrated* article by Tim Layden called, "The Hustle."

45 JonBenét Ramsey was a child beauty queen who was found dead in her parent's basement in Colorado in 1996. Is this a dated reference? Maybe. Tough. I felt like JonBenét Ramsey that night.

"What sort of fines are we talking about?" I asked.

"Oh, $185," he answered, as a woman peddling a sponsored tuck-tuck waved and said, "Hi, Richard!"

"Wow, that's a lot of money. How many times do you get fined?"

"Three times in the last month, and probably ten times this season so far," he said.

"What? That's $1,850. C'mon, that's crazy."

"Oh yeah," he shot back. "It's a lot, but we make a lot out here. I've been doing this twelve years, and believe me if I had known about this twenty years ago, I'd be up with the big guys now. It's good money."

Hmmm. This sounded kind of like the ice-cream van outside my office in London. Every day it parks illegally, gets two to three tickets and a slap on the wrist, but the money for selling that swirly to tourists who don't know the exchange rate more than makes up for the fines. In both cases I wonder if they bother to pay those citations anyway.

Back outside the Toyota Center, beside a well-lit outdoor court, we find a young scalper who's got two lowers, one in the corner and one behind the basket. I knock him down to $40 for the corner sixteen rows up, but there's a big elephant in the room. Richard. One of us, either me or the scalper, has the onus of paying Richard's fee, and since I supposedly knocked this guy down so much, he wanted the burden to fall on me.

As we were now buddies, I relented and agreed to sort Richard out. Of course, I had nothing smaller than a $10 bill on me, and he wasn't about to give back any change. So after hugging it out, $50 it was, for a corner seat to a game between two mediocre teams in an arena that was nowhere near sold out. I'm not going to pretend like that was a great deal, nor do I have the benefit of a face value on the ticket to know exactly how to measure it. For the first time in memory, I bought a ticket that had no price on it. Not even a "Price $0" sign. Nothing.

But going by the team's website (which was selling a first-row center seat behind the scorer's table for $285 an hour before the game), it was worth $60 (plus another $8.25 in fees). But even though I technically saved 28 percent off the face value, I still paid way too much. Maybe NBA games have become a quotidian ritual for me, but I would argue that watching a good movie on a huge screen for $15 would have offered more value than watching the Rockets and the 76ers last night.

Once inside, though, I grabbed my customary light beer ($8.25) and sat on my two-hour rental seat. By the end of the first quarter, the place was solidly half empty, so I moved down six rows and had a very good view of a fairly competitive game. To my right, twenty rows behind the basket, was the Rockets' designated cheering section. The Red Rowdies are a pack of crazies with horns, drums, tambourines, and other distracting objects all dressed in some fashion of red. My favorite was the guy in a red jumpsuit and Mexican wrestler mask with a bolt of red lightning across it.

It does say a lot about the Rockets, however, that they can section off ten rows in the lower tier for a cheering squad. Once they traded Tracy McGrady and lost Yao Ming, their seven-foot, six-inch Chinese center, to yet another foot injury, the team's marketability completely evaporated. Remaining are Luis Scola, a giant Argentinean who looks like a reject from *Conan the Barbarian*, and Kyle Lowry, an undersized, scrappy player who had the game of his life. Lowry ducked and dived on the way to a career-high thirty-six points.

But that wasn't nearly enough. The 76ers were a superior team, more athletic and talented, and pulled away for an easy ten-point victory. Walking away from the center, looking for a place to get a bite in downtown Houston at 10:00 p.m., I felt a weird mixture of accomplishment and lament. There was a good reason for this.

To complete this frantic series of ten games in twenty days, I had to forgo my tickets to the biggest soccer game of the year in London: Arsenal, the team I have supported fervently for over a decade, versus Barcelona, widely anointed as the best team ever assembled. Not only was I thousands of miles from the match, but I was also flying to Houston just minutes after kickoff. Naturally, the Southwest flight did not offer Wi-Fi or any kind of connectivity to the outside world, so I had no way of following the score.

As it turned out, Arsenal pulled off a stunning upset in the last twenty minutes, coming back from a 1–0 deficit. To cap things off, the winning goal was celebrated inches away from my seats. Kill me with a corkscrew.

On the one hand, I felt like a sheepish whore for selling my tickets to what's already been hailed as the greatest victory for Arsenal in the past fifteen years, but on the other hand, I have to pat myself on the back for the determination to finish off this streak, which was planned months before I knew about that matchup.

Stepping back and taking stock of this, though, I'm sure people must wonder what the hell I'm doing—going around following overgrown men bouncing balls, and flying back to watch undersized men kicking balls. Why bother? They're all just overhyped kids' games, right? Heck, on the flight back to London (always a good time to ponder the meaning of life), I wonder the same thing.

But I already know the answer. It's way more than bouncing balls. It's about dedication, sacrifice, team play, competition, upholding the spirit of the games, and the artistry that goes on between two goal posts. From a fan's perspective, I have great admiration for these aspects of sports; even a Vince Carter, who's making his oodles of millions and is often criticized for not giving it his all, has put in thousands of hours toward honing his skills and keeping his body in peak shape to be at the very pinnacle of his sport. Being close to that level of performance when everything is clicking is a thrill and an addiction that I'm certainly not ashamed of.

On to London.

```
FACE: $60
PAID: $50
DISCOUNT: 17%
```

PART THREE

LONDON: MARCH 4, 2011

NETS 116
RAPTORS 103
ATTENDANCE: 18,689 (sellout)

"I am such a fucking moron."

Those were my exact words to the girl whom I sprayed a Diet Coke on at Friday night's game. I'd like to say it wasn't my fault, but it was entirely my fault. I was trying to balance one of those stupid cardboard trays with two plastic cups filled with ice, two bottles of soda, and a bag of chips thrown in the middle. As I squeezed to get to my seat, one of the Diet Coke bottles slipped, torpedoed to the floor, and detonated a fizzy shower all over the poor woman and me.

It was one of those slow-motion situations where you can't do anything but watch and hope. And then, for a split second before you face the music, you pray that your victim has a sense of humor. Mercifully she laughed it off. Still, is there any possible way to feel like more of an ass in public?

"How bad did you get her?" asked Nat, the Raptors diehard fan and über blogger to whom I owe a big thanks for the awesome seat.[46]

"Bad. All over her," I answered, drying my hair and cleaning my sticky eyelashes.

"Yeah, she's wiping off her shoes," Nat told me.

Urgh. Once the halftime buzzer sounded, I ran around the concourse looking for a Raptors t-shirt as a gesture of goodwill for this woman who, as it turned out, was on a date. The £20 for the souvenir served me well; we exchanged pleasantries, and she thanked me. I was off the hook—or just enough to focus back on the game.[47]

In the interest of full disclosure, I'd been suffering through a shocking hangover all day. The kind where you can't pay for anything in cash because counting change is like solving the quadratic equation.

The night before I'd been to a glam birthday party, where copious amounts of champagne had been consumed. I lost count after ten glasses. So, battling sickness, I came home from work early and tried to nap. Can anyone else verify that jackhammer drilling outside your apartment only takes place when you're trying to sleep off a hangover? So much fun, right?

No matter, I had to shake it off. There was a big game to gear up for: the first-ever NBA regular-season matchup held outside North America. So even though the weekend double-header pitted two struggling teams against each other, the games were a huge deal.

Tickets were not quite sold out for the Friday night game, but they were completely gone for Saturday's matchup (surprisingly, both were home games sacrificed by the New Jersey Nets, a sign that they can't fill their arena, and that the Toronto Raptors can). I dragged my lifelong buddy Damon to the game, eager to see what kind of deal we could fetch on the streets of Greenwich.

---

46   Check her out on @nat77

47   At the time of writing the exchange rate was $1.59 to £1, making that a $32 apology.

What we didn't realize is that the O2 has a zero-tolerance policy toward scalpers, or touts as they call them in England. There was not a single one around. We checked all over, near the tube station, outside the massive Millennium Dome, and inside of it where the O2 sits. Absolutely nothing.

I bumped into six young Americans who were also banking on scalpers and desperate for seats. For a second they looked at me like I was their savior, but then recoiled once I asked them if they had a spare.

There were still tickets on sale at the box office, but the line was long, and by the time it was Damon's turn, all 18,689 seats were gone. It was officially a sellout.

This business of banning scalpers is a first for me. I've been to concerts and sporting events all around the world, and there's always someone outside working the aftermarket. English scalpers are particularly resilient, so the fact that the O2 successfully drove them away must mean they have a legal right they can uphold. There were security guys lurking about with flashlights, and I've read online that scalpers get arrested on the spot.[48]

But I was lucky. Nat had planned early (a new concept for me). A season ticketholder, she'd flown in all the way from Toronto. Our seats were row A, just beyond press row and behind the basket. The face value said £40 plus a £4 service charge, which sounded low since the nosebleeds were going for £55. Most of the lower-tier seats were going for over £100. Fans flying in from North America, it seemed, were given a hefty break on ticket prices for the matchup.

There was really only one marquee player on the floor Friday night: Deron Williams. Yes, the same Deron Williams who supposedly drove Jerry Sloan out of town in Utah after twenty-five years of service. Williams had been in London in the preseason with Utah, and

---

48   Police were on full alert for scalpers all over London that weekend in a practice run to curb the street trade for the Summer Olympics in 2012. The following week the UK Home Office announced a £20,000 fine for all "touts" selling Olympics tickets ("London Olympics 2012 Ticket Touts Face £20,000 Fine" (bbc.co.uk), March 10, 2011).

he learned about this trip soon after his surprise trade last week. He is built like a small SUV—top-heavy and bulky, but with great handle. At one point he put a fake on Raptors' guard Sonny Weems that left him sprawled out on the floor.

Although the Raptors boast players from Spain, France, and Italy, the crowd was probably more familiar with the Nets' Kris Humphries, the latest squeeze of Kim Kardashian.[49] Alas, Kim was not in the house last night, as far as we knew.

However, many of the gimmicks used in NBA games did make the trip, including the kiss-cam, the ubiquitous "everybody clap your hands" Busta Rhymes sound bite, the cheerleaders, and the mascots. But certain Briticisms also crept into the game, like the "Mexican wave," as they call it in the United Kingdom.

Another local treat: long lines at the concession stands. Whereas in the United States, cashiers are generally taught to move the line quickly and speed up service, the staff at the O2 operates in slow-mo. The crappy service triggered what I like to call my own version of Tourette syndrome. It's what often happens when I'm hungover, tired, and impatient on a line that's not moving. I flail and curse at no one in particular, like an old bag lady. Not good.

Toward the end of the game, Brook Lopez, the Nets' seven-footer, got tangled up in a messy altercation with Amir Johnson, a rugged defender from Los Angeles. Unlike most NBA shoving matches, this one looked like it could break out into a real fight, and for two seconds the arena held its breath. I could feel NBA commissioner David Stern's heart pumping from my seat. Could there be any potentially worse situation for the league than to see a big fight break out on the court at the inaugural international NBA game?

But cooler heads prevailed, and Lopez had to be looked at for a long scratch down the side of his arm. During a break in the action, Raptors superfan Nav Bhatia bolted out of his courtside seat to talk trash to

---

49 We know how that went. The courtship became the precursor to the most famous seventy-two days in reality television history.

Deron. Bhatia spends $80,000 per year on season tickets and attends every home game. The president of a Toronto Hyundai dealership, he's constantly in the opposition's ear, to the point where he's been dubbed, "The Turbanator."

Alas, the superfan's work was not finished Friday night, as Deron pulled out his first win in a Nets uniform. But there is no doubt that on Saturday night, during the Raptors' triple-overtime loss, the Turbanator was back.

FACE VALUE: £44 (invited)

NEWARK: MARCH 17, 2011

That's Sully's beer in the foreground.

```
BULLS 84
NETS 73
ATTENDANCE: 18,351
CAPACITY: 18,711
```

Kicking off my second trip, I'd flown in from London just in time to catch the Nets-Bulls matchup, which was tipping off at an early 7:00

p.m. timeslot Thursday night. Rushing, I headed to the game with two of my oldest friends in the world, Sully and Sylvester. We've known each other since preschool, at age four. That was fitting since this expedition started off with a male-bonding road trip to Newark, New Jersey.

After thirty years of wallowing at a listless arena in the Meadowlands, the Nets' Russian billionaire owner Mikhail Prokhorov decided to move the team into Newark's Prudential Center, a full ten miles farther out from New York, before their big move to Brooklyn in 2012. But ten miles on a weekday at 6:00 p.m. spells an extra forty minutes of driving, and we ended up missing the entire first quarter.

We were annoyed, and that's not how you want to arrive at an NBA game—especially if you're shelling out for floor seats. Sully's a lifelong Manhattanite who, like me, just cannot support the Knicks (the reasons are too many to list). So for better or for worse, we're Nets fans. And one of Sully's vices is to subscribe to a half-season package of courtside seats.

Ahh, courtside. The best analogy I can find to sitting courtside after a lifetime of sitting everywhere else is that it's like flying on a Gulfstream after thinking business class was the pinnacle of air travel. You almost shouldn't do it, because sitting back where you used to loses its luster fast.

Tonight we've got what the Nets call "Hollywood AAA" tickets, meaning they are not only floor seats, but positioned elbow to elbow with the opposing players' bench. Ever watch those clips where you hear what coaches say to players in timeouts? Imagine that the entire game, with no bleeps.

Jay-Z isn't in the house tonight, but he and Beyonce have the same tickets as Sully, only on the Nets side of the court. I'm guessing since he owns somewhere between 1.5 and .15 percent of the team (Jay-Z disputes the lower figure) that he gets his on the house.[50]

---

50   In April 2013, it was announced that Jay-Z was exiting his ownership stake in the Nets in order to qualify as an NBA agent.

Sully hands me my ticket, and I can't help but notice the face value: $2,170. Yes, the same price of a banged-up Toyota to watch a subpar NBA team defend itself in March. Granted, these are the best seats in the house. Sully is sitting elbow to elbow with Luol Deng, but really, why drop over $4k on a pair of seats to watch the Nets play in Newark?

"Yeah, they're expensive, but I like hearing the players talk shit; it's a highlight. You can also hear them complaining to the coaches and refs…and you always hear them make fun of the Nets," he tells me. "You don't get that experience in the $20 seats."

There's no arguing with that. There are certain experiences you just can't put a price on. It's also true that the Nets VIP personnel know how to treat their clientele. In the spring of 2010 they flew Sully out on the team's private plane—along with the players—to watch the Nets take on the Cavs (who were a hot ticket with LeBron), all on the house. They did something similar for other courtsiders when the team made a trip to China to play exhibition games later that year (though Sully was not invited; he thinks it's because he offered too much "constructive criticism" to Nets staffers).

Indeed, that same night, the Nets comped Sully an extra courtside seat for Sylvester, worth another $500 (cheaper because it was on the baseline behind the basket). It was a nice touch.

On the other hand, browsing through StubHub, I found courtside seats for $800 a pop (not the "Hollywood AAA" seats Sully favors beside the team's bench, but ones that are directly on the other side of the court). On Ticketmaster, the same seats were listed for $1,600 each, including fees. Taking into account StubHub's surcharges, you're still looking at 45 percent off. Even Filene's Basement couldn't match that (well, maybe they could make those kinds of deals…but that's how the company went bust).

There's no other way to say this about first-year Bulls coach Tom Thibodeau, but he's one annoying blowhard. I've never seen a coach who barks commands at his players multiple times during every single possession. At one point *in the middle of a possession,* he yelled at one of his guards to pass the ball to a specific player. This was like watching your buddy play *NBA Live*, only with real players on the court instead of their avatars. If he doesn't have a heart attack before his fifth season in the league, I'll be shocked.

To be clear, Thibodeau can coach, and he was even praised by Bulls fan Barack Obama for reaching the top of the Eastern Conference.[51] But if he sticks to his niggling ways, he's risking getting tuned out by Derrick Rose. If the MVP candidate decides he's heard enough, Thibodeau's days in Chicago could be short-lived.

But back to courtside. From our seats we could not only hear the players talking smack to one another (at one point Carlos Boozer, who was not even in uniform for the Bulls, yelled, "You can't play!" to Sasha Vujacic, to which Vujacic replied, "Well, you can't guard me"[52]), but you can also talk to the players yourself. Some are more social with the crowd than others. Brian Scalabrine, the ginger-haired permasub known as "White Mamba," would only smile and shake or nod his head when talked to, like a kid who didn't want to get in trouble with his teacher. Whereas Joakim Noah, the son of tennis great Yannick, fist-bumped Sully, who told him that we also went to the United Nations International School. How can you put a price on that?[53]

---

51   He would go on to win the Coach of the Year award in 2011.

52   Though Vujacic is one of the greatest overreachers in the history of celebrity couples (via his engagement to Maria Sharapova), he was right. If a guy like Boozer can't even stay healthy enough to get on the court, then he shouldn't be talking smack. Maybe it's something to do with Eastern European guys being easy targets, because even the mild-mannered Scalabrine got in on the act with a hilarious head-fake impersonation of Vujacic on the back of the exchange with Boozer. [Update: Sharapova and Vujacic broke up in the spring of 2012 while he was playing in Turkey. Though he was absent from her box at the French Open, Wimbledon, and the Olympics, their breakup was such an afterthought that no one bothered to ask her until the US Open in September.]

53   Sully's proudest moment as an interactive fan took place years ago at a Lakers-Knicks game in LA. Sitting courtside at the Staples Center, he yelled at Knicks guard Chris Childs to pass the ball. Childs promptly stopped dribbling, shot Sully a look and told him to "Shut the fuck up."

It was tempting to accidentally on purpose spill our drinks on the Bulls' horrid green uniforms in celebration of St. Patrick's Day. While he was trying to guard an inbounds pass, Kyle Korver told us they had to wear them for the next two games.

The game was surprisingly well attended (18,351, though that's probably bloated), considering it was a late-season game for the Nets, who are wallowing at the bottom of the Eastern Conference. Absent again was the aforementioned Kim Kardashian, although many in her entourage were there, like her reality show sidekick and PR guru Jonathan Cheban, along with rapper Bow Wow.

Though the Prudential Center seats fewer fans than the Izod Center (eighteen thousand versus twenty thousand), it's a newer, plusher facility. Luxury boxes were plentiful, and premium-seat holders enjoy access to a private bar and dining room with complimentary drinks and food (the sushi was surprisingly good).

In the second half, the Bulls clamped down on defense and pulled away for the win. Deron Williams's effectiveness was limited to only five points and eleven assists. Rose continues to impress in showdowns against the league's other elite guards, including Dwyane Wade (the best-dressed player in the NBA) and Rajon Rondo (a glitzy passer and floor leader with a subpar jump shot).

The only detriment to sitting so close to the action was that the ref blocked my view of the play of the night, a monstrous Rose slam. I had to replay it online later that night.

Outside, cop cars with flashing lights sectioned off the street in front of the Pru, as they do for every game. Newark is a city with a high crime rate and not much else of note, aside from its mammoth airport. Most people want to get out of there as soon as possible. A fall 2012 move to a lush complex in Brooklyn awaits, at which point everything about the Nets will be different.[54]

"They are going to be a lot better in Brooklyn," Sully tells me. "They definitely make an effort [with their VIP season ticketholders] and take very good care of them. But they had to try harder because of that fucked-up arena," he says, referring to the Izod Center in the Meadowlands.

The catch is that to move to the new gleaming facility known as the Barclays Center, they asked their courtside season ticketholders to pony up for the first three seasons in advance, according to Sully. By depositing10k in monthly installments starting in 2010, he would have dropped $660,000 on his pair of seats to secure them. "I thought that was offensive, considering they just broke the record for most losses," he said, pointing to their record-breaking 0–18 start in 2009.

Needless to say, he didn't take the Nets up on their offer.

On to D.C., where I get to watch the Nets for the third game in a row in two different countries.

FACE VALUE: $2,170 (Invited by season ticketholder; the team threw in a $500 third ticket for free)

---

54   Everything is different, especially Nets ticket prices, which have more than doubled since the move to Brooklyn. They went from the third cheapest in the league to the eighth most expensive at an average of $86 for the 2012–2013 season, according to secondary-ticket aggregator SeatGeek.

WASHINGTON D.C.: MARCH 20, 2011

For some NBA players, there's no better time to eye-
surf for babes than during the national anthem.

```
WIZARDS 98
NETS 92
ATTENDANCE: 17,761 (can't be true)
CAPACITY: 20,278
```

I could get used to floor seats. There's really no equivalent in other sports, sitting so close to the action that you're liable to get injured. Where else but in the NBA can you hear the bitching among players, coaches, and refs and have the chance to join in the conversation? Where else can your date get eyed up by a genuine NBA player?[55]

The closest comparison might be ringside in boxing, where you'll see Hollywood A-listers and corporate big shots littered around the first few rows. But those high-profile matchups, say a Manny Pacquiao and Oscar De La Hoya, happen maybe once every eighteen months. On any given night in Los Angeles, New York, or Miami, however, you can find the likes of Jack Nicholson, Madonna, Paris Hilton, Mark Wahlberg, Matt Damon, or Lil Wayne fist-bumping players on the sidelines. Yes, these personalities all express an allegiance to certain teams (or in the high-profile cases of some, the players), but the face time on camera also presents a seductive thrill. Celebs will show up to other sporting events, but not en masse and with the same regularity. For hedge-fund managers in New York and Boston, courtside offers prestige. While they compete for everything, from the latest Ferrari to the length of their yachts, sitting slightly closer to half court can provide a psychological boost.

In LA the enterprise is more commercial, where super-agent Ari Emmanuel (the same guy Ari in *Entourage* is based on) owns four seats alongside the Lakers' bench. He pays close to half a million dollars a year for the privilege, though hardly ever shows up himself. Instead, he passes them on to his high-profile clients to soak up free exposure before a movie opening.

During the finals in 2010, Phil Jackson told off a sideline reporter while she interviewed Chris Rock steps away from him. Maybe it's because he'd had enough of Rock trying to break the ice with Kobe

---

55   This actually happened to Rebecca during the singing of the National Anthem. One of the Wizards practically undressed her with his stare. Thinking about it, it really is the best time for the players to go eye cruising around the crowd for hotties.

Bryant during the game. Check out the YouTube clip of this; it's a must see.

But there's the glamorous courtside experience as well as the more pedestrian one, a la Washington D.C. The Wizards have sucked for so long it's a wonder they can get anyone to commit to paying $20 a seat, much less $1,000. The game at the Verizon Center tipped off early, at 1:00 p.m., and showcased two of the weakest teams in the NBA. To make matters worse, the only All-Star on either team, Deron Williams, was out with a sprained wrist. Adding competition to the mix, a bracket of the NCAA tournament was being held nearby at Georgetown University. And to top it all off, it was a gloriously sunny day. All these factors conspired on my side, working the premium tickets' prices like stocks on the Egyptian bourse in 2011.[56]

Scanning Craigslist and StubHub on Saturday evening, I found a few good deals on offer. Some seats in the front row of the lower bowl, both center and around the basket, for about 50 percent off. Still, there was no reason to jump the gun. In cases like this, the better seats you shoot for, the bigger the deal you're likely to rope in. So every hour I'd refresh Craigslist until I saw this listing:

"Two seats in Gold Section—VIP parking, VIP food, and courtside tickets. $300 for everything."

I fired off an email. Were the tix still available? Yes, they were.

Excellent, where exactly are they? Gold, North, AAA.

Indeed, they were first row on the floor. I offered $160 for the pair but got no response. Shoot, not good—maybe I pissed the guy off. I came back to him, saying if they were close to center court I could stretch myself. He said they were just off center, so I raised the offer to $200, told him that was my limit but that I had "cash in hand," and crossed my fingers.

---

56 Wizards tickets performed even worse than Egyptian stocks, which were down a relatively paltry 50 percent in 2011.

The response: "$200 for these seats is a steal, but as long as you have cash that is cool."[57]

Sweet, I'd just bagged $900 seats for $100 each! It was a total savings of $1,600, not including the onerous fees of $100 each on Ticketmaster. No matter when the game's played or what teams are involved, it's still a courtside center seat to an NBA game.

Once my friend Rebecca (a huge Cavs fan) and I sat down to watch the teams warm up, we knew we were in for a treat. A seventysomething waitress came and took our orders (food and drink complimentary), and sipping our light beers we grinned. It felt like we'd snuck into first class without the stewardess noticing.

The game turned out to be very tight. The Wizards went down by seventeen in the first half, only to come blazing back and tie the game. John Wall, the Wiz's lightning-quick rookie, was showing off his skills against a Nets understudy. Jordan Farmar, the league's only half African American, half Jewish player, had a solid game with ten points and seventeen assists, but he struggled to contain Wall's speed.[58] On the other end of the court, seven-foot slam-dunk contestant JaVale McGee went body to body with Nets center Brook Lopez.[59]

At halftime, we retreated to the Courtside Club, where a buffet and draft beers awaited us. The spread was decent, with a turkey carving, mac and cheese, and ice cream on offer, but the space itself was a dump. It was a roped-off section under the stands, near a collapsed

---

57   The mention of holding cash is an effective—yet entirely illogical—way to help your cause. Of course you're going to be holding cash. What's he going to take, traveler's checks?

58   Farmar, who is not religious, once ran a basketball camp in Israel where Israeli and Palestinian kids played on the same teams, a notable cause. In 2012 he signed a three year deal to play in Turkey.

59   McGee can do amazing things, like dunk three basketballs at once (a world record), but is generally recognized as the most boneheaded player in the NBA. There are over a million YouTube hits of various McGaffs, including him running the wrong way during a play and celebrating a triple-double with his team down by twenty points.

basket, a deflated gimmick rocket, and a forklift. This was nowhere near as nice as the wood-paneled room and sushi bar the Nets offer their VIPs.

The most frantic cheer of the day came during a break in the second half. Tin-foiled burritos were being thrown into the stands. It was like the Beatles were back on the *Ed Sullivan Show*. Even the guy next to us, who had access to free food and drink, was jumping out of his seat for one. Maybe they put Scooby Snacks in those things. Who knows?

John Wall took the game over in the last five minutes, finishing with twenty-six points as the Wiz pulled out a rare win. Back outside, the sun was still shining, and there was plenty of time to walk around and hit a downtown sports bar (The Redline) for some gourmet bar food and March Madness. Alas, Syracuse lost to Marquette in a thrilling upset. I wonder if those Syracuse players heading to the pros realize their careers may have just peaked. Alumni cheer for everything. Wizards fans prefer burritos.

On to New York for the Knicks-Celtics matchup tonight.

FACE: $900
PAID: $100
DISCOUNT: 89%

NEW YORK, MARCH 21, 2011

Only the Mecca of Basketball riding on those shoulders.

```
CELTICS 96
KNICKS 86
ATTENDANCE: 19,763 (sellout)
```

The Mecca of Basketball: That's what New Yorkers call Madison Square Garden. They also bill it as the World's Most Famous Arena. Both are technically not true; the Knicks have been abysmal for most of the past decade, while other arenas, including LA's Staples Center and London's O2, have probably eclipsed MSG in notoriety.

For this marquee matchup, however, the Mecca was in full pilgrimage mode. The city is still abuzz over the Carmelo Anthony trade, and the star-studded Celtics are their biggest traditional rivals.

All of this was evident way before tipoff. Walking into MSG involved twenty minutes of navigation through a scrum of thousands, something I hadn't seen there over a lifetime of attending everything from Ringling Brothers Circus shows, the Ice Capades, Big East tournaments, and Knicks playoff games. Without a doubt, this was the biggest buzz I'd seen at a New York basketball game live, even surpassing the heyday of Ewing and Starks.

This was strange and unexpected on a number of levels. The Knicks have been one of the worst-run franchises in all of team sports, making mistake after costly mistake for the past twelve years while charging some of the highest ticket prices in America. Yet sellouts are the norm, as actors, directors, rappers, and corporate bigwigs turn up in droves. That's the power of New York.

Shuffling in, I could see the scalper trade in full bloom and overheard an exchange where a third-bowl ticket was quoted for $100. Anything lower would have gone in the multiple hundreds or higher. I saw an older white guy ask, "How much to just get in and sit anywhere?" to a scalper, who just shook his head. StubHub's prices for courtside were going for $4,000, and I'd heard Spike Lee was offering $5,000 to get some more of his crew in. It's safe to say this was a night where discounts to face value were not on offer.

Once Knicks diehard Ganesh and I finally got inside, we parked ourselves into his courtside seats on the very far end by the baseline (huge thanks to Ganesh, who has been going to Knicks games for twenty years and aggressively worked his way up the season-ticket ladder four seasons ago). About ten seats to my right sat Lee (in full orange regalia) next to Ray Allen's mom (wearing a Celtics "Mom Allen" jersey).

Meanwhile, Donald Trump, aka "The Donald," was seated perpendicular to my left. True to form, he scowled the whole night (how many times was he dying to say, "You're fired" to the Knicks players?), and like his personality, his hair never wavered.

Before the game a waiter took our drink orders, and I was surprised to see there was a charge for concessions. How can Washington afford to offer its courtsiders free food and drinks while the Knicks—whose pricing is exactly double that of the Wizards—refuse to? The answer is that starting next season the generosity finally kicks in. The beer-and-nacho fairy will make its way down to courtside...after a nifty 60 percent price hike.

So even though the face value on my ticket showed a startling $1,900 it was, by definition, undervalued. It was undervalued in a sense that there were more people willing to pay $1,900 to buy the ticket than there were people willing to sell at that price. Ganesh knows this and has a pool of fellow courtside-seat holders' numbers that he can call on when he can't make a game. They never go unused. "On balance, the tickets are usually worth what we pay for them," he tells me. "The downside is limited." (Which is more than you can say for the stock of Cablevision, which is also majority owned by the Dolans.)

Executives at the Madison Square Garden Company are fully aware of the high demand for premium seats in New York, which is why they were confident enough to splash out $1 billion on a refurb. They figure if prices are at times going for double face value at courtside, they want a piece of that action, and they're going to use the money to improve their facility so that they can justify the increase to the fans. Makes perfect business sense.

As one disgruntled season ticketholder told the *New York Post*, "I could go to a basketball game and feed myself. I don't need a $1,200 meal." One assumes that for the extra charge, VIPs will finally have the ability to retreat to a private club with separate restrooms, unlike the current situation. I waited until most of halftime was over to climb up to the first level and line up with forty others. Is that really what Spike Lee or notorious germaphobe Donald Trump go through?

To be fair, the Garden is an archaic arena (forty-four years, second oldest in the NBA) and is in desperate need of a facelift. Knicks' parent MSG, now owned by public shareholders, has already laid out the first $800 million in its refurbishment plan. Its crux is to add new luxury suits, while beefing up existing ones, a few of which will go for well over $1 million a year (though they would include all MSG events, including hockey and concerts).

Presumably, part of the regeneration project is to upgrade the team too. Though it is far too early to judge the Carmelo trade, adding big names has not yet translated into big performances, and this game was no exception.

The first half started out well enough, with the STAT (Amar'e Stoudemire's nickname: Standing Tall and Talented) and Melo (Carmelo Anthony) show in full effect. They were passing back and forth while scoring at will. The Celtics seemed stuck in first gear, losing possessions as Rajon Rondo (their dazzling but mercurial point guard) and Ray Allen (the all-time three-point shooting leader) missed open shots. DJ Fatman Scoop spun tunes and hyped up the crowd while the Knicks went up by fifteen points.

But the Knicks are not a defensive team, and they were on a streak of five losses in six games against weak opposition. I turned to Ganesh and offered $5 that the Celtics would tie the game. I rarely bet on sports, so for me this was showing some conviction. True to form, the Knicks melted in the second half under a physical Celtics onslaught. Ray Allen suffered a bloodied head and later said that playing for the Celtics is sometimes like playing in the NFL.

Despite his shooting lapses, the best player on the floor was Rondo. He's one of those "one step ahead of everyone else" athletes, whizzing passes no one else on the floor could have dreamed of. The jaw-dropping moment was neither a score nor an assist, however. It came on a crucial possession the Celtics were about to lose; rather than let the ball go out of bounds, Rondo zipped from one sideline to the other, dived, and knocked the ball off a Knick. I could have sworn two seconds earlier he was on my side of the floor.

It was a startling display of quickness, and one that was best appreciated live. The difference between Rondo's speed and that of everyone else on the court gets watered down on TV. But Rondo still has some work to do to be considered one of the elites, namely developing a dependable jump shot. The obvious scouting report on him is to give him room to shoot. Once he makes defenders pay, however, he'll be blowing by them and dominating games from end to end.

Boston scored the final ten points of the game, and Knicks fans walked out quiet and dejected, facing the prospect of a quick first-round playoff series against this same Boston team.[60] How long Knicks fans will stay quiet remains to be seen. If the rumbling gets louder in the press and in the stands, the Carmelo situation could get ugly in a hurry.[61]

Ganesh is understandably annoyed at the Knicks' lack of mettle, and we cross the street over to Stout NYC for some drinks to cool off. "After a while you get tired of cheering for a team that's not going anywhere," he confides.

Will this change his view on splashing out so much money on tickets every season? Even with the big refurb coming?

"If you have premium drinks, who cares? If you have a nicer lounge, who cares? Fans want to pay for winning. Yes, there's always the option of getting cheaper seats or going a la cart..."

The conversation drifts off, and we order another round, along with some sweet potato fries. Ganesh will go on to renew his season tickets.

---

60   Boston swept the Knicks in the first round of the 2011 playoffs.

61   And it did, with the apex of anti-Melo sentiment forming during a seven-game February 2012 winning streak with Melo out and Jeremy Lin in. Suddenly, "team" was not a four-letter word in New York.

Of course he would. You can buy anything you want in New York, but hope…hope is free.

On to LA where the Clippers-Wizards game beckons on Wednesday.

FACE VALUE: $1,900 (invited by season ticketholder)

LOS ANGELES: MARCH 23, 2011

```
CLIPPERS 127
WIZARDS 119
ATTENDANCE: 19,060 (sellout)
```

Even though I grew up in New York, I have an open affinity for Los Angeles. The beaches, palm trees, gorgeous scenery, and perfect climate all suit me just fine.

What gets swept under the rug, however, is one unavoidable LA rite of passage: getting lost and winding up in the ghetto. Although the advent of GPS has curbed the frequency of these tense experiences, it hasn't eliminated it by any means. Without fail, during every visit to LA there's a point at which I think I'm heading to Beverly Hills, only to wind up on streets that are familiar only because of NWA lyrics. Crenshaw Boulevard and Slauson Avenue are two favorites.

Another rite of passage is getting stuck in ungodly traffic at the worst possible time. It's counterintuitive, but taking the freeway only makes things worse.[62] So when my friend Demetria picked me up at 7:00 p.m. from my Santa Monica hotel for a 7:30 p.m. tipoff in downtown LA, I figured we'd be fashionably late.

Demetria, a lifelong Angelino and former beat writer for the Lakers and Clippers, navigated us through the backstreets on the way to the Staples Center. An hour and fifteen minutes later, we crawled into a parking lot ($10) by the finest arena in the NBA I've seen. The area surrounding the Staples Center has come a long way since I attended the 2008 finals. Back then it was a construction site. Nearly three years later, and it's a booming playground, complete with two five-star hotels and a half dozen giant restaurant/bars.

But we had no time for pregame drinks or a wander around. The first quarter was already over, yet we were ticketless and relying on whatever spare inventory was left on the streets. It's good to get to a game close to tipoff or slightly after to pick up last-minute deals, but if you're one of the last people to arrive, you run the risk of all the decent seats selling out.

While Demetria changed from her flats to high-heeled boots, I struck up a conversation with one of only two scalpers still lingering. I told him I was looking for a pair of lowers, and he asked how much I wanted to spend. He was talking to a college-age white girl who I thought was also looking. It turned out the tickets were hers, and she wanted to unload them at $30 each (face value was $70, excluding fees). They were in a corner, so not ideal, but they were the best seats on offer. I countered with $50 for a pair, arguing the game had started

---

62   I've learned to ignore the sat nav at rush hour, or turn the settings to "avoid highways." Otherwise, you're on the 405 for a half hour just to move a mile.

long ago. Amazingly, she wouldn't budge. "I have too much pride," she told me. "These are my seats, and they're good. I'll wait."

"But there's no one else here," I explained. "You're not going to sell them."

"Then I'll keep them. I just can't sell them for $25 each."

Wow, pride's a strange thing. It'll get in the way of a sure $50 sometimes. And after all the cities I'd been to, and all the ex-cons and goons I'd had to deal with to get premium seating, I'd never really run across pride in this way. No one selling actually feels like he or she owns the tickets; it's purely business. They either just bought them from someone who had spares, or they got them from a big-ticket broker looking to recoup some capital.

And that's how this fresh-faced nineteen-year-old had me in a corner. I had no way of appealing to her business acumen when emotions were involved. To my credit, I quickly realized this and plucked down $60 for the pair. It was still a big savings, though we'd missed out on most of the first half.

The seats turned out to be pretty good. Unlike center seats, corner lowers are available as spares for most games. They're always at a big discount compared to centers, for obvious reasons, but I don't mind them so much anymore. The views are not that bad, and you're still close to the action; for the discounts they're worth it.

This was my first opportunity to watch Blake Griffin perform live. I say perform because what he does is truly a performance, and you don't have to like basketball to appreciate it. Last month Griffin made headlines for bunny-hopping a car on the way to winning the slam-dunk title.[63] On this night we weren't privy to anything quite as

---

63   He jumped over the bonnet of a Kia. There are probably dozens of NBA players who can do that. But it's Blake Griffin, so the dunk is more thunderous, explosive, and cooler than if anyone else tried it. Personally, I think Javale McGee got screwed out of the slam-dunk title because dunking two balls on two rims *at the same time* is a much more original and difficult task. But All-Star weekend 2011 was in Los Angeles, and there was no way a local player was not going to take that trophy.

spectacular, though every time he touched the ball there was a hushed sense of electricity that ran through the crowd.

It should be explained that the LA Clippers are one of the sorriest franchises in the league, with only four playoff berths in twenty-seven years since moving to LA. Before Griffin, attendance was poor. Now, not only are most home games sellouts, but they are also sold out *on the road*. That's one mean feat, and I can't really think of anyone on a losing team who could draw that kind of crowd since Michael Jordan sprang into the league in 1984. Maybe LeBron James, but I doubt that even he had this kind of pull as a rookie.

At halftime, we walked around the concourse looking for a snack. This is the only arena in the NBA shared by two teams, and everything—all the merchandise in the gift shops and the banners around the court—has to be changed as soon as the games are over. We noticed a McDonald's, which is the first I'd seen in an arena, though the prices were double what they charge outside. Other concessions on offer were sushi (though arena sushi is usually a bad idea) and a fantastic roast carving station that I'd tried before (though that's only accessible on the club level in the second tier). We settled on a bag of organic caramel popcorn to tide us over until dinner.

I was also thirsty and asked a soft-drink vendor if he had any water. He'd sold out, but—out of nowhere—a man with a really grimy Lakers string bag full of Dasani bottles overheard and flashed me his stash.

"$5," he said.

"What?"

"Ok, $4."

"Huh? Are these legit?"

"No, I got 'em for free. But at least I'm being honest. Ok, $3."

As I handed over the $3 (normal price $4.25), he opened up the satchel bursting with chocolate bars and popcorn. He even had a candied apple. It was weird. Sealed bottled water is one thing, but I'm not buying contraband candied apples off anyone.

As the second half played on, the Wizards and Clippers traded leads, bucket for bucket. John Wall and JaVale McGee continued to impress me, as they had back in D.C. As the game clock wound its way down to less than a minute to go, it was close to 10:00 p.m., and neither Demetria nor I had eaten all day. We were close to fainting from hunger and wary of kitchen closing times in downtown LA (mostly 11:00 p.m.).

So with twenty seconds to go, and the Clippers up by a point with two free throws to ice the game, it was our cue.

Now, prior to the game, Cavs fan extraordinaire Rebecca and I traded text messages. I'd mentioned that I may bag early to grab dinner, and she wrote back, "Good thing you're not with me. I never leave a game early. Maybe that's part of being a Cleveland fan. You just don't do that."

Clippers fans agreed. It may have been a result of watching so many leads evaporate over the years, but they were staying put. A guy in a Griffin jersey even chased us out to the concourse and asked if we were coming back. No, we weren't.

"Great, we'll take your seats then if that's ok," he said.

"There are only twenty seconds left!" I said, chuckling. What a joke, I thought. He ran to ask us if he can sit in our seats for the dying seconds of the game?

Fast forward sixteen hours.

I'm flicking through the sports section of the *LA Times*, and buried on the third page (this is still the Clippers, after all) was this headline:

"Clippers Need Two Overtimes as Griffin Posts First Career Triple-Double."

Shit.

That kid who took our seats was smarter than I thought. Apparently, Eric Gordon missed the back end of the two free throws, and John Wall rushed the court to score a last-second layup, sending the game into overtime.

Lesson learned. Going forward, I'm abiding by the Cleveland fan handbook. I just hope this doesn't mean I've given up all hope of ever rooting for a championship team again.

We did eat well, though. Bottega Louie is a massive downtown brasserie that plays hip-hop. It's a good thing they weren't showing the game. It would have killed my dinner.

```
FACE: $70
PAID: $30
DISCOUNT: 57%
```

LOS ANGELES: MARCH 25, 2011

```
LAKERS 112
CLIPPERS 104
ATTENDANCE: 18,997 (sellout; Lakers capacity
is slightly less than that of Clippers games
due to a different seating configuration)
```

Yet another LA rite of passage is bumping into actors and athletes around town that you forgot existed. The last few times I've been to the City of Angels I've spotted the likes of 1980s action hero Dolph Lundgren, Seth Green (Scott Evil in *Austin Powers*), Olympian Maurice Greene, reality bible thumper Stephen Baldwin, and retired Wimbledon champ Pete Sampras (ok, we never forgot him). That bizarre potpourri of personalities rolled right off the top of my head.

But for true, hardcore celeb spotting, there is no place better than at a Lakers game in the Staples. Jack, Becks, Denzel, Penny, Leo, Flea. They're always around, and it's always fun recounting the who's who to your friends the next day. But believe me, they don't help matters when you're trying to find a good deal on a ticket.

Combine the celeb factor with the hype of the Lakers, two-time defending champs, playing their fellow arena-mates in a home game. It was a huge deal, and ticket prices online were going for $350 and up in the lower section. It was safe to say I'd have to pony up more than $30 for a ticket this time around.

I stumbled onto a $5 parking lot only two blocks from the arena (on Eleventh and Hope). Maybe this was a good omen, I thought, as I walked toward the LA Live complex, which sits across from the Staples Center. I was meeting up with an old high-school buddy, Amer, and his lovely wife Brigitte, two diehard Lakers fans. They had their seats taken care of in advance.

I was another story.

While they checked out the impressive ESPN Zone sports bar, I put out some feelers with a burly scalper in a Lakers jacket. He quoted me $300 for a lower-bowl ticket and then went down to $250. I balked, saying it was too much. He asked what I was willing to spend, and I said $80.

"Man, what? $80! Man, I'm wasting my time with you. Who the fuck do you think we are?"

Wow, that was not exactly the reaction I was hoping for.

"You cannot get anything for $80, not even at the top. Man, these are the Lakers!"

Yikes. I'd better up my $100 budget, I thought, looking for an ATM. Over dinner at Trader Vic's, Amer—who often buys off the streets himself—told me to expect to pay $200.

Post-meal, I got back into a scrum of scalpers, none of whom were going below $200 for a second-tier corner seat. Thoughts came to mind of what I could do with that $200 instead of attending yet another basketball game. Tipoff had come and gone, but the street trade was in full effect. There were plenty of people willing to pay more than me, which is never a good thing. I was half watching the first quarter on ESPN's giant HD screen and half keeping an eye out on the street trade.

A hired policeman was working security outside the bar, so I asked him whether scalping was legal in LA. He shook his head and said no. It was definitely a crime, though you have to catch them in the act using particular wording. He compared it to prostitution, where you can't just bust a hooker for being on the streets. There's a certain lingo they use to circumvent the law; therefore, it's mainly vice squads or undercover cops who handle these types of crimes.

Interesting, I thought. Then I made my way back to the pack. Prices still weren't dropping, but I noticed an Indian guy who was also looking for a single. I approached him and asked if he wanted to double up, so that we could buy a pair and make it easier on ourselves. He seemed receptive to the idea and asked what I was willing to spend. "$150 for something decent," I replied. Then I retreated back to watch the game through the giant paned glass. In truth, by that point I was so done with sitting through NBA games that watching from the comfy seats of the ESPN Zone and saving the cash was looking very appealing.

And just when I was about to call it a night, my fellow ticket searcher came up to me and said he talked the guy down to $375 for the second-tier pair. Hmm, still too high, I thought.

"Man, you're wasting your time with this guy," said the scalper, who could have been mistaken for the rapper Ludacris if I didn't know any better. "He doesn't want to go to the game."

He was right. I couldn't be bothered. But somewhere in the commotion I'd agreed to put up $160. I don't know exactly what happened with the math, but I handed my money over to my partner RJ, and he took over.

As we walked toward the arena and he handed me a ticket, I told him I felt like I'd just been mugged.

"No, you're fine, man; that was the best deal out there. Believe me," he said.

The face value said $115. It was the first time I'd willingly paid above face for any event since a sold-out Lenny Kravitz gig in London years ago. And that was a one-off in a tiny venue. The concert ended up getting postponed, and the guy who sold them to me asked if he could buy them back (I declined).

That wasn't happening tonight. But once I sat down, it became completely obvious why I had paid so much. Blake Griffin slammed a monstrous dunk that had the entire crowd oohing and aahing. People gasped. They cheered. They laughed in that giddy way, knowing they'd witnessed something up close that only a few are able to see. And those were the Lakers fans!

He repeated the feat two more times in the quarter, each dunk more thunderous, explosive, and awesome than the last. The third was an alley-oop off a pass that looked way behind him. No matter—he's like a dunk magnet. Throw the ball within five feet of his radius, and he's bringing it home.

There are only a few athletes on Earth who are worth the price of admission regardless of the competition. In other words, you're walking in just to gawk at their skills and physical ability, never mind the actual game. Although he's at the tail end of his career, the Lakers' Kobe Bryant is one of the few who still commands that kind of attention. LeBron is the third and final member of that club in the NBA. Dwight Howard, who at six-foot, eleven-inches and 240-pounds is probably the most chiseled player in the league, may also be in there because no other player is so huge and agile. In soccer, Lionel Messi of Barcelona is a good comparison. Watching him live is an unreal experience. Maybe Roger Federer in tennis. And if you can focus for ten seconds, Usain Bolt is another example.

List: short.

And here tonight I was in the presence of two of these physical specimens. If it weren't the case that they'll both tally well over $100 million for the duration of their careers, they'd be in that freak circus show on Venice Beach I walked by yesterday, alongside the wolf boy and the two-headed turtle.

I discussed this with RJ, as we talked supply and demand of various tickets.

RJ, it turned out, was an ex-Lakers season ticketholder who dumped his subscription for the flexibility of the street trade. On Friday night he knew exactly what he was doing, having regularly bought tickets off the core five scalpers who work the area. Normally, discounts are on offer, but he explained that the intercity rivalry, Lakers cachet, and showcasing of Griffin versus Kobe was enough to pump up pricing.

I picked the right guy to pair up with; he did all the work. A few weeks ago he even bagged a ticket to the All-Star Game at a $350 markdown from face value. It was like sitting next to a member of a secret club. He totally got it.

In the second half I moved and sat beside Amer and Brigitte in the lower bowl just behind the Clippers basket (I borrowed Brigitte's ticket to show the usher, an old but faithful tactic). That was more like it. Now I felt like I really got my money's worth. That is, until I had beer splashed all over my new jeans, the only clean pair I had left on the trip. Serves me right for looking high and low for good deals and then squandering any savings at True Religion![64]

As the Lakers pulled away for a win, Chris Kaman, the seven-foot Clippers center with a combover (who one blog compared to Ork from *Lord of the Rings*), and Derek Fisher, the diminutive Lakers co-captain, exchanged unpleasantries. As Kaman got ejected, he motioned for Fisher to meet him in the parking lot after the game. Now *that* would be a ticket worth paying for.

And that's it for now. Second leg of trip over. Tally so far: thirty days, sixteen games, fifteen cities, and two countries.

---

64   I now realize how duped I was into paying $280 plus tax for a pair of overstitched jeans. Who am I kidding? I've always been more of a Levi's guy.

The funny thing is, I don't know when I'll be able to attend my next game. There's a lockout looming at this end of this season in June. Players and owners are embroiled in a faceoff about pay, which is likely to turn ugly and cancel at least part of next season. Meanwhile, a bulk of the business model is supported by overpaying fans. Something's got to give.

FACE VALUE: $115
PAID: $160
PREMIUM: 39%

PART FOUR

MY TAKE ON THE 2011 NBA LOCKOUT

Kenny Anderson is a good man. Well groomed with a college de-gree, he is, by all accounts, kind and polite. He's just not very good with money. By thirty-five, an age where many slug it out in middle management, Anderson had already made a cool $63 million over his career. Yet, somehow, he was filing for bankruptcy.

Antoine Walker, paunchy with a penchant for tailored suits and out-rageous bling, accrued a whopping $108 million when he retired at thirty-three. But there he was at a Harrah's Casino in 2009, handcuffed for writing bad checks and slipping into $4 million of bad debt.

Eddy Curry was even younger. At just twenty-nine, the giant with braids and endless body art made $69 million over a ten-year span in a career that, ironically, has been labelled a flop.[65] But in 2010 a Manhattan court ordered him to pay $75,000 *a month* in interest for personal loans on which he'd defaulted.

The former New Jersey Nets forward Jayson Williams had a short-lived—but spectacular—working life by most people's standards.

---

65   Curry experienced some redemption as a twelfth man for the 2012 championship Miami Heat team. For that season he was paid $1,229,255 and totalled twelve field goals.

Despite being in the labor pool for only nine years, the outspoken charmer with a knack for New York's nightlife racked up a kitty of $87 million. At thirty-two, he'd written his life story and retired to a twenty-seven-thousand-square-foot mansion in New Jersey. By forty, he was broke, suicidal, and pleading his case in a murder trial.

In what walk of life can men so young, with such little understanding of how to handle wealth, be paid so much? Even in the hedge-fund capitals of Manhattan and Greenwich, you'd be hard pressed to find Harvard Business School grads in their twenties making $10 million a year on basic salaries.

The answer, of course, is professional basketball. Specifically, the National Basketball Association, where an incredibly fortunate 450 players make an average of $4.5 million a year.[66] No other job on the planet pays as well.

And no other people lose their money as quickly.

Within five years of retirement, 60 percent of NBA players go broke, according to *Sports Illustrated*. The list of reasons has a long tail, but a short head. Players run into many of the same pitfalls time and again.

"You know the old saying: History repeats itself," says Tom Ajamie, a lawyer specializing in financial fraud who has represented five NBA players. "No one is either taught or learned from the generation that has preceded him."

Kenny Anderson, the gifted point guard from New York, fathered seven kids from five different women, costing him tens of thousands in child support a month. And like many in the league, he supported old friends and hangers-on with monthly payouts. He also had a penchant for diamond jewellery and kept a fleet of eleven cars. Anderson

---

66 The figure went from $5.2 million in 2011-2012 to approximately $4.5 million for the 2012–2013 season, after the new collective bargaining agreement was signed. (*Forbes*, "NBA Owners Win Big with New Collective Bargaining Agreement," November 28, 2011, by Patrick Rishe).

now has his feet back on the ground coaching high school basketball, but not before hitting rock bottom.

Walker's main vice was gambling, but he also fuelled an entourage of seventy, according to his mom. Flashing around his money led to repeated gunpoint robberies (once for $100,000 in jewellery outside a Chicago nightclub). Curry, who wallowed through weight problems, injury, and depression with the Knicks, blew his money on gambling, cars, and legal fees defending bizarre lawsuits.[67]

Williams lost most of his fortune defending himself in court after he accidentally shot and killed his chauffer in a drunken spell at his mansion. He was enjoying an early retirement after blowing out his knee just halfway through the first of his guaranteed six-season $100 million contract with the New Jersey Nets. Racking in $13 million to $14 million over the next few years with little to do other than toy around with guns and go out bar hopping, he was a disaster waiting to happen.

But not all professional athletes' financial entanglements stem from vices. Ajamie stresses that the clients he handled were not big partiers, just victims of bad advice who spent on causes that made no financial sense.

One tried to revamp his hard-luck hometown in the Midwest by buying up vacant downtown office blocks. "A laudable goal but a black hole," says Ajamie. "You know it's good hearted, trying to give to charities and develop cities, but it just sort of goes away then."

Well intentioned or not, pitfalls are more the norm than the exception once NBA players sign their first big paychecks. The money starts

---

67   In 2009 his male chauffer accused him of sexual harassment. NBA players are prime targets for all kinds of lawsuits, especially rape and harassment cases, because they are often settled out of court for big sums.

Ajamie recalled a story where the Sacramento Kings hired him to stand on their sidelines during a game. One of their players had been stalked by an ex-housekeeper; she was suing him based on a forged contract promising her a high salary, and the team received a tip that she'd create a scene on the court. The scene was avoided.

disappearing even before the taxes (which start at 35 percent) agent's fees (up to 4 percent) and inevitable bad investments.

"I don't want to be critical of players in any way because they don't have a business background—nor should we expect them to. That's not their forte," Ajamie explains.

"So they often turn to people they've known a long time or trust to manage large sums of money. The problem is those people normally don't have business acumen either. But they will say that they do.[68] So the financial advisors are making very poor investment decisions, and sometimes they end up just being dishonest."

One advisor who fell into the dishonest camp was an ex-player himself. Perhaps that's how former New Jersey Net Tate George sensed a golden opportunity and raised $2 million for his Ponzi scheme. Telling NBA players he was investing in a vast real estate portfolio, he used the money to fund his lifestyle and child-support payments. (Is stealing to pay child support morally defensible? It doesn't feel like it in this case.) He was arrested in September 2011 and is currently facing up to twenty years in prison.

All this profligate behavior is possible because of a cunning labor agreement negotiated by players' association executive Billy Hunter in 1998, which guaranteed NBA players 57 percent of the league's revenue.[69] Amazingly, NBA owners caved to this point with no regard for their own team's profitability. Nearly half the season was lost that winter before terms were met (and renegotiated in 2011 after a bitter lockout that also wiped out 20 percent of the season). The NBA

---

68   The poster child for this situation is LeBron's business manager, Maverick Carter. Though Carter sounds like he has a great head on his shoulders and has backed LeBron on some very lucrative sponsorship deals, he was also responsible for organizing the disastrous ESPN show *The Decision* where LeBron publicly shat on every NBA fan in Ohio.

69   The new agreement brought that revenue split down to 49 – 51 percent for the players, which is still a hell of a deal.

claimed it was collectively losing $300 million because of hard economic times and inflated salaries, with half the teams in the red.[70]

In what other business have employees been guaranteed a majority of the revenues with no regard to profit? Certainly not at Goldman Sachs, Exxon, or any other public company; there would be a shareholder revolt.

That agreement expired in June 2011, leaving the team owners looking to rein in a situation that had spiralled out of control. By the summer of 2011, an endless recessionary environment had four or five teams in serious financial difficulty (one, New Orleans, had to be rescued by the league before its owner went bust), and others scraping by. Costs could be cut across the board, but the glaring expenses that needed reduction were the players' salaries.

So here's a reality check to NBA players following the path of Shawn Kemp, who fathered at least seven kids from six different women, and—naturally—had nothing to show for his stellar fourteen-year career: When it comes to the next labor agreement in 2022 (or 2017 if either side exercises its right to opt out), stop focusing on what slice of the league's revenue you're getting and start cutting out some of the ridiculous spending.

In his heyday, Shaq spent $875,000 *a month*, including $24,300 on gas and $17,000 on clothes. Surely he can cut down on the gasoline

---

70   In truth, it's likely that five or six teams were really bleeding money (New Orleans, Sacramento, Charlotte, Atlanta, and New Jersey, which has a billionaire Russian owner). And maybe Memphis, Milwaukee, and Detroit too.

Earlier in the 2011 season LeBron James made waves when he kind of sort of said the league should contract. Whatever he said, he was definitely onto something before he realized how many people he pissed off. Basketball in the 1980s and early 1990s was a lot more competitive. Take out the two worst-attended teams in the league, and you've probably solved the most crippling part of the league's finances. Of course, you're also shelving the jobs of thirty NBA players and another twenty coaches, countless trainers, equipment people, and arena staff. So it ain't gonna happen, but if the league is hell-bent on continued expansion, players have the right to kick up a storm if the league balks that it is losing money.

now that he's retired. And Kris Humphries, who made $3.2 million in the 2010–2011 season and blew at least $750,000 of it on that infamous 20.5-carat engagement ring to Kim Kardashian, has hopefully learned his lesson and will tighten the screws going forward.[71] Would Kardashian not have married him if the ring were only worth, say, $500,000? Actually, never mind.

What exactly was the point of David Stern and Billy Hunter negotiating for thirty hours over three days in an October 2011 marathon session, when most players are so good at blowing it all anyway?[72] Even Scottie Pippen, one of the fifty greatest players of all time, had to make an ill-advised comeback when he burned through his entire $120 million fortune and couldn't afford the upkeep on his Gulfstream jet.

As it turned out, Stern and Hunter were all too aware of the fate of so many former NBA players. The new agreement provisions 1 percent of the league's "basketball-related income" to be placed in a pension fund every year ("A great idea," says Ajamie). It also encourages them to contribute up to 10 percent of their salaries to the retirement scheme, which kicks in at fifty. Let's hope most players use their heads and decide not to opt out.

Along with the prudence of the pension scheme, the union managed to hold on to terms that would still afford NBA players a standard of living in the ninety-ninth percentile of all Americans. The average reduction of approximately $412,000 each per year—after taxes and in real terms—equates to one Maybach, one very big night out in Vegas,

---

71   The headline figure on the Lorraine Schwartz ring was $2 million, though it was allegedly purchased wholesale at $750,000 (Huffington Post, March 15, 2012). Either way, Humphries was not getting it back, according to Kim's mom. "I hate an Indian giver," said Kris Jenner on *Good Morning America.*

72   Ironically, Billy Hunter was fired as head legal counsel of the NBA players association in February 2013, after allegedly passing his $15 million contract without proper approval, and trying to get the association to invest in a failing bank that his son sat on the board of. (Adrian Wojnarowski, "Players Vote to Oust Billy Hunter as Union Executive Director," (*sports.yahoo. com*), February 16, 2013).

or ten months of child support. Not to mention, NBA players are still living in five-star hotels for the better part of eight months and flying on private jets.

It sure beats sitting out a season and taking a crash course in frugal living.

PART FIVE

PRE-TRIP THOUGHTS: FEBRUARY 11, 2012

BA Flight from Heathrow to Chicago

I'm terrified. Well, severely daunted might be more accurate than terrified. Or scared shitless. I mean, I'll survive the subfreezing temperatures I'm about to brave in the February Midwest, though it won't be easy.

I'm heading to Chicago, Milwaukee, Minneapolis, and Cleveland on a bone-crushing jaunt through four NBA arenas in Middle America. The forecast before I left ranged between thirty-two degrees and ten degrees Fahrenheit in each city. It ain't gonna be fun hitting the sidewalks of Wisconsin and Minnesota in search of game tickets, but again, it will be my task. A year ago this week I was shuffling through Memphis, Oklahoma City, Denver, and Salt Lake City through what was one of the worst cold fronts that the South and Rocky Mountains had seen in decades. Apparently, last year's punishment wasn't enough for me, or I simply forgot how frozen over I felt. Twelve months later, as I make my way to Milwaukee I wonder how the 2012 strike-shortened season is affecting the supply-demand curve for NBA ticket sales.

On the one hand, there are far too many games a week (squeezing a sixty-six-game season into eighteen weeks has teams playing four and sometimes five games a week), meaning weekly supply is up.

Pricing, on average, is up too. For this 2012 strike-shortened season, ticket prices have managed to rise 1.7 percent on average, according to the AP. That's because even though thirteen teams actually cut their prices, the seven that jacked them up did so heavily.

New York, Miami, Chicago, and LA are the most affluent and price-elastic markets out there. They can afford to squeeze as much as they can out of their fans with the knowledge that the demand will still be there, and they did. Heck, they even sell out most games when they play on the road.

In terms of entertainment, marquee players are getting injured left and right due to the physical demands of the more intense season. And although matchups have been tremendously exciting in certain cities (the Knicks with the emergence of Taiwanese-American sensation Jeremy Lin and the Clippers with the Chris Paul/Blake Griffin duo are the two biggest draws in the league), the quality of the product on the court has to be questioned.

So, in theory, supply is way up, and demand may be crimped. And therefore—in theory—this should mean that season ticketholders will be dumping their tickets onto the secondary market more often than in previous seasons.

But in reality, I have no idea if it will be harder or easier to get NBA tickets at under face value in 2012. I was wildly successful last season, if I do say so myself, having meaningfully paid over face only once. Will it be so easy once again? I have no way of knowing. I'll just have to go out there and see.

And with that, here are the challenges I'm facing:

February 13—Miami at Milwaukee

The Heat are always a tough ticket and are probably the biggest road show in town this year. It will be subfreezing outside. I will also be pairing up with a friend of a friend who's a local, so we're looking for a pair. Milwaukee is also a small-market town, and since baseball's Brewers and football's Packers are in their offseasons, this game will be a big deal. My confidence rating is about a 4/10 to get something below face, and a 6/10 to pay face value for a good seat.

February 15—Charlotte at Minnesota

Minneapolis is a slightly larger-market town, but one with a team in recent resurgence with the Rubio/Love twosome (you know I'm dying to say Love triangle…can't they have one more good player to throw in the mix?). The pairing of a baby-faced Catalan passing freak and the rapidly improving power forward gives Minnesotans something to cheer about for the first time since the team's demise after braided firecracker Latrell Sprewell chocked then-Coach PJ Carlesimo.

I will be hitting the game on my own, which should make things easier, and I plan to go back to the basics by standing outside the arena with a wad of $20 bills, hoping to strike potluck. Minnesota's opponent, Charlotte, is the worst team in the league, after all. Although, I have yet to face cold the way I will likely be confronted with it on that night.

Confidence rating: 7.5/10

February 16—Boston at Chicago

These two teams must know each other really well by now. They boast two of my favorite players in the league, Derrick Rose and Rajon Rondo, and are both storied franchises.

My friend Sami in Chicago is a joint-season ticketholder and is "working on good seats." Half of me feels sheepish about joining him in the corporate good seats, but the other half wants no part of freezing outside the United Center looking for a good deal (though that is the whole point of this exercise).

So I'll compromise. I'll also look for a good deal online and see if I can pry tickets out of the hands of an uninterested season ticketholder, while hoping Sami can come through with the aforementioned good seats. The Bulls' Rose is in and out of the lineup due to injury. If he's not playing—who knows—demand could dip very quickly.

Confidence rating for availability of seats below face: 6/10

February 17—Miami at Cleveland

This is certainly the toughest challenge of this suite of four games. We all know the story. Spurned lovers, the Cavs fans, nervously anticipate the return of their glorious ex, LeBron James.

The boo-dometer will be off the charts. The secondary market for this game, viewed through the online ticket aggregators, is sky high. Tickets are going for multiples above face value—$185 seats for $800 and so on.

But there's a trading opportunity (call it a loophole) that's emerged from this mess. Because Cleveland went from having sold-out arenas and tons of season ticketholders during the LeBron era to a dearth of season ticketholders for a team coming off a last-place finish, tickets can be found through the Cavs' online box office at face value.

The night before my trip, seats were going for between $450 and $800 in "center lowers" on StubHub, but combing through the Cavs' site I miraculously found floor seats going for below $400. Now, $400 is no giveaway either; that is well understood. But LeBron James is one of the athletes in the NBA who can genuinely be called a freak of nature, and watching him live—preferably as close to the floor as possible—is worth breaking the bank for. Only Blake Griffin can command that much awe from spectators in today's NBA.

In fact, on the same day that Blake had that monstrous throw down over Kendrick Perkins that will be etched in NBA lore (some say as the greatest dunk of all time), LeBron had one nearly as exhilarating. He leapfrogged over another player on the way to an alley-oop. He practically checked his wristwatch for the time on the way to the rim; that's how easy he made it look.[73]

At any rate, this circumstance—the ability to put a commodity on a seller's market for far above it's "fair value" (or "par" if this were a bond) while *simultaneously* finding the commodity on the buyer's market at half the price—is known as "arbitrage." What a seasoned trader would do is immediately buy up all the spare tickets for this game on the Cavs' website, then turn around and sell them on Stub-Hub for double the price.

Sure, the trader is taking a risk that he may not turn the tickets around at a profit, but it is a calculated gamble. Traders can point to the last few games in which the Heat have played in Cleveland and study buyers' behavior to gauge their chances of flipping the tickets at a profit. The game is also being held on a Friday night, which would not taper off demand.

Though I'm not acting as a trader, I can appreciate the trader's mentality, and I scooped up two center floor seats in the fourth row off the Cavs' website for $350 each, including fees. On this countrywide journey I haven't paid anything close to that price as of yet, but a deal is still a deal. Loophole aside, my confidence level would have been a 2/10.

---

73   Youtube LeBron and Griffin's gobsmacking dunks from January 30, 2012 and decide which was more impressive.

MILWAUKEE: FEBRUARY 13, 2012

Can't decide if this 'Fear the Deer' float is creepy, cool or both.

```
HEAT 114
BUCKS 96
ATTENDANCE: 16,749
CAPACITY: 18,717
```

My first time ever in the Midwest! Of all my years traveling through this great country, I've yet to dip into the region of the Great Lakes, jumbo sausages, and yard-long beers.

But here I am, in cold and overcast Milwaukee. Tonight I had the good fortune of pairing up with a local. Marcus is a friend of a friend who's been living in Wisconsin his entire life and is a die-hard Brewers, Packers, and Bucks fan. His six-year-old daughter even wants a red Brandon Jennings jersey for her birthday; it's got to be the Gumby haircut Jennings has been partial to that won her loyalty.

But back to the task at hand, which is to produce a pair of tickets for tonight's big game, preferably in the lower-bowl center for under face value. As it turned out, it shouldn't have been nearly as big a challenge as we let it be. Pouring over Craigslist, I noticed at least three season ticketholders (or possibly ticket agents) offering their seats for under face value. The one that caught my eye was a pair on an aisle facing the free-throw line. They were advertised for $100 each O.B.O. (with face being $122 each). I offered $150 for the pair, and the seller quickly shot back an offer of $180.

That's where the negotiations stalled and never recovered. But the bottom line is the opportunity was there, and I could have nabbed the pair at a discount of 26 percent. Marcus, on the other hand, was content to go either way. Rather than snapping up the Craigslist deal, we opted to "play the scalper game," as he put it. His thinking was that on a Monday night, spares would be plentiful, even for a game featuring a marquee attraction like LeBron James and the Miami Heat.

And with that, we converged at Major Goolsby's, a Milwaukee institution three blocks from the Bradley Center. Its infamous claim to fame is that it once named a seven-foot-long piggybank (created for charity) after frequenter Charles Barkley, with the power forward's blessing.

It's a very cool dive, with big plasmas spread around the bar, but without the uber-sleekness of many of today's sports bars. Milwaukee is known for its beers (duh), especially the Miller Brewing Company, but it also boasts a slew of microbreweries like Sprecher.

And like all other cities in the Midwest, Milwaukee is a sports-crazy town. Highest in the pecking order are the storied Green Bay Packers (a two-hour drive north) and then come the Milwaukee Brewers, who went far into the Major League Baseball playoffs in 2011, quite an achievement for a market of only six hundred thousand. Additionally, the Bucks and Marquette have their own cult basketball following, and there is no greater fan than the guy locals call Freeway.

An African American in his forties, Freeway is autistic,[74] and legend has it a bus hit him early in his life, which led to a lifetime offer of season tickets to the local sports teams as a fig leaf from the city (this is likely just an urban myth, but one that locals enjoy telling).

As luck would have it, while hanging at Major Goolsby's, I met the one and only Freeway. After a quick hello from Marcus, Freeway immediately proclaimed that he was "now on Facebook" and asked if Marcus and I were on Facebook too. Kind of an awkward situation, but a quick, "Oh, I don't do Facebook, never have the time," was Marcus's sharp reply. He then flashed a look at me and asked, "Are you on Facebook?" to which Marcus jumped in and said, "No, Freeway, he doesn't do Facebook either." A minute later he peered back at Marcus's Blackberry and said, "Hey, it looks like you're on Facebook there. I can see it."

I want to come back to Milwaukee just to hang with Freeway.

Though the scalpers all converged at the corner around Goolsby's, we chose to ignore them until ten minutes to tipoff. That wasn't the brightest idea and went against all my lessons learned last year. But hey, I'm rusty.[75]

So by the time we walked out of the bar, all that were left were seats in the upper deck. We didn't even ask how much. Instead, Marcus called a scalper buddy of his who was skiing in Utah to find us a deal. And a phone call later, we were set up with two lower-bowl seats facing the baseline at $100 each (which, by the way, was a worse

---

74   According to his sister, who is trying to raise money for a documentary about him. There's a poorly made YouTube video featuring Freeway dancing wildly in the aisles of a Bucks game.

75   Very rusty, as I would come to realize later on that leg.

deal than the one I had been offered on Craigslist). Or so we thought. We waited for ten minutes in the cold, and the guy never showed up. Scalpers are a bit like drug dealers; they ain't the most reliable cats on the planet. It turned out that on his way to us the guy unloaded them at $150 each.

The story would have ended there if it weren't for the kindness of a long-serving waitress at Major Goolsby's. Knowing Marcus for years, she comped us two tickets that were sitting behind the bar. Even though she was hoping to sell them, it didn't seem like she bothered to ask anyone if they were looking for spares. Thankfully, Marcus asked on a whim and—poof—we had $47 face value seats in our hands for free. It helps when you've been going to the same bar for twenty years and the staff turnover is low. That's America's heartland for you. I grew very fond of those Midwestern values on my trip.

The Bradley Center reminded me a lot of Energy Solutions Arena in Salt Lake City, only I liked it a lot more. It was old school in the same way, yet felt a lot cozier; even in the upper deck I never felt that far from the action. In fact, though we were sitting baseline in the thirteenth row of the uppers, the view was more than adequate. The one downside was that half of my view was watched through a protective Plexiglas pane (though the row in front of us was empty, the usher insisted we move to our seats). No matter, it didn't deter me from watching LeBron score thirty-five in the first three quarters before he sat out the rest of the blowout. I have to reiterate how much of a consistently great show he puts on. Expect to get your money's worth with King James in the house.

The Bucks' plan to cover him with Carlos Delfino was never really going to work either. It was hilarious, though, to hear the Argentine's baskets greeted with Madonna yelping, "Don't cry for me, Argentina!" on the PA system. Another Bradley Center quirk was the Squad 6 cheering section, courtesy of Andrew Bogut. The Aussie shelled out for one hundred lower-level seats for some of Milwaukee's rowdiest fans. Typically for Bucks fans, he was lost for three months with an ankle injury early in the season, leaving Squad 6 with very little to cheer about.[76]

After the game Marcus and I took in some cocktails downtown at the roof bar of the Pfister Hotel. Though it could use a facelift, you can tell that the hotel is as grand as they come in Brew City. And with that one-hundred-year-old classic design come certain amenities. In my case they were spotty heat and hot water (nonexistent my first night).

In the case of many baseball players making their way through town, it's ghosts. Some Dodgers players refuse to spend the night alone in their rooms, according to local station WISN. Other guests claimed to have seen the ghost of Charles Pfister overlooking the sweeping staircase. If I'd seen him I would have complained about my shabby heating, which had me freezing the first night, but I took it up with the manager instead, who comped me a night's stay.

Free room, free game. I could get used to this Midwestern hospitality. On to Minneapolis.

```
FACE: $47
PAID: $0 (comped by bartender)
```

---

[76] Squad 6 had even less to cheer about a month later when Bogut got traded to Golden State for Monta Ellis, leaving the future of the cheering section in doubt.

MINNEAPOLIS: FEBRUARY 15, 2012

```
TIMBERWOLVES 102
BOBCATS 90
ATTENDANCE: 15,139
CAPACITY: 19,356
```

Minneapolis is known for a few things: cold weather, Prince, the Vikings, the Twins, gorgeous tall blondes of Nordic origin, and um, that's pretty much it.

So when I found myself in Minneapolis surrounded by Somalis, I was kind of surprised. Well, not hugely surprised. Nearly every cab driver I'd ridden with in the past year was born outside of the United States. In Memphis my airport cabbie was Somali too. But Minneapolis is their stronghold. Somalis first arrived at the start of their civil war in 1991, with thirty thousand of them eventually settling in Minneapolis because of Minnesota's strong programs for refugee assistance.

Indeed, it seemed like every cab driver and airport employee (and even an emaciated stripper) was Somali. I found that they were very friendly, honest, and punctual. I gave two of the cabbies repeat business and cut discounted deals with them to downtown and the airport.

Along with its Somali population, Minnesota is overlooked for its microbrews. Like Milwaukee it boasts quite a selection. Downing a few tasters across from the Target Center at Gluek's Restaurant and Bar was a treat. They even had taster-size portions ($1.25 for four-ounce shots), which was a godsend for someone like me with little time to spare. Out of the five I sampled, my favorite was Gluek Red, an amber lager with a 5.8 percent alcohol content.

The Target Center is in the heart of downtown Minneapolis, flanked by pubs and strip joints. It's also right across the street from the music venue First Avenue, made famous by Prince in his epic biopic *Purple Rain*. On my first night in the Twin Cities there was a popular underground band called Polica playing. My friend Robert and I tried to make our way in, only to be told that the $12 door tickets were sold out. So naturally, we went looking for the scalper trade. Remarkably, we were offered two tickets for a $100 each. Out of shock I let out a nervous laugh, and not losing a beat, the scalper mocked my shrill and did an about face. It felt like a bad omen for the next day's game.

Luckily for me, Minneapolis was going through a very "mild" winter, and the temperature was only in the twenties.[77] Unluckily for me, the Wolves were enjoying a great resurgence behind one of the most dynamic duos in the league (Rubio and Love) and were enjoying a newfound Love affair with the city (in case you're wondering, Kevin Love is the nephew of Mike Love of the Beach Boys). Rising from the doldrums, they were now in the middle of the pack of the NBA's attendance report, at 88 percent capacity for home games.

My Somali friend dropped me off a block from the arena, and I made my way toward the street hustle. You can always tell when you're

---

77 The winter of 2012 was the fourth warmest in recorded history for the lower forty-eight states, according to the National Climactic Data Center.

in a state that's tolerant toward scalping when you see guys carrying laminated signs that say, "I need tickets," along with laminated seating charts (that was actually a first). So that put me slightly at ease. I felt my way around the trade and put one guy on an assignment (fat white guy, we'll call him FWG) to fetch me a single in the lower tier. In the meantime, another scalper (stubbly black guy, SBG) approached me and said he had a great single. It was section 129, row A. I checked the chart on my Blackberry, and it showed up as a baseline seat. He started at $100, and I countered at $40. He insisted on $60 ("C'mon, man, these are front row, $300 seats!"), but I stood at $55 and wasn't going to budge.

At this point FWG came back with a seat for me, fueling a little tension between the two street hustlers. "Hey, I got him!" said SBG.

Now, I have no loyalty with scalpers, and neither should anyone. They'll sell their grandmothers for an extra $10, as witnessed in Milwaukee when our sure thing unloaded his seats on the way to meeting Marcus and me. So I entertained the offer from FWG, asking him where his seat was, and for how much. It was dead center on the bottom circle but in row X, not nearly as good as SBG's row A on the baseline.

FWG wanted $50. So I leveraged my position by turning back to SBG and *lowering* my original offer to $50 for the better ticket. I was in the power position, with two choices for decent seats, and SBG knew it. And that's why he quickly relented, swapping my wad of bills for the ticket in one quick motion.

Once inside I was delighted with my purchase. Row Λ was only five rows from the floor and directly behind the Bobcats' bench. I could see the players warming up and chatting with their beleaguered coach, Paul Silas. Charlotte was coming into the game riding a sixteen-game losing streak. Though the team is owned by the greatest player who ever lived, Michael Jordan, it is the most pathetic one assembled in the NBA. Their best player, Boris Diaw, looks like he spent a year locked in sumo-wrestling camp. His ass must take up two private-jetliner seats on the team's Gulfstream. He still has some moves driving to the basket, but they're in slow-mo. Their second-best player, Corry Maggette, is on his fifth team and never met a shot he didn't like.

Conversely, their coach, Paul Silas, looks like the NBA's version of Sidney Poitier. He's all class. Unfortunately, he's also as soft-spoken as Poitier and looks nearly as old. He barely calls plays, and during timeouts he resorts to dropping his face in his hands, shaking his head back and forth and wiping his eyes for a full minute. Not exactly inspiring stuff when your best player is looking around to see if anyone left a spare Twinkie under the bench.

Speaking of things under the bench, fearing the Minnesota cold, I dressed in five layers, leaving me baking once I settled into my seat. Once my neighbor showed up, I tried stuffing my ginormous Arsenal puffy jacket under my collapsible chair. That turned into a big joke and had me rethink my game wardrobes going down the road. Anything under a seat is bound to get messed up with beer, popcorn, peanut shells, and the like.

But if there was any beer to spill it would likely have been Miller Lite ($8.50 for a pint) as there were none of the great microbrew beers I'd sampled available. In fact, the arena was pretty uninspiring, save for the location and my great view.

Halfway through the first quarter I asked the mild-mannered, sixtysomething, white Minnesotan to my left if he was a season ticketholder. He replied that he was and that I was sitting in his spare. We then went through the usual routine of me getting asked how much I coughed up for the seat. He had sold his spare for just $10, so he was shell-shocked when I told him I paid $50.

"$50, as in five-zero?"

"Yeah, $50," I deadpanned.

He explained that his cost as a season ticketholder was $65 for that game (the lowest price on a tiered-game system), and single-game holders would have to cough up $85. He also emphasized that he had the best deal in the house, since the very next row in front of him is part of another section with seats that run 46 percent higher in price.

So just five rows from the basket, I managed to bag the best season-ticket deal in the house, which I paid even less for on the open trade outside. Now, I wonder, why was he so astounded that I paid $50 for his seat? Perhaps because he only sold it for $10, but his bad business didn't make the ticket any less valuable to me.

By early in the fourth quarter the Wolves were up by sixteen on the back of Kevin Love's thirty points and eighteen rebounds and giant Montenegrin Nikola Pekovic's twenty-one points and eleven boards. Minnesota's cheering section, Darko's Swat Team, was chanting, "We want Darko!" For the past few years, calling for the long-suffering journeyman Serb has been a way for NBA fans to say the fat lady has sung.

And with that, I met my friend Robert for a drink, and we took in some happy-hour sushi rolls at Zake Lounge, some salsa dancing at Fogo De Chao, and some topless dancing at one of the many for-gettable gentlemen's clubs nearby. At $20 a lap dance for some very average-looking strippers, I can safely say there was a lot more value for money on offer at the Target Center.

On to Chicago.

```
FACE: $65
PAID: $50
DISCOUNT: 23%
```

CHICAGO: FEBRUARY 16, 2012

How cool is that?

```
BULLS 89
CELTICS 80
ATTENDANCE: 22,592
CAPACITY: 23,129 (figures include
standing room of approximately 2,200)
```

Before I say anything about Chicago, let me start by noting that the United Center is shockingly awesome. It is an arena befitting of the greatest basketball player who ever lived, whose statue welcomes fans outside the doors of West Monroe Street with a reminder of who was in charge here for the glory years of six championships.

If you include standing room up top, the House that Michael Jordan Built is the largest arena in the NBA in terms of size and capacity. The lights and slew of championship banners along the layers upon layers of seats and luxury boxes (169 in total!) are truly worthy of gawking at.

As we walked into the arena, my friend Sami, a twelve-year Chi-town resident, handed me a printout ticket that he'd bought off of StubHub. I had no idea he was going that route (his invitation was an extremely gracious example of Midwestern hospitality at work), or else I would have objected and insisted we roam the streets around the arena in search of the scalper trade. But he was convinced that the tactic would have not yielded us a good result, as a game against the Celtics on a Thursday night was going to be in very high demand.

So we cozied into our fifth-row center-court seats, offering us probably the best view in the house. One row in front of us and a few seats to the left was Mayor Rahm Emanuel, President Obama's former chief of staff, who was whooping and hollering throughout the evening. There was a definite who's who familiarity to section 112. Everyone was on a first-name basis, with a few guys shuffling back and forth between other sections while patting Sami on the back along the way.

That may have to do with Chicago being a "small big city," if that makes any sense. It's a financial hub with ample business to pay for all those luxury boxes, but it's still not New York or London. Most of the movers and shakers with even a passing interest in sports know that Bulls games are the place to be, especially on cold winter evenings. Regularly cozying up to the likes of Rahm Emanuel before tipoff is access that can't be duplicated elsewhere.

So with that said, we were in good company when the lights went off and the arena began its famous electronic music buzz (now shamelessly copied by so many other teams). Once PA announcer Tommy

Edwards began his intros with "Annnd nowww!" the goose bumps took shape, and the Madhouse on Madison was ready to roll.

The game itself went down to the wire, with the aging Celtic "Big Three" putting up a valiant fight until the fourth quarter. The problem with the Celtics is that they're not only old, but they have no depth whatsoever. They traded away their two best role players in Big Baby Davis[78] and Kendrick Perkins (who then lost thirty-one pounds in the offseason by cutting Gatorade out of his diet), and they lost Jeff Green to a season-ending injury. Including Rajon Rondo (who still can't shoot a jump shot) there are only four guys on the entire team who can score. On the opposite end, the Bulls were playing great team ball even without reigning league MVP Derrick Rose. Carlos Boozer and Joakim Noah combined for thirty-eight points and thirty-one rebounds to pull out the win.

The tremendous energy and atmosphere at the United Center had me befuddled as to why the Bulls are not a team that attracts a lot of big-name free agents. While Carmelo Anthony and LeBron James bolted to New York and Miami, and other stars clamor for Los Angeles, no one gave Chicago so much as a sniff. I don't get it. They have an awesome fan base and a fantastic arena that's filled to the rim every night, and they are based in a bustling city with great restaurants and a nightlife that's just cool enough so that no one gawks at the celebrities.

In fact, after the game Sami and I headed straight to the Paris Club on Hubbard for drinks, when about two minutes later the Bulls' seven-foot Turkish center Omar Asik walked in with his girlfriend. We wondered how on Earth he managed to get there at the same time as us, when he was just playing in the game. Coach Thibodeau must not be one for postgame speeches.

On to Cleveland (or so I thought).

FACE: $160 with fees (invited)

---

78   Glen Davis really does look like a six-foot-eight, 300-pound big baby.

CLEVELAND: FEBRUARY 17, 2012

View from standing area. Sign behind scoreboards says 'Welcome to the Madhouse.'

HEAT 111
CAVS 87
ATTENDANCE: 20,562 (sellout)

CHICAGO: FEBRUARY 18, 2012

```
NETS 97
BULLS 85
ATTENDANCE: 22,300
CAPACITY: 23,129 (includes standing room)
```

Leaving the game in Chicago on Thursday night, I got a call from a friend whom I was supposed to meet in Cleveland the next day to join me at the game. Unfortunately, due to a family emergency, she was not going to make it.

I had a choice to make. I could still take the trip to Cleveland and look to unload one of my two floor seats, which I had splashed out $350 on in anticipation of a crazy, in-demand matchup. Or I could simply sell both of my seats, stay in Chicago, and perhaps go to another Bulls game by testing my bargaining prowess.

I decided that night that I would list them on the Cavs' official ticket seller, Flashseats.com, which I must say, is a very convenient way to unload seats. It also afforded me a great amount of flexibility after shelling out $703.68 on the pair from across the Atlantic. Using the service was exactly the same idea as eBay. You put your item up and have a "buy it now" price, and then you wait for bids to roll in. Once they do, you can accept a lower bid or wait for someone to come in with your "buy it now" price.

Since the service takes a cut off the top, I elected to put my seats up at $400 each, ensuring me my full purchase price back if someone bit. That was 12:30 a.m. Exactly eleven minutes later I got my first bid, albeit for only $100 each. I soon passed out for the night and woke up to a flurry of other bids that took place overnight. Clevelanders must be night owls. The best of the lot were for $350, each posted at 3:00 a.m. I figured things were looking pretty bright at that point, and it was clear that I had probably posted them at too low a trigger price. Sure enough, by 10:30 a.m., my tickets were gone, and I was credited $756.90 after fees by Flashseats.

So after everything was said and done, I made a profit of $53.22 from the game in Cleveland without even having set foot in the birthplace of rock and roll. My pre-trip hunch was correct; the face value seats I bought actually were undervalued, even at $350 a pop. There's a decent chance that had I posted them at $500 to $600 each I could have walked away with a handsome profit. In the meantime, I hope the IRS does not come knocking for that $53. As for the game, the Heat busted out of the gate with a twenty-one-point lead in the first quarter, allowing LeBron to rest for most of the second half. Unless the person who bought my seats was a big LeBron fan, and not a Cavs fan, he must have felt pretty let down by halftime.

With the tickets out of my hands, I was feeling rather cozy in Chicago and elected to stay in town for the weekend. The Windy City boasts a very charming downtown, with great restaurants and nightlife. Besides, I never got to test my negotiating skillz on the big bad streets of Chicago. The Bulls-Nets game the next day posted a challenge, and I don't like to back away from challenges.

Ordinarily, a 3:00 p.m. tipoff on a Saturday presents a lot of opportunity for floating excess tickets in the NBA. I nabbed my 90 percent discounted courtside seats in Washington in a similar situation (in fact, the awful Nets were the visiting team on that occasion too). So I was feeling pretty upbeat about my chances to snatch a pair of quality seats to this matchup at a cut-rate price.

My accomplice was Bridget, a local Chicagoan who had somehow never been to a Bulls game. We rolled into Adams Street, right in between the giant parking lots facing the United Center, at 2:30 p.m. First guy I see is wearing a black faded Bulls jacket and yelling, "Tickets? Tickets?" at every passing car. I approached him and asked what he had. He was holding a wad of printout paper tickets, neatly folded in squares with a rubber band piling them together.

"I've got eleventh row in the center," he said. "These are $150 seats, but I can't go lower than $75 each."

I told him that I wasn't interested in printouts, and that there could be a hundred copies of those floating around.

"Oh, you want season tickets? I ain't got none of those," he said and shrugged. "I'm working for somebody, man."

My ticket agent contact in New York did tell me that they sell their excess inventory through street scalpers at the last minute. It was not at all unusual to see scalpers in most cities flogging printout seats, though I can't remember ever buying any in the past. It's a major red flag.

But something happened after dozens of successful transactions with scalpers, city after city: I got complacent.

And I started to trust the system, for there is definitely a system in place and one that requires trust. In nearly every city I've bought tickets in, including my current hometown of London, the scalpers who congregate around a venue are there day after day and all know each other. They generally will not risk screwing someone over because they will be back at the same corner the next day and won't want to be branded as scammers. Besides, the best customers are repeat customers.

At any rate, I left the guy and sprinted towards Wood and Madison, seeing a couple of scalpers at the corner. One was talking to two young Bulls fans who walked away from him; the other asked if I had any tickets. I asked him the same question back, but he was completely dry. "There ain't nothing out here. I ain't had my hand on a ticket all day," he said, shaking his head.

Hmm, the situation was not looking good. Maybe the Nets as the visiting team with the allure of booing newly crowned "Most Hated Player in the NBA" Kris Humphries was a bigger draw than I thought. Or maybe the fact that the Bulls have a 100 percent sellout rate this season should have told me this was not going to be an easy task. Chicago is, after all, a huge sports town. And with fewer winter attractions than New York, LA, or Miami, going to a Bulls or Blackhawks hockey game on a weekend is one of the best options in town.

All of a sudden my first option of buying those eleventh-row tickets for below face value was looking pretty tasty. I sprinted right back to Adam Street (I had told Bridget to wait by the arena entrance) and found the same guy in the Bulls jacket still looking for a buyer. I offered him $50 a pop for those eleventh-row center seats (I double checked the location on a seating chart on my BlackBerry).

"Ok, $60, $60, how 'bout $60?" he countered.

"$100 for the pair; that's all I got," was my reply.

"Awwwww, maaan. Shoot. I'm gonna call my boss, and I know what he gonna say. He gonna say there's nothing for me then. I gotta make something!!"

And with that he took out his cell phone and called his boss. "Yeah, yeah, I got this guy here, he says he only got $50 for each. I know, I told him. Yeah, yeah, yeah, all right."

He hung up and said, "Shoot, man, you can have 'em, but I gotta make something for myself too. C'mon, man, gimme another $20. I been out here all day, man."

This guy was good. He managed to squeeze another crumpled $5 out of my pocket, while I told him this was a game against the Nets, and that paying $100 for seats was bad enough. It's not like this was a game against the Heat.

"Awwww, man, I'm pissed off that you know basketball, man," he said, massaging my inflated ego as I left him to cut through the parking lot and wave my unbelievable deal at Bridget. I was feeling great about myself.

"I got us awesome seats at less than half price," I gloated. "It's always a great sign when the scalper is pissed off after the sale," I said, teaching this newbie the tricks of the trade.

We worked our way toward the turnstiles, through the mosh pit at the entrance. Finally, after getting frisked, it was time for our tickets to be scanned.

Instead of the short beep it was making for everyone else's ticket, mine got a high-pitched BEEEEEP, like leaving a Sears with the security tag of your Levi's still clipped on.

Oops. Oh, it's got to be a mistake, I thought. But then Bridget's ticket made the same sound. That was not good news. I knew in the pit of my stomach we'd been screwed.

"Something's not right with these," said the security woman. "Go to the problem counter at Gate 1." And so we did.

The woman at the problem counter took one look at our tickets and said, "These are not real. Did you buy them outside?"

"How can you tell?" I asked.

"Because we've seen fifty of these today."

Ouch, $105 flushed down the toilet. I had an empty feeling, like I'd been punched in the gut. Half of it was from wasting all that money, but the other half was definitely a pride thing. I had painstakingly explained my project to Bridget, and how I'd been buying tickets off the street trade for the better part of my life. I branded myself as an expert unlikely to get duped. That was partially the exercise of this whole book—to show people that you can buy tickets through the aftermarket and not get ripped off as long as you know what you're doing.

Well, I got what I deserved. I completely ignored the obvious warning sign that the tickets were printouts (I even verbalized this to the guy and walked away once), and instead I put faith in someone whom I had absolutely no business in putting any faith in.

The system had worked like a charm for me over the past year, and I let my guard down. It was nobody's fault but mine (cue Blind Willie Johnson). I ran back to the spot of the sale, in a half-baked attempt to get my money back, but he was long gone. As Bridget rightfully pointed out later, what did I think was going to happen? He knew he sold me fakes; I was more likely to get a bloody nose than a money-back guarantee.

In retrospect, here's what I should have caught as a red flag (other than the printed-out tickets): He was willing to drop the price far below face value right off the bat, even with a good twenty minutes to tipoff and no other sellers in sight. The phone call was a little too dramatic and convenient too. Granted, he could have won an Emmy with that performance. I have to tip my hat to the guy; he did an excellent job.

But I was in a predicament. I had no tickets to the game, and Bridget had called her brother on the way, excited that she was going to her first Bulls game. I couldn't just leave us hanging in this situation. So I opted for our last resort: I waltzed up to the ticket counter and asked if there were any seats left.

"Lemme see," said the ticket guy. "Looks like we're all sold out, except for standing-room seats. $25 each."

I asked Bridget if she was up for standing, and we both figured, what the hey. We'd come that far. So another $50 later (no extra fees tacked on), we got through the turnstiles without any drama.

This time my view of the court was vastly different from the one I shared with Rahm Emanuel. It seemed like we were walking upstairs forever, up a Stairway to Heaven, if you will. Only this heaven had a bunch of bars and very little walkway room. It was crowded with hardcore fans who had arrived early and finagled some elbow room on the rails, leaving everyone else to peer over them.

Peering over a crowd when you're looking up, like at an outdoor rock concert, is one thing. But when you're trying to view a court the size of a matchbox from three hundred feet in the air with a forty-five-degree angle, it's anything but comfortable. I'm six-foot, three-inches, so it didn't bother me all that much, but five-foot, four-inch Bridget may as well been at home, even in her heels.

She did manage to curve her neck under someone's armpit for long enough to get a quick glance at Kris Humphries, though, which as a fan of the Kardashian reality series, set her alight.

On top of everything, the game was pretty awful too. The Bulls were getting smoked on their home court by a woeful team. By the end of the third quarter the Bulls were down by seventeen, and we made our way down that long stairway toward the exits. Hump finished with twenty-four points and eighteen rebounds, thoroughly outplaying Chicago's heralded big men, who had done such a great job against Boston only two days earlier.

So my grand outlay leading up to watch those two and a half quarters of average basketball from the heavens was $703.68 for a pair of tickets to the Cleveland-Miami game (of which I received back $756.90), $105 to Jim the evil bastard scalper in front of the United Center, and a further $50 on two standing-room seats. Net spend: $101.78.

Bad? Yes.

A disaster? Maybe.

Morally crushing? Without a doubt. Getting scammed in Chicago was the lowest point of my trip so far, by a million miles.

Just to keep the theme of the day going, my steaks at Gibson's that night were nearly on the same level of rip-off contention. Paying $37.75 for a chewy ten-ounce filet mignon, I was thoroughly underwhelmed.

And onto the next leg of my journey, $100 poorer, a million times wiser.

FACE: $25 (for each standing-room ticket)
NET SPEND: $50.89 each
PREMIUM: 104%

PART
SIX

THE SCALPER INTERVIEW

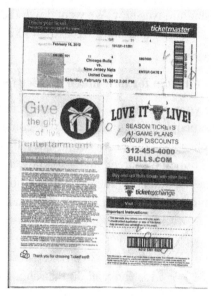

Beware of paying for one of these. Overacting
by the scalper is a dead giveaway.

*By way of my connections in Milwaukee, I procured a phone inter-
view with a national scalper who has ten years of experience under
his belt. The scalper—we'll call him "Jay"—is a Midwesterner based
in Salt Lake City. The hour-long conversation provided ample insight
into the psyche and lifestyle of a scalper, along with some valuable tips
for the discerning fan. Here's how it went:*

Me: How did you get started in all of this?

Jay: I went to Marquette University, and I graduated in 2003, but in 2001, a guy who used to cut my hair for years, he used to always go down to work tickets at the Brewers, and he'd leave and come back with $400, $500, $600, and I didn't believe him. I said, "No way you're making that kind of money."

I was a typical broke college student, and one day he said, "Hey, let's go down to Miller Park." [Where the Milwaukee Brewers play.] That's when the stadium was new. We went down there with $25, and when everything was said and done we had $400 or $500. So I was hooked after that.

So do you have a formula for how much to offer for a spare ticket?

You got to feel your market out. A lot of scalpers are a little more sophisticated than people may think. They will contact the box office and see what the cheapest ticket is to get in. They'll also know if there are a lot of tickets out on the street, and also know what StubHub and Craigslist look like. At that point they'll at least know what [the minimum the fans] have to pay to get in if they don't have tickets.

For instance, I'm working a Jazz versus Minnesota Timberwolves game tonight. They probably have $10 to $20 seats left at the window, so the most I'm gonna pay is $5 or $6 a ticket, cos I can turn around and sell 'em for $10 or $15, and you do that enough times, and you make some decent money. I save [the fan] some money and actually make a profit.

So ultimately, the guy who's buying off you, he's coming out ahead too, right?

Absolutely. You know the resale of tickets has a bad reputation. And "scalping" is obviously a word that has a negative association. People think that scalping is charging someone above face value, but [that's really only if] it's a huge event and it's sold out. Ninety-eight to 99 percent of the time, no matter where you go in the country or what type of event it is, the guys who you'll deal with on the street will give you a better deal than you will get at the window.

I rarely sell tickets at face value. I would have to be at a Packers game or Bears game or a national championship or something like that. For the most part fans [with extras] want to recoup a few dollars. They don't know what the market is, and they're not interested in being out there [selling tickets on the streets], so you offer them $5 a ticket on a $20 seat, and most of the time they will take it. And then you turn around and sell it, saying, "Hey, the cheapest ticket at the window is $30 bucks, gimme $20." That's how you make your money.

Yes, that's exactly how I've been operating around the country, buying at a fraction under face while leaving some margin for the scalper. One of the only places it didn't work was Salt Lake City. I had one of my worst experiences there. The scalpers are hardcore and not easy to bargain with.

The thing is, unlike in a lot of cities, the Jazz have a history of winning; they have a strong basketball following. For so long they've had forty, fifty, sixty wins. I've only been here since September, but I've noticed that too. The demand is so great here, 'cos they don't have professional football or baseball either, that the scalpers know they are going to get the money they're asking for. It's supply-and-demand driven, and they have a strong Jazz following.

Yes, I noticed that they weren't competing against each other; they were all in collusion.

Well, a lot of the guys you see selling in Salt Lake, they are brokers; they have jobs. They're a little bit more organized, whereas if you go to some of these other places like Chicago or New York or Milwaukee, there are a lot of guys who are desperate; this is all they do for a living. This is how they make their money. So you'll sense a lot more desperation. Guys [in other cities] will haggle with each other. You could be getting a deal done, and [other scalpers will] jump right in the middle of it; they don't have any respect for each other. But the guys in Salt Lake are a little better off, so they don't have to take lower prices.

Yeah, it also seems like the culture in SLC is that people don't mind just rocking up there and looking for tickets at the last minute on the street.

Yeah, that happens even with the internet. You know, years ago we worried about StubHub and Craigslist and how online would affect the ticket market, but from 2002 'till now I still do about the same business on the street every year.

So the scalping business is not going to go away in the next five years?

I don't think so. You're always going to have people who buy tickets who can't make it. You're always going to have a daughter, brother, son, friend who can't make the game, so they got extras. So there will always be some kind of street market for tickets.

You know, I've got buddies who put $200,000, $300,000, $400,000 a year into inventory, and they flip it, and they're killing it, you know. They work from home. I've got two buddies who started this in 2004, I think they put in $30,000 combined, and they bought into the Brewers, and they started putting more and more in, and now they put about $300,000 a year into just the Brewers alone, and all they do is sit at home on StubHub, and they just sell these tickets. They mark 'em up, and they hedge certain games that they know are going to be good, and they do really well.[79]

---

79   Fascinating—this is pure arbitrage trading at work. If there is a price disparity between marketplaces, the situation will be exploited by someone for big profits. That is a certainty in today's world of efficient markets.

Wow, so they don't even bother going on the street.

No, you rarely see 'em. They're buying so heavily, and they know what games to buy for, and they turn around, and they sell 'em on StubHub.

So you've got the guys on the street making their $30,000 to $50,000 a year, just grinding out events, and you get guys who are kind of independent. They work out of their office or at home on the computer. And some of those guys are making a few hundred grand. And then you've got the big brokerages like Gold Coast Tickets or Ticket King.

Do they ever call and ask you to get rid of their spares on the street?

Absolutely. In fact, I've got a relationship [with a big broker] who probably stocks three to four hundred tickets for every Brewers game. The day before or the morning of, I will call them, and they will typically give me whatever they have left, because they won't go out on the street with them. So I might buy a hundred of their $15 upper-level seats for $2 to $3 apiece, and me and my buddy will go out there and sell 'em all for $10 to $15 a ticket on the streets. You know, it works out well when you build a relationship with some of these brokerages because they will wholesale you stuff. Because the last thing they want to do when they're in the office all day selling tickets is to go out on the streets.

What about the potential for sports teams to go entirely with paperless tickets or swipe cards for entry?

If I had a product that I bought, I would be pretty irate that I couldn't resell it. Who are they to tell me that I can't go out there and sell it on the secondary market? It's a free market right? In a capitalist society you buy a product, that's your property, and you're free to do what you want with it.[80]

---

80   Jay has a valid point, one that is being debated at the highest levels of US legislation. No less a figure than the president of the American Antitrust Institute, Albert A. Foer, backs him

Some teams and venues are now trying to play the secondary market because they know about all the money that's involved. They know what the market is doing, and if they see that people are buying tickets for three to four times face value, they're bothered by that [and want a piece of the action].

Have you ever been harassed by cops?

Oh, absolutely! It's part of the game, but for the most part it's minimal. Milwaukee laws have changed back and forth over the years. For a while they didn't want you within a certain amount of feet from the box office; you'd get a citation for trespassing.

The worst harassment is in Chicago. In a lot of cities, if they see you, and you're not supposed to be selling tickets, they just say, "Hey, you're not supposed to be here," or "Get off this property." Chicago is one of those places where you will get arrested.

I've been arrested over the years a few times when they've taken all my money. They clean you out, and you don't get it back. They keep it as evidence. And they have a lot of undercovers there. So I've worked Bears games where I've had $1,000, $1,300 on me, and I get caught, and they take the money, and I just chalk it up as part of the game. I go to jail for a few hours and get a ticket. But over an eight-game season I probably average $1,000 per game. So if I get caught one game a year, it still pays for itself.

Philly's really rough. They have a lot of undercover. You need a permit for everything out there. Peanuts, shirts, tickets. The one time I was selling tickets out there I might have picked up six seats; it was a Giants-Eagles game. I think they caught me within ten minutes.

But I have to say, out of everywhere I go Chicago is probably the roughest place to hustle tickets. I work there, but I'm always on edge.

up. In a January 19, 2012 *New York Times* op-ed piece, "Who Owns My Ticket?" Foer cites an AAI report that says the restrictions on the reselling of tickets through technology "depart from bedrock market principles by unjustifiably limiting consumer choice and suppressing free competition. They also might violate federal and state antitrust and consumer protection laws."

Where other cities do you hit?

I go all over the country. I've been everywhere doing tickets like on a weekly or monthly basis.

I do mortgages full time since 2003, but I've been working tickets every day for the most part. I might miss a day a week, but I'm working the Jazz tonight. Tomorrow, Miranda Lambert is here.

I do concerts, NASCAR, the Kentucky Derby, soccer, the home opener to Real Salt Lake, you name it. I do a lot of Bears games, a lot of Packers.

I did the Super Bowl in Tampa in 2007, and I was at the Super Bowl [in 2012] down in Indianapolis.

Was that a tough one?

It was strong before, but believe it or not, the day of the game there were a lot of tickets out there. I think brokers bought in a bit too heavy, and the market was saturated. The market fell to a point where you could get into the Super Bowl for $600 or $700.

If there are too many tickets out there and the guys start getting nervous, the prices come down.

Are you conscious of the laws in each state? Do you know what's legal and what's not everywhere you go? Do you study that stuff or just wing it when you get there?

I've been doing this for ten years at a lot of the same venues, so every year it's the same thing. After you go a few times you know the ins and outs; you know what the rules are.

In Miami the cops were cracking down, but in Orlando it was totally out there in the open.

Yeah, I was out there in Orlando for the [NBA] All-Star Game. I was down in Daytona for the Daytona 500, and I went to the All-Star Game three hours beforehand. I planned on working it for a while and going in, but it was just so saturated with guys selling tickets, and I saw what was going on out there, so I just bought my ticket and went in.

But Orlando, you know it was illegal for a while, and they opened it back up, so now you'll see guys from all over the country. And it's weird 'cos you're at these events…it doesn't matter if you're in LA, Chicago, or New York, you'll see all the same guys. When I went to Orlando I probably saw twenty guys who I knew from all over the country.

What? Really?

Well, for a lot of these guys, this is all they have. They travel and work events every day. So they catch planes, or four or five of them will drive together from event to event. And I know it sounds crazy, but these street guys that you see, they probably make $40,000, $45,000, $50,000 in cash every year. They're working events every day; that's all they do.

Aren't there local guys too? Don't they give you a hard time? Like, say, in Atlanta?

Atlanta's a weird place too. You know Atlanta, Chicago, and certain cities, the cities that you see where you can't buy and resell tickets, it's because the guys there have pretty much messed it up. Meaning they sell fake tickets. They manufacture their own fake tickets—some of them look good, some look like crap—and what happens is fans get burned so much that they turn to the sports teams, saying, "This is ridiculous. What are you going to do about it?" And they have to change the policy, because in these bigger cities the guys are a little more brutal about the way they do things.

Even in Chicago…Chicago is a pretty ghetto city. If they didn't have the law put in place I would not be surprised if some fans got mugged or beat up, especially at the White Sox [games] on the south side of Chicago. If they weren't cracking down on that, it would be a free-for-all. You'd have fake tickets everywhere.

So you've never been involved in violence from other scalpers because it's their territory?

You know, I've been doing this since 2001, and I can honestly say that I've never been in a physical altercation. You'll get some looks from guys if you're in different cities, but for the most part they won't approach you. They'll just look at you like in a "Who the heck are you?" sort of way.

They just get used to it. At the end of the day it's a free market. You can go out and work those tickets if you want, though I would assume in some cities like New York and LA or Oakland, maybe it does get violent, and they try and run you off. But I think a lot of it is just beating on their chest because, at the end of the day, if another scalper does something to you, if they hit you or touch you, they know that they are pretty much screwed. If police get involved that jeopardizes their chance at selling tickets, and that is their livelihood.

Chicago was the worst for me. It's the only time in my entire life I've been completely ripped off.

Chicago is brutal. I haven't worked as many Bulls games, but I've worked the White Sox and the Bears, and the thing about Chicago is that it's typically illegal to sell out there. And the ticket prices are pretty high for Bears games. So there's more incentive to a scalper to manufacture fake tickets or sell stolen tickets, because they figure if they sell five or ten of 'em, they will get their money, and they can get out of there.

Chicago is a rough place. You got to know what you're doing there. Every Bears game you see people being had for $1,000, $1,200 for four tickets. I see it every game that I work. They make fake tickets.

So do you have a policy of avoiding paper tickets?

You have to use your discretion. A lot of times those paper tickets do work. But often, even if they do work, they are stolen. What a lot of these [crooked scalpers] do is that they use stolen credit cards. They will create a Yahoo! or Hotmail account, pay for the tickets with the stolen card, then go to a Kinko's and print them out and sell 'em. By the time the person who's been burnt gets the credit card statement at the end of the month, the tickets have been long gone and sold, and they've made their money.

I typically want the hard tickets. They are easier to sell. There are people who still don't know that paper tickets and bar codes [are easily faked]. So when it's an average or small event and I'm not paying a whole lot for 'em, I'll buy 'em. If it's a big event, and let's just say tickets for a Bears game are going for $250 to $300, and somebody's got two [then I would be cautious, because more money's on the line]....And I definitely don't buy 'em from the [other] scalpers.

But then the fans...I'm a bit leery [of them] too, because you never know. I've seen fans who have the hard tickets, but then somehow they also have the same tickets on email, and [they] sell the email version and then go in with the hard ticket. I've seen sneaky fans. I've seen them even do it in Salt Lake.

You've got to go with your gut feeling. A lot of times you just look at the person you're buying the tickets from, and you see how they're acting. If you're a fan and you're buying paper tickets, hey, why not safeguard yourself and ask him to walk you to the door? You can say, "I'll let my friend or my wife go in first, and if that one works, I'll give you the money for both of them." Sometimes they won't want to do it if they're at a parking lot and the stadium is far, but at a basketball arena they should have no problem with that. If they don't want to walk you to the door, then you know [they're likely fake].

Have you ever unknowingly sold a fake ticket to a fan who has come back to you?

There have been times that I have bought tickets that I didn't know were fake. I bought them off the secondary market and sold them to the customer, and it's rare, but they didn't work. And they came back huffing and puffing, and I said, "Hey, if I had known they were fake

I'd be long gone by now. Here's your money back." That's how it goes sometimes.

So what do you think the percentage is of scalpers who are legit?

I would say 97 percent of the guys out there are pretty legit. When I say legit, I mean 1 percent of these guys may grab your money and run or do anything physical to you. But for the most part even the ghetto guys from the inner city understand this is how they make their money. A lot of these guys are felons; they can't get regular jobs. You got some guys, though, who just don't care. They're in it for a quick buck; they'll do the stolen tickets and fake tickets. But it's a small percentage.

I agree, which is how I ended up trusting this guy in Chicago. I figured he was out there every day and has his regulars. And if he thinks that I'm local he won't rip me off. But fuck, he did anyway.

Yeah, but some of these guys are traveling guys. They might be in a city and figure they might not be back for a year. So you'll find some of the guys who travel around all of the time will say, "Hey, I'm not from here anyway. I'll screw this person over 'cos I'm not going to see him again."

Do you have any tips for fans? Best time to approach a scalper? Right before tipoff or right after?

Every event is going to be a little bit different. You've got some fans who think they're going to wait it out, but you really have to have a good understanding of the market. Most of the time if you wait until an hour before game time, you've got more buying power. You're going to be able to wheel and deal a little bit better because hustlers have got their only money invested in these tickets. So the last thing they want to do is lose money.

But sometimes when these events are sold out I've seen people say, "Hey, I'm going to wait it out," and they don't get in. Or they might not get the seats in the lower levels that they want.

For a typical game where there's not a huge draw, and it's nowhere near being sold out, I wouldn't buy tickets until a half hour to an hour before, and then really start looking.

When do the prices really start to sink? Around tipoff?

I'd say tipoff or fifteen minutes after tipoff you get prices coming down. Actually, the advice I would give...Actually, I wouldn't give a whole lot of advice because this is how I make money!

But if I were sending a friend or family member I would say don't get overanxious. For most events, even if they're sold out, you're going to find tickets. And for the most part you're probably going to do okay getting 'em from a scalper. People get anxious, and they buy into all the hype and end up paying three times what the tickets are worth on StubHub two weeks prior. I always tell people don't get too emotional about it; you'll find tickets out there.

Should we avoid the scalpers right outside the subway? They're trying to hit you up before you know what the prices are, right?

Exactly. It's the smart thing to do from the scalper's standpoint. If you get on the outskirts, you're away from guys who you gotta compete with who are gonna throw their tickets in the mix when you come up to a sale. And you're also catching people who don't know the market. You can say, "Hey, there are not a lot of tickets out here," and they haven't had a chance to walk through everything to feel it out.

Yeah, so I would definitely recommend to take your time, walk through the crowd, don't get too emotional about it. Fear will put you in a position where you will end up paying way too much. But again that's how we make money!

I also found that when you do a walk around, tell someone what you're looking for and then go away; it kind of helps. When you come back they will rush you and say they found what you need.

Yeah, yeah, 'cos that gives [the scalpers] time to pick up seats from the people who are walking by them. To put everything into perspective, these guys do put work in. A lot of these guys get out there two to three hours in advance, invest their money into it, and they play this [ticket] market like any other market. You might get a fan who shows up thirty minutes prior, but [the scalper] was out there two to three hours prior. He's wheeling and dealing, and he happens to be good at buying low and selling high. You know, it's a skillset that some people don't have.[81]

Well, you've been going all around the country; you're probably getting a feel for how to do this. You know what to say, and you're probably starting to feel out what these markets are when you get to a game.

A little bit. And obviously leave the designer clothes at home, don't shave, and look a little bit rough.

Yeah, yeah, because if they see you and they think you have a lot of money, they're going to throw a big price at you.

Yeah, you got to look a bit street, like be one of the guys. And what I've found is that if I look a little bit rough, fans will think that I'm a scalper, and they'll come up to me. It's happened once or twice where I've bought off a fan, and I get a scalper price instead.

You know what I would do? Between you and me, is if I were in your situation and just traveling around, I would never buy from scalpers. I would go out there an hour or two before, and I would walk around, and if you're dressed clean and looking nice, all you have to do is put

---

81   This is fundamentally true. Not everyone can just hit the streets and hustle fans for their tickets at pennies on the dollar and then turn them around at a 100 percent margin in five minutes. It's definitely a skillset. If everyone could do it, they would.

your hand up, like two fingers, and be like, "Hey, anybody got an extra pair of tickets?" And when a fan comes up just be like, "Hey, I'm not a scalper. I just want an extra pair of tickets to go in." And offer 'em scalper prices, 'cos that's all we're doing. If they're giving us their tickets at [a certain] price I'm sure they would be just as inclined to sell you those tickets at that price—if not less because you know you're going in with them.[82]

I would definitely play the game. What would it be to get there half an hour or forty-five minutes prior and talk to fans just like scalpers do?

You see that a lot. But at the bigger events, one way or the other you're going to have to spend some money to get those tickets.

This industry—if you want to call it that—is fascinating, man.

---

82 This practice is easier said than done, in my experience. I'm always wary of crossing a line and encroaching on scalpers' territories, especially in cities I'm unfamiliar with. I have found bargaining directly with fans has resulted in confrontations with scalpers in London. Never physical, but menacing. There is a psychological barrier you have to break through to deal directly with other fans. Signs might be a good solution. Let your cardboard sign do the talking instead of you.

PART SEVEN

EAST COAST SWING, PRE-TRIP THOUGHTS AND JITTERS

March 18, 2012

Written flying from Washington D.C. to Raleigh/Durham, NC

I'm launching leg two of my basketball travels for 2012, and leg four in total. I'm hoping to put my newfound wisdom gained from Jay the scalper to use over the next week. Here are the games I'm targeting:

March 19, 2012—Philadelphia at Charlotte

Charlotte fields a horrible team, perhaps the worst I've ever seen. UNC could easily kick their asses. Watching them play in Minnesota last month was painful. I cannot imagine why any local would bother to turn up to one of their games against a visiting team with no star power, like Philly.

Bagging a good seat off an agent or season ticketholder at the last minute is probably a good bet. Otherwise, the street trade can't be that hard to work. I'm tempted to pay no more than $10 to get in. Even if we're in the uppers, I'm sure we could walk down right to the tip of the terrace like in Atlanta.

Chances: 9/10

March 21, 2012—New York at Philadelphia

Jay told me Philly is a very tough town to scalp in. The police are apparently pretty ruthless. NY is a hated rival in all sports to Philly fans, and the Knicks are a big away draw with their star power and the emergence of Jeremy Lin among Asian Americans.

I have no idea what to do in this case, but I may just turn up and discreetly ask fans walking in if they have spares...otherwise, StubHub is going to be insane. Craigslist will be worth a look. This is definitely my toughest test on the campaign.

Chances: 4/10

March 23, 2012—New York at Toronto

The last time the Knicks played in Toronto, it was a sellout and a virtual home game for the Knicks. The fans went bananas as Lin stepped back and launched a last-second game-winning three. The atmosphere will be equally crazy, and I have no idea what operating the streets in Canada will be like (hopefully civilized and polite, like everything else Canadian).

Chances 3/10

CHARLOTTE: MARCH 19, 2012

Yeah, I know, it's totally wrong. But let's face it, it's a cool shot.

```
UNIVERSITY OF NORTH CAROLINA 87
CREIGHTON 73

XAVIER 70
LEHIGH 58

ATTENDANCE: 18,722
CAPACITY: 23,500
```

BOBCATS 80
SIXERS 105
ATTENDANCE: 12,792 (6,000 is far more realistic)
CAPACITY: 19,077

This trip spans four basketball arenas and three games in two days; that's a pretty tall order even for me. But I'm in North Carolina after all, one of the world's greatest basketball centers.

Though this is an NBA-minded trip, what makes North Carolina special is its rich history steeped in college basketball, primarily the rivalry between the University of North Carolina, Chapel Hill (UNC) and Duke. As luck would have it, I have cousins attending grad schools at each of the storied campuses.

As they explained it to me, the arch-rivalry is perceived as class warfare. UNC is a public school with a student body of nearly thirty thousand. Duke's students total half that figure, most of who come from well-to-do backgrounds. Both schools boast very high academic standards, labeling the area of Raleigh/Durham/Chapel Hill as the Research Triangle.

Duke's campus is more picturesque, with colonial-style buildings nestled around plush lawn space. The highlight there was the visit to the Krzyzewskiville, the plot of land outside Cameron Indoor Stadium. The space is named after Duke's revered head coach, Mike Krzyzewski, and it's where campus kids camp out to get tickets. There is a strict system in place whereby sirens ring every hour, and students have to wake up and sign something to prove they've been alert throughout the night. This sort of thing is not unusual in college basketball. My cousin Big Mo camped out for three days straight as an undergrad to catch Michigan State games.

Remarkably, the doors to Duke's "indoor stadium" were flung wide open for us to walk in. As much of a Duke basketball hater as I've been over the years, I was completely in awe. The place is absolutely tiny, looking more like a big high school gym than the arena of a perennial national-title contender and factory of many NBA players to be. Visions of all the huge games I've seen on television crossed my mind as I walked around the hallowed floor. I must have taken a hundred pictures of all the banners, before posing on the Duke bench and simulating a tipoff at the center circle (cheesy, I know, but you'd do it too). I didn't actually watch a game there, but it was certainly a very cool experience to savor.

Though the Dean Dome at UNC is a lot bigger than its cousin at Duke, it was also pretty inspiring. Carolina blue covers all the seats and banners, which include the honored jerseys of Michael Jordan, Sam Perkins, James Worthy, Vince Carter, Rasheed Wallace, Jerry Stackhouse, and dozens of others. Out of those forty-seven honored numbers, eight of them are actually retired, the most recent being Tyler Hansbrough's number 50.

The day before making the trip to these twin pillars of college basketball greatness, Big Mo and I drove for forty-five minutes to watch back-to-back NCAA Basketball Tournament games in Greensboro. The tournament, better known as March Madness, links the top sixty-eight teams in college basketball every year for a loser-goes-home knockout tournament. The last team standing after seven rounds is crowned national champion. Duke and UNC hold nine of the seventy-three titles in history.

On this day UNC was playing tiny Creighton in the first game, followed by giant-slayers Lehigh against Xavier, a small private Jesuit school in Ohio.

Big Mo and I scoped out Craigslist before heading out, and we just missed out on two lower-level seats at $100 a pop over the phone. Never mind, we thought, at least we have a ceiling price now. And so, after paying $5 to park behind a trailer park minutes from the coliseum, we rolled up looking for tickets.

We found two scalpers who had a pair of lower-level seats on the baseline; their first offer was $200 each. We countered with $100 each, and the guy wasn't having it. Finally, he caved and said he'd give them to us at such a great price because we were "a little bit darker skinned," a shade or two closer to him than the hundreds of predominately white fans in Carolina blue making their way into the arena. Big Mo and I cracked up. It was a cheesy line, and one that left us in just enough doubt that we were getting had. We told him we'd think about it and walked away.

Ten seconds later we saw two Carolina fans approach the same guy, and quicker than you can say, "Duke Sucks!" our tickets were gone. By the time we went back to him with ten rolled-up $20 bills, the only lower-level tickets he had were sold. Big Mo and I were left pretty annoyed, and we were in one of those, *Damn! We should have taken them!* moments.

To be fair, I should have pushed to snatch them up. After all, this was a game with four sets of rabid college alumni attending. Though Mo is a UNC grad student, he has no allegiance to the team, so our price threshold was lower than most of the attendees decorated in their school's regalia.

We took a long walk around the Greensboro Coliseum and found two other scalpers, though much rougher looking and less inclined to offer us any "deals," no matter the shades of our skin. Lower-level seats, in the corners with a $75 face value, were being offered at $125. We left those behind and kept circling…and circling. To the point where we just didn't see any more scalpers on the streets.

All the stuff Jay told me was playing out. We should have showed up earlier and approached UNC fans with two fingers in the air, signaling we needed a pair. By the time we got there, though, a dozen fans were doing the exact same thing, seemingly with no luck.

So I eventually reverted to Jay's other suggestion, which was to go straight to the box office and see if it had any returns. And lo and behold, we found two center-court seats in the uppers. Way in the uppers, but dead center at $70 each. Honestly, we were happy with the result. We walked in just as intros were going on, and we watched the first game pretty comfortably perched up in the nosebleeds. Thankfully,

Greensboro is an old arena, and so there are no layers of luxury boxes that render seats in the uppers unwatchable territory. The view was actually pretty damn good.

The UNC game was a blowout, but that didn't stop the enthusiasm of the Tar Heel faithful. Every basket, including free throws, was cheered for. It was a stark reminder that college and NBA fans show appreciation on an entirely different level.

During the break between games, an announcement on the PA system reminded fans that tickets were not to be exchanged or sold for over face value. That was strange; I'd never heard an announcement like that at any sporting event anywhere. That rule, incidentally, makes it impossible to patrol scalpers. The police would have to be standing over their shoulders to know whether they're breaking the law. Going undercover would seem like the only way to catch a scalper in action, and an argument could be made that it's not even worth police time.

By the time the Lehigh and Xavier players were warming up for the second game, thousands of UNC fans had evacuated, allowing us to stroll down fifteen rows to get a prime spot for the much more competitive of the two games.

Unsurprisingly, Lehigh could not pull off its magic twice in a row, and it blew a fifteen-point first-half lead to fall to the bigger and more athletic Xavier team. By the time the thrilling finish was playing out, we had moved to the lower section and joined three other UNC MBA students from Mo's class.

The whole experience worked out really well, except that I showed up on an empty stomach. The food offerings at Greensboro were pretty pathetic (I settled on a very bland taco salad and a pretzel), and on top of that there was no beer served (a disappointing NCAA rule). After over five hours in that arena I was itching to get out.

The very next morning the search for tickets to the Bobcats' NBA game was on. This time we recruited my other cousin Fahad and his friend Marques to our expedition, making us a group of four. StubHub listings were unrealistically high, so I kept hitting the "search" button on Craigslist until a listing for four lowers in the corner showed up. They were only a few rows up from the Bobcats' bench. The season ticketholder even had a blurry picture of Michael Jordan signing photos in front of him. It's kind of sad that the selling point of seeing a Bobcats game is possibly getting to see their owner rather than anything going on with the team. But hey, they are a putrid team, and their players don't hold a candle to their owner in terms of star power.

They were on offer for $75 each, including parking, so $300 in total. I shot him an email offering $200. The reply came back ten minutes later. "That's too low; these are premium seats."

That's where the conversation should have ended. The seats were great, but the product on the court was dog shit. Getting a front-row seat to a non-event should cost little to nothing. In the same way that one thousand multiplied by zero is still zero.

The problem in this case was we were driving 150 miles to get to Charlotte for the game. Did I really want to chance it by strolling up to the arena after that kind of drive, and not find four decent seats together? There's no doubt our somewhat negative experience with the scalpers in Greensboro paved the way to take the safer route.

So with that in mind, I emailed back saying we could scrape together $240, or $60 each. The face value was $85 plus fees, but again, face value meant very little in this situation. Plopping down $240 was more than generous, and frankly, I doubt there were any other takers out there. The Bobcats were a .162 team at that point, and the Sixers were slightly above .500 with almost no star power. On a Monday night, this game was strictly for the diehards or those who were given freebies. We didn't fall into either category.

At any rate, an hour went by, and there was no reply. This guy was clearly holding out for a better offer. So I emailed him again, saying we were hitting the road. He finally replied, saying, "Call me." We hashed out the details on where to meet, and after a quick pulled-beef sandwich with fried okra at the Original Q Shack in Durham, we were on the road.

After two and a half hours of AOR rock-radio listening, we rolled up into the specified parking lot and met the guy with the tickets. He was a white guy in his mid to late thirties who looked fairly well to do. He mentioned that he worked for an insurer who sponsored the Bobcats and that these were the company seats. Effectively, this must have been his turn to get dibs, and he simply cashed out. Indeed, there was no price on the tickets.

He was a nice enough guy, and he walked us around the shopping and hotel complexes that connected the parking structure to the Time Warner Cable Arena, but I couldn't help but feel annoyed. I have no doubt he would have taken $200 had I held my ground. Honestly, who in their right mind would have gone to the game instead of us? I'm still pissed about it, even as I sit and write this on the train ride to Philly two days later.

What rubbed it in even more was the plethora of tickets available from scalpers soliciting right at the door of the TWC Arena (or the Cable Box, as it's known locally). A guy offered us four uppers together at $15 each. I'm sure we could have talked him down to $50 for all four, if not less. We held the tix in our hands, though Marques insisted they were fakes since they had no wording or barcode on the back. I didn't have a good look myself so I can't be sure, but it's doubtful. Why bother printing fakes for a Bobcats game for God's sake when there are so many spares floating around? The Bulls or Knicks, they ain't.

But once we walked in and secured some premium beers (Yuengling was very tasty) at one of the many bars dotted around the concourse, I couldn't resist breaking into a smile. The seats—in the sixth row diagonally behind the Bobcats' bench—were actually awesome, and four of us sitting together with that kind of proximity to the court was pretty special.

The arena itself is also a joy to be in. Aesthetically, the steel-grey color scheme complements it well, adding a modernist taste to the place. It also feels and looks brand spanking new. Plus, the four Daktronics flat screens measuring sixteen by eighteen feet on each side of the scoreboard were the coolest I'd seen. They are, in fact, the biggest screens of any indoor arena, perhaps contributing to the decision to host the 2012 Democratic National Convention in Charlotte.

Now that Charlotte has its arena sorted out, all it needs is a real team. What they put out on the court is a disgrace, quite frankly. It's even more appalling because the team's owner is none other than Michael Jordan. Air Jordan didn't bother to show up to the game that night (his seat by the home team's bench was only a few rows down from ours), and he is probably more a frequenter of the casinos and golf courses than the TWC Arena these days.

An arena, incidentally, that has an inordinate number of luxury suites to cater to a city the size of Charlotte. I counted eight suites boarded up (I'd never seen that before; it reminded me of the vacant stores at the Memphis shopping mall), and a further sixteen were empty on that night. The Bobcats must be bleeding money, and I don't see a way out any time soon. It's no wonder previous owner Robert Johnson sold the team at a loss just to get out.[83]

Nevertheless, what the crowd lacked in size, it made up for in enthusiasm. Despite their team's awfulness, they cheered loudly. But those cheers rose a billion decibels when it came time for cheerleaders to shoot t-shirts into the crowd, and the same goes for the kiss-cam, dance-cam, or any other crowd cam that night. It's a little pathetic that these crappy gimmicks work city to city. I couldn't help but notice that the college teams didn't need to resort to that kind of lameness to get the crowd going.

The Bobcats did make a go at keeping it somewhat competitive, down by just two at the half. And this without their two "premier" players of Boris Diaw (the fat-ass I discussed at length in Minnesota) and well-traveled ball hog Corey Maggette. Come to think of it, it makes a lot of sense that they were playing better.

---

83   The Bobcats lost $200 million over their first eight years, according to Peter Lauria's article in *The Daily Beast* ("Michael Jordan Bails out a Billionaire," March 31, 2010).

"Better" is a relative term, though; they still looked like a collection of individuals rather than a team, and just like in Minneapolis, coach Paul Silas did more burying his hands in his face than coaching.

The congenial African American season-ticket holding couple next to me remarked that Silas was known for his offensive rebounding in his heyday as a Celtics player. In that case, it must make it even more painful for him to watch his team lack any sense of rebounding positioning or defensive intensity. Before getting here I proclaimed that UNC's college team could have whooped their asses, but after the last two days, I think Lehigh could give them a run for their money too. Alas, the 76ers would have to do.

We left with the 'Cats down by twenty with less than seven minutes to go. Even if His Airness suddenly bolted out of the tunnel, took off his sweats, and started raining threes, there'd be no hope for these losers. Hopefully next year provides a high draft pick and new hope. "But we've been waiting for a great draft pick for the last three years now," my neighbor reminded me. Indeed, this is true.[84]

On the way back to Durham we hit a sushi place awesomely called the Cowfish Sushi Burger Bar a few miles outside of town. The rolls were great (but the sake and wine were awful) and stuffed us just enough for our hip-hop blazing ride home.

On to Philadelphia to watch the Sixers battle the Knicks.

FACE: $85
PAID: $60
DISCOUNT: 29%

---

84   Charlotte would draft second in 2012, narrowly missing out on the Anthony Davis sweepstakes. Instead they landed his Kentucky teammate Michael Kidd-Gilchrist, a far less impactful player.

PHILADELPHIA, MARCH 21, 2012

Bobby Jones, Dr. J, Billy Cunningham, and a disco ball. My youth encapsulated.

KNICKS 82
SIXERS 79
ATTENDANCE: 20,470 (sellout)

"I'll bet you today there are gonna be lots of Asians who don't know a single thing about basketball," said a pudgy Chinese American in a tight Jeremy Lin jersey as he walked toward Philadelphia's Wells Fargo Center. Indeed, there were hundreds, maybe thousands of Asian Americans making their way to the big Atlantic Division showdown. In fact, I'm pretty sure some were not exactly Asian American, but actual youth from various parts of the Far East who were in Philly and wanted to watch the Great Asian Hope up close.

I took the train in from New York, along with a flock of others ready to cheer on the Knicks. In the interest of full disclosure I should admit that as a New Yorker, I dislike Philly with a passion. I hate their teams, especially the Eagles, and I don't particularly care for the city either. It's windy as hell, and there doesn't seem to be any point to it aside from being a ninety-minute train ride to New York.[85]

That said, I got to the City of Brotherly Love as efficiently as possible, taking a train into Union Station that would give me a full hour before tipoff to sniff around for a bargain.

Taking the subway to the game (with a bunch of fans in Knicks jerseys), I had the number forty etched in my brain. That was going to be my soft budget for the evening. Anytime one of the scalpers would ask what I wanted to pay, I planned to hit back with $40, and that's that. I'm sure this had something to do with feeling like I got ripped off back in Charlotte, and then aching to make up the difference by bagging an unbelievable deal.[86]

Well, the $40 mantra may not have gotten me very far, but it did put out an alert to the scalpers that I was a cheapo. It also gave me an idea of what pricing was looking like. An hour before tipoff anything in the lower section was going for $100, and uppers were $40 to $50. I was

---

85   I realize that I'm glancing over the Liberty Bell and Ben Franklin, but this ain't a history book.

86   This is a common pitfall for inexperienced stock traders. A bad investment leaves them wanting to make up the loss by aggressively seeking a higher risk and a potentially higher reward trade. It can lead to a quick downward spiral.

quoted $175 for a lower-bowl seat in one of the center sections, which made me gag.

In reality, I shouldn't have been surprised. The whole exercise of this book is to show that normal NBA ticket pricing is utterly unreflective of the supply-demand curve, and that a fan with a bit of knowhow can expose this pricing disparity to his or her benefit. The aftermarket, just like off-hours stock market pricing, is often a far better reflection of that ticket's value.

In the case of the stock market, a "pre-market price" reflects the difference in demand in the stock from the time of the market's close the previous day to that moment. The usual example is when a company, say McDonald's, announces its earnings after the market closes. If it sold way more hamburgers than the market anticipated that quarter, the stock will shoot up in the pre-market (because of secondary market activity), giving a good indication of how the stock will open the next day.

With tickets, the difference in time between when the price is set and when demand is most important (on game day) can be up to ten months away. Today, the ticket prices were acting like stocks that had been priced at a close before the Fed announced it was lowering rates by fifty basis points.

Though the Knicks are probably in the top tier of the Sixers' ticket-pricing scheme, the pricing was done before the advent of Linsanity, the worldwide phenomenon that took off when this ordinary-looking Taiwanese kid from Harvard scored thirty-eight points on the Lakers and singlehandedly rescued the Knicks' season. Though the news coverage has cooled off since last month's All Lin All The Time media blitz, Lin is still an enormous draw to any arena.[87] So much so that it renders any home team's advantage nearly useless, especially in cities with large Asian communities. Philadelphia not only has a large Asian

---

87   David Stern on Linsanity: "I haven't done a computation, but it's fair to say that no player has created the interest and the frenzy in this short period of time, in any sport, that I'm aware of like Jeremy Lin has." ("David Stern Fascinated by Jeremy Lin," AP, February 24, 2012).

community, but it's bursting with a load of transplanted New Yorkers too. It made for a very testy atmosphere with "playoff basketball intensity," as the cliché goes.

But back to the parking lot. I had a ticket to procure and a big game to hit. I had walked back and forth around the arena. I spoke to about a dozen scalpers. Jay had warned me that Philly was a very tough place for him to work, though it totally did not appear as such. Scalpers in droves were out in plain view of cops—the same Philly cops who had been known to bust scalpers on a whim from time to time. I had one kid offer me his upper-tier seat with a $10 face for $20. Yup, I was offered the worst seats in the house at a 100 percent markup.

I even resorted to Twitter and found a Temple student selling a fifth-row seat behind the basket for $150. I offered $70, and needless to say, the conversation didn't go much further.

By 6:45 p.m., the subway exit had cleared out, and all the scalpers moved elsewhere. In the parking lot, I succumbed to a bait-and-switch routine: One guy who lured me then called over the other guy with the ticket. The trouble is that the ticket was a dreaded StubHub printout. I talked him down to $60 on the proviso that I get walked in (another tip from Jay). He was negging on the walking-me-in part, saying it was too risky to exchange money so close to the turnstile. And in the heat of bickering about it, I heard a female voice projecting toward me.

"Are you looking for one in the lowers?" asked a middle-aged blonde woman. "I got one right here."

My ears went on alert, like a Doberman's reacting to a dog whistle. I figured this woman is a good ol' squeaky-clean housewife, a Sixers fan who was just trying to get rid of her spare and ready to be had. Hers was a lower on the corner in the tenth row (really fifteenth row after the floor seats). A decent ticket, I'd give a 6/10 in the grand scheme of things. Its face was $65, and she was asking $75. "I have to get back what I paid," she told me.

I countered with $60, but she didn't even entertain the idea. Instead, she took a call and started barking the ticket's section and row into her cell. That was enough for me; after circling the arena for an hour I finally capitulated and gave her four rolled-up $20 bills. She claimed she had no change, but when I threatened to pull the deal she unleashed a crazy wad of $20, $10, $5, and $1 bills to give me change. Wait a minute, this was no housewife!

She was a scalper in her own right and a damn good one too. She got to the point, offered me a fair price, and didn't budge. She may have even had her own ticket business for all I know, and just hit the streets with her excess. There's a chance, though, that I may just be saying that because she was white, and 95 percent of the scalpers out on the streets of Philly were black, many of whom had probably seen better days.

Earlier in the day I had read an article in a Philadelphia newspaper about the local ticket trade. In it, a white scalper claimed he got more business because the fans he dealt with were racist (his words), often walking straight by his black competitors to him.

Did I just do the same thing? The black guy I had been squabbling over walking me to the door with his printout thought so. I heard him say, "You didn't ask her to walk you to the gate." And then a sly "Fuck you" under his breath.

Honestly, not asking her to walk me to the gate had nothing to do with her being white; it was because the ticket was not a printout. Hers was a classic-looking ticket, agent issue with a bar code. But did I ease up on my bargaining prowess because she was white and a woman? Did I subconsciously feel like I was less likely to be screwed over because of the combination of those two features?

I'd be lying if I said that didn't come into play at all. This blonde woman could have been an axe murderer just released from the state pen, and I wouldn't have known any better. But as soon as I heard her yell in my direction, I dropped the deal I was engaged in and walked straight over. The black scalpers must see this all the time and lose their shit.

But the fact of the matter is I've been doing this for years, and I've dealt with both scummy white people and black guys who have been super respectable. At the end of the day my choice of scalper is down to one thing: whoever can get me the best deal.

And after my last debacle in Chicago, I was not about to get duped twice on that printout garbage. No way, not a chance in hell. For $75 I was paying just a sliver above the face value of $64 plus the $9.12 extra in hypothetical booking fees, which was fair enough for me.

In fact, the cheapest ticket left at the arena's ticket booth was going for $99 for a seat up in the rafters. So my deal was a no-brainer, even on the off-chance that I could have squeezed a better one had I waited it out.

The truth is, though, that the scalping game is a grind, and after an hour of circling the Wells Fargo Arena and speaking to nearly every scalper out there—all of whom vociferously labeled me a cheapass—I had nearly had enough. And like the situation in Charlotte, the long journey made the stakes to get in unnaturally high. I had taken a ninety-minute train ride into Philly from New York, with the roundtrip costing me $100.

Had I been a local, I'd be rocking up around tipoff and seeing what deals were out there with little to lose. So for any locals reading, you would be wise to do the same. If you don't get a deal, your downside is going to a bar or back home to watch it on a big screen. I'd have three hours to wait for my train ride and a lame story to tell.

In the end, I'm glad I did go in, because I saw a terrific game. A game that had the proverbial "playoff intensity," or perhaps Lin-tensity, if you'll allow me the indulgence. The intros were eyebrow raising because it was the first time I'd seen a visiting team introduced in the spotlight, player by player, rather than the usual under-the-breath mumblings of "andatguardnumbertwenty-fourKobeBryant." If the hosts did this because half the crowd was dressed in Knicks regalia, then it was a strange act of hospitality. Why hype up the enemy?

Jeremy Lin walked out first to a chorus of cheers. Even if Lin-sanity has been branded as "over" (by no less an authority than *Sports Illustrated*, which put him on the cover two weeks in a row), he's still a huge fan favorite. Heck, I was excited to see him. It was my first glance at him live, after all the highlights and hoopla I'd seen on ESPN over the past month.

My first reaction is that he's not very big, but that he is quick and drives to the hoop with gutsy determination. I wish I'd seen him in the midst of the D'Antoni days, but hey, I'll take what I can get.

Philly native and Sixers investor Will Smith sat beside the Knicks' bench, yapping with New York homie Spike all game. The contest started out ugly, with Philly missing its first fourteen shots, but it was tight most of the way. Lin eventually scored sixteen of his eighteen points in the final quarter to pull out the win.

The New York crowd, who had been cheering louder than the home fans, broke into a "Let's Go, Knicks!" chant on the way out. And it's no wonder; as the New Yorker sitting next to me pointed out, it's a lot cheaper to come to Philly to watch the Knicks play than try to get a ticket back at the Garden. It's no exaggeration; the equivalent to my $75 ticket in Philly is chasing $134 plus fees on StubHub for a game against the Magic in New York.

One last word about Philly: Its arena has by far the best food I've tasted around the country. Philly is known for its steak sandwiches, which luckily translate well to the kitchenettes that dominate sporting events. There were loads of different types of subs, along with crab fries (no crab, just Old Bay seasoning). I went for the braised short rib sandwich with a side of potato chips ($12.50) and a Bud Light to wash it down ($7.50). It was absolutely scrumptious. Hats off to Philly, you guys sure know how to feed your fans.

I hope my visit to watch the Giants play the Eagles one day will be equally as welcoming. Somehow, though, I doubt Eagles fans would be quite as passive about fans in their stadium cheering for a New York team. I just don't see it happening.

On to Toronto to see the Knicks take on the Raptors.

```
FACE: $64
PAID: $75
PREMIUM: 8.8%
```

TORONTO, MARCH 23, 2012

Linsane artwork

```
RAPTORS 96
KNICKS 79
ATTENDANCE: 19,800 (alleged sellout)
```

Toronto is known as Hollywood North because of its popularity with US production companies looking for Canadian production subsidies. It is also known as White Vegas in NBA circles, mainly for its strip clubs and decadent parties thrown by Egyptian-Canadian Mona Halem.

In fact, former Raptors forward Antoine Wright credited Mona for getting the team fifteen Sunday wins a year due to her legendary Saturday night bashes that wore down visiting teams. Much of the partying takes place in downtown Toronto, which converted from an industrial zone into a hotspot in just the last few years. It is also where all three professional sports teams converge, with the Air Canada Centre and Rogers Centre within walking distance from each other. Mimicking a model ran by Comcast Corporation in Philly, Rogers Communications gobbled up the Maple Leafs (who rule Toronto), Raptors, and Blue Jays along with their two arenas before building a regional sports network.

More importantly (to me), they also built a fantastic sports bar by the Air Canada Centre called Real Sports Bar & Grill. Its lighting, food, service, sound, and well-positioned HD screens make it a winner, turning the Kentucky routing of Baylor in the Sweet Sixteen into a treat.

Before that, though, there was a game to see between the visiting Knicks and Raptors. Evidently, the Knicks were up all night at one of Mona's parties, because they certainly played like it. It was either that, or it was simply the fatigue of playing in five out of eight nights in the unreasonable strike-shortened schedule. New York came out toothless, and Toronto made them pay for it.[88] The last time they met turned into an instant ESPN Classic game in February, when Jeremy Lin solidified his credentials by sinking a game-winning three over Jose Calderon with the shot clock at zero.

On this night, Lin was off, scoring only six points and generally looking tired and overmatched. His teammates were not that much better either, getting outplayed by the likes of seven-foot Italian Andrea Bargnani along the way. My viewing partner that evening was the lovely Natasha, a Raptors superfan, and sometimes official team blogger, who procured us a pair of seats from her boss for the evening. They were twelfth-row corners with $109 price tags on them. It was

---

88   In a March 29, 2012, podcast with ESPN's Bill Simmons, Steve Nash called the schedule "ridiculous," then added, "There are a lot of people with [their] hands out, including the players, who are trying to make as much as they can, and we can't really do that without playing. I don't know if there's an alternative…the schedule is almost detrimental to the sport."

mighty generous of her boss, a real estate mogul who once rented the entire Air Canada Center for pickup games on his birthday, and I was not about to turn down the offer after shelling out to watch games in Greensboro, Charlotte, and Philly over the past week. There was not much to prove anyway, because procuring a good deal—one well under face value—would not have been an issue.

Craigslist was bursting at the seams with advertisements for tickets "way below face!" Most were about 50 percent off; tickets with face values of $178 were going for $80 each, others with $75 stamps were going for $40, and so on. As I rolled out of my cab fifteen minutes before game time, I heard the chirping of "Tickets, tickets!" all around the arena.

I quizzed one of the scalpers working by the door on what the going rates were. He was completely open and cooperative. "Prices are about to start sinking in five minutes," he deadpanned, holding a deck of Raptors tickets out like a royal flush at a poker tournament.

They had face values of $349 each on them, a huge sum of money to spend on watching a home team with a 16–32 record. He was hoping to get $200 each for them, but they were likely going to fetch no more than $100 or so. Although Toronto is a basketball town, unlike the rest of Canada, it still isn't New York or Philly. If those were tickets to a Maple Leafs hockey game instead, he'd have fetched over face value easily. Leafs games are the toughest tickets in town.

We nodded in agreement about how overpriced season tickets were, and I asked him if he got a hard time from the police. The scalper, who was a white, well-dressed Canadian, said he did not. Perhaps the egregious overpricing of Raptors seats contributes to a blind eye on the rampancy of ticket scalping outside the arena. At the end of the day, an empty arena benefits no one, and the scalpers are there helping put bums in seats, as they say in England.

Once I settled into my chair, I hit it off with a nearby fan who had recently given up her pair of season tickets after splashing out a total of $70,000 Canadian over five years.[89] Fourteen thousand dollars was simply too much money to throw down annually, and she now buys a la carte on discount via an Iranian scalper.

She explained that Toronto is a city of immigrants, and the newcomers adopted the Raptors as their team once they entered the league in 1995, leaving the Maple Leafs, and their handed-down tickets from one generation to the next, to the white Canadians. Successful immigrants like Nav Bhatia, the sharp-dressed Sikh I'd mentioned in the section on the London game, pledge all loyalty to the Raptors. Toronto's highest-profile fan was there in his usual behind-the-basket floor seat, perfectly placed to wreak havoc on the refs.

Somehow, however, instead of busting their chops, he charmed a ref into giving him a game ball during a timeout. When I say he gave him the ball, I mean the ref wasn't expecting it back, leaving Bhatia and his courtside friends to bounce it near their seats for the rest of the game. I'd never seen that level of camaraderie between a fan and ref before, in any sport.

"It's his arena; we're just guests tonight," Nat clarified. Ahhh, I got it. Maybe it's a Toronto thing. It's a big town with a small-town feel, so the few high rollers there tend to rule like kings. Chicago felt the same way.

Given that it's the only true NBA arena outside the United States, it wasn't surprising that the Air Canada Centre offered some quirks I hadn't seen before. Roaming the concourse at halftime, we stumbled on a microbrew complete with viewable brass beer tanks and pipes. I sampled the Rickard's Red, an amber beer under the umbrella of Molson Breweries of Canada. The beer tasted fine, though at Canadian $10.50 for about two-thirds of a pint, it was expensive.

Furthermore, all beers at the Air Canada Centre are served with a snow-cone-style plastic cap that doesn't come off. I spent ten minutes trying to pry that thing off before realizing it was designed that way to

89   The exchange rate is nearly $1 US to $1 Canadian at the time of this writing.

avoid spillage (probably a good thing given my history). But sipping beer through a plastic hole takes a lot of the joy out of it, and I saw a few other guys also (hilariously) struggling with the cap before succumbing to defeat.

Alongside the microbrew a DJ spun some tunes with a full mixing board at his fingertips. I've come to realize that the worse the teams, the more distractions you find at arenas. Atlanta's in-arena sports bar was more popular than watching the Hawks, Charlotte had a ton of food and bar options, and Toronto had a DJ trying to lift the microbrewery into a club-like frenzy.

Original food options were also in the mix, including, bizarrely, an organic fruit stand. I try to avoid eating most of the trash at sports arenas, but an apple or banana isn't really the snack I want to wash down with my beer either. What next, Whole Foods Market sponsoring an arena? If the giant organic-food chain's home of Austin, Texas, ever hosts a pro sports team, America better be ready for packs of kale and soybeans replacing popcorn and fries.

Back on the court, the star of the evening was unquestionably DeMar DeRozan. The twenty-two-year-old from Compton, California, has one of the best vertical leaps in the game, and he showed it off with a variety of alley-oops and dunks to finish with thirty points. Drafted at nineteen, the story goes that DeRozan ordered chocolate milk at team dinners until a teammate alerted him that the drinking age in Canada is actually nineteen. Someone in the Raptors organization probably wishes DeRozan never found out.

As the Raptors closed out the win, I heard two very attractive, young Asian women flanked in Knicks regalia bicker on the way out. "Your guy sucked tonight!" one said to the other about Jeremy Lin. "Only six points!"

My, how quickly sentiment turns in the world of sports; a month ago the Taiwanese American sensation brought the house down in Canada. On this night, even though he attracted a barrage of homemade signs—including one with his likeness shooting a basketball above a biblical scripture (he is an open Christian)—he was pelted with boos (and then cheers, oddly) and had no impact on the night.

After the game, I doubt Lin took in the delights over at the Brass Rail, the notorious strip joint in the Yorkville area of town. But I did. I had to catch a glimpse of the place out of sheer curiosity (and because Canadian strip clubs are, on average, better quality than their rivals in London or New York), but it turned out to be a dud. It was just way too crowded, no doubt because there's no cover charge. With no place to sit and fewer women freelancing than I'd expected, I lasted only five minutes before retreating back to my hotel. I had one last day in Toronto to go, and I wanted to make the best of it.

I faced a crucial decision the next morning: I could either go back to Real Sports to watch Louisville take on Florida in the Elite Eight, or rent a car and drive to Niagara Falls. My head said seize the opportunity and go to the falls, which was only a ninety-minute drive away, but my heart wanted to plant myself in the sports bar, drink beer, and watch a great college hoops game.

Ultimately, I did what all men do when they are faced with indecision: I asked a woman to make up my mind for me. So the hotel concierge gave me the whole spiel about how you have to get this off your checklist because who knows when I'll be in town next, yada yada yada. Though the weather in Toronto was menacingly grey, she assured me I'd be all right once I got to Niagara. "It's always misty there anyway, but you'll be fine when you get there."

She was, of course, totally wrong. One rental car and a ninety-minute drive later in pelting rain, I caught a five-minute glimpse of pure fog and a sliver of a waterfall. It was nearly enough to make me grab a barrel and jump off.

Lesson learned: follow your heart.

So long, Canada!

FACE: Canadian $109 (invited)

PART EIGHT

TRIP FIVE, PRE-TRIP THOUGHTS AND JITTERS: APRIL 19, 2012

And here I go on my fifth trip in this series, trying to tie up all the loose ends that I haven't yet covered on my four previous excursions. I've got exactly one week left of the regular season, along with another ten days of playoff action to tinker with before heading back to London.

With so little time left in this strike-shortened season, I've had to cut out one team that had nothing to play for and whose tickets had been trading for next to nothing on StubHub in the past few weeks. It was none other than the Detroit Pistons.

As mentioned early in this book, Detroit plays in the biggest-capacity arena in the league and wallows twenty-eighth out of thirty in home attendance, so the readily available deals were no surprise. For the sake of thoroughness, however, I engaged in a mock transaction for the April 22, 2012 game against the Raptors. I simulated purchasing a pair of upper-level tickets for $35.95, including fees on StubHub. The same tickets went for $60 with fees on the Pistons website, a 67 percent premium to the open market, and it was probably even higher versus the street trade outside of the Palace of Auburn Hills. I'll get to Detroit at some point in its more competitive future, but now isn't the time.

Meanwhile, I have four regular-season games to look forward to next week: two in Texas, spanning a road trip from Dallas to San Antonio, and two in the Bay Area, affording me a scenic drive from Oakland with stops in San Francisco, Berkeley and up to Sacramento.

Here are my pre-trip thoughts on each of the matchups:

April 20, 2012—Golden State at Dallas

It's been well-documented that the Golden State Warriors are tanking their asses off in a desperate effort to get a leg up on the NBA lottery.[90] Meanwhile, Dallas is sleepwalking into the playoffs as the likely seventh or eighth seed, seemingly uninterested or maybe just unconvinced that it has any shot of defending its championship.

I can't imagine there will be huge turnout to see a fairly uninteresting matchup with a lowly team that's benching the few marquee names it's got, so I'm going with a 7/10 in likelihood of scoring a good ticket on the cheap.

April 23, 2012—Portland at San Antonio

The Spurs are cherished in San Antonio, not just for their four championships but for exhibiting all the local charm and graciousness that the city is known for. Like Golden State, Portland is really playing to lose at this point. I give this a 7/10 too.

April 24 2012—New Orleans at Golden State

This gets a solid 10/10. And to boot, I'll put a $5 cap on my ticket price for that night.

---

90   In the April 17, 2012, *Grantland* article "NBA Tankonia!" Jay Caspian Kang ranked the top (or, um, bottom) eight NBA tanking clubs.

April 26, 2012—Lakers at Sacramento

This will be the last day of the regular season, and possibly the last NBA game to be played in Sacramento for a very long time. The team has been threatening to move, though that talk has dissipated as of late. Sacramento is known for its crazy loyal fans. On the other side are the Lakers, who always attract their own fans nationwide. This matchup brings back memories of the Sacramento glory years of Divac and Webber in the early 2000s and their battles with the Shaq-led Lakers. Sadly, those are just memories.

There is a 5/10 likelihood of a cheap tick.

DALLAS: APRIL 20, 2012

I could lie and tell you this was the best seat in the house…

MAVERICKS 104
WARRIORS 94
ATTENDANCE: 17,929 (oddly, the official
attendance figure seems low).
CAPACITY: 19,200 and up to 21,146
with standing room.

Three is a magic number. Yes it is, it's a magic number
—Bob Dorough

Well, according to many who sang those illustrious lyrics of Bob Dorough, it is, but in reality it ain't, especially when it comes to buying seated tickets to an event. Dallas was the first stop on my fifth and final tour of the United States, completing my NBA sojourn.

By now I'd attended twenty-two games in three countries. I'd interviewed a national scalper extensively, and I dealt with countless street hustlers and season ticketholders. I should know what I'm doing, right?

Wrong.

If this game were a *Friends* episode, it would be "The One Where I Didn't Get In."

Yeah, painful.

The evening started out promisingly enough. Armed with a block of cardboard and a sharpie, I fashioned a sign a full ninety minutes before tipoff to get the ball rolling. My friend Wahab and I were staying at the W Hotel across the street from American Airlines arena.

The sign said, "I need three tickets, please."

Didn't help.

Thousands of people walked by. Not one was selling.

Though Dallas was playing the lowly Golden State Warriors, winner of the *Grantland* Tankapalooza award, this was the defending champion Mavs' last home game of the season. Demand for seeing a game against a low-level team openly losing for a better position in the draft was unexpectedly high.

In Wahab's postgame analysis, with a nod to Texan Dubya speak, we'd "Misunderestimated the appetite for this game and the availability of tickets. And there were three of us, which was never going to be easy if we weren't willing to split up."

A quick perusal through the online secondary market should have told me all I needed to know. Not much was left on StubHub, with the cheapest prices to get in starting at $32.95 plus fees for the upper corners. One person on Craigslist had a pair of lowers below face at $70 each, and another pair four rows from the corner behind the Mavs' bench at $100 each. But again, these were pairs on offer, and along with Wahab and Sam, two great buddies of mine from high school, we were a group of three. It was a reunion that necessitated three decent seats next to each other, not a disjointed pairing in the upper bowl.

It appeared pretty likely we were going to have to scour the bustling street trade outside the W Hotel to come up with our goods. At least a dozen scalpers were hovering around the corner opposite the main entrance to Dallas's AA Arena.

We were first offered prime seats, in the center lowers for $150 each, a slight discount off the $180 cover price. Still, it was early in the night, and we weren't willing to splurge that much. Our budget was closer to $100 for all three.

There were other offers out there but nothing too promising, so we bided our time by circling the arena. Eventually, we came across a young Latino-looking guy with three tickets on the 200 level. He explained that they were not together, yet it was the part of the arena with bars and a restaurant where people stand together and watch the games from the raised tables.

I offered $30 each, and he countered at $40, and we didn't budge from there. We were splitting hairs at this point, so in hindsight this was a silly tactic. With so much at stake (who knows when the three of us would get together again with the timing right to watch an NBA game) I should have just gone with it. But I had a point to prove, and we had it in our minds that prices would sink close to game time.

So we circled and circled some more, but prices were holding firm. Eventually, I went back to our guy with the seats in the 200s, offering him his asking price. The problem was prices had now gone up! He wasn't letting them go for under $50 each. It was a textbook case of dynamic pricing at work. One that the NBA should take notes on.

Again, we bargained, and a $45 offer for each ticket was on the table. While I rolled up $120 in my right hand, thinking the allure of quick cash would be too much to pass on, a group of three guys walked by. In a flash they scooped them up, probably for $50 apiece or more. And just like that, our tickets were gone. In fact, all night it seemed like whenever we were in a bargaining position, a group of three would fall out of the sky and move in on our deal.

Sometimes the chips aren't falling. It took a while to get to this point, but after a hell of a run it happened. Our last stand was an offer for three upper-bowl tickets with a face of $30 for $75 each just after tipoff.

Instead, we passed and retreated to the W bar, where we sat outside and watched the street trade while sipping on beers. Eventually, Sam managed to stream the game on his Samsung Android Galaxy phone, and we put together a stand made out of the cardboard sign to prop the phone up. At least it served some kind of purpose that night.

We watched the street trade thin out, like the sand in an hourglass slipping away.

A blonde woman with two impeccably dressed blonde kids under the age of seven strolled up and was offered the same seats we'd declined.

A Scottish telecoms consultant and his Asian coworker scooped up a pair for $40 each (face of $31) while finishing their cocktails on the bar's patio. "Prices are going down evv-a-rrrreee five minutes," he told me. Which was true, but there were only pairs of seats left, as far as I could tell.

Then three Mexican teenagers scooped up the last set of three for $40 each at the end of the first quarter. And that was that. The only things left to scalp that night were parking passes, which the remaining scalpers were flogging to any car stopped at the intersection.

Our hearts were just not into it, and I kept thinking of how that $120 would buy a hell of a cabernet to go along with our steaks that night. We had a table waiting for us at Bob's Steak & Chop House, an alluring alternative.

By halftime, we'd given up. We settled on not going to the game and jumped in the W's courtesy car instead, headed toward the massive Omni Hotel. Next to Bob's was a trendy sports bar (a new theme in North America, I've noticed) that we settled in to watch the end of the Dallas game, along with the Lakers game on the neighboring giant HD projector screen.

I'm not going to get all cliché and say that the experience at the sports bar was better and cheaper than it would have been at the game, because that clearly wasn't the case. The game was a nail biter all the way until the fourth quarter, when the Mavs' experience and might was too much for the upstart Warriors to handle. And the crowd reaction at the AA center was loud, joyous, and evidently optimistic for their playoff hopes after a pretty lackluster regular season. It would have been great to hit the game, and I had a sick feeling in my stomach that I let my friends down. After all, I was supposed to be the expert (I felt the same way after the incident in Chicago).

Instead, we finished off the game and headed to Bob's, where some prime cuts of fillet mignon awaited us. Brad, our waiter, pushed a cabernet on me that I wasn't familiar with at a $36 discount. I bit and ended up regretting it—$99 for an average bottle of wine that was way overwhelmingly powerful on the palate was a rip-off. The Mavs game at $120 for three average seats would have provided better value. It's a tradeoff and a gamble. I just hedged the wrong way on that night and had some two-way buyer's remorse going on. I should've bought the tickets, and I shouldn't have been suckered into the wine.

On to San Antonio.

No ticket, no face value.

SAN ANTONIO: APRIL 23, 2012

Understated and awesome.

```
SPURS 124
TRAIL BLAZERS 89
ATTENDANCE: 18,581 (sellout)
```

A road trip through Texas with a stop in Austin was just what the doctor ordered to wash away the bad memories of Dallas. Hey, I'm a New Yorker anyway. We don't like Dallas; it was only fitting that my experience there sucked. I didn't want to get too familiar and gushy about that place anyway. I'll come back for a Giants-Cowboys game and take my frustrations out on Dallas that way. But that's another chapter for another book someday.

This one's about San Antonio and its annual Fiesta, which Wahab and I happened to stumble upon. It's their equivalent of Mardi Gras, only it's just called, "Festival" in Spanish. Although its tradition bears a generic name, San Antonio is not a town without character. In fact, I was very pleasantly surprised. It's a great place to spend a day or two, with a scenic downtown crowned by the flow of the tiny San Antonio River, engulfed by a slew of bars and restaurants.

It's also the home of the San Antonio Spurs, the best basketball team in the Western Conference this season, and along with the Lakers, the most successful NBA franchise over the past fifteen seasons. Not coincidentally, that's also when their coach, former US Air Force enlistee Gregg Popovich, took over.

On this night, the Spurs were capping off their home stand against the Portland Trail Blazers. It was a similar situation to what we saw in Dallas: a final home game in the season against a team playing for nothing. San Antonio needed this win to clinch its position as the first seed in the West, locking up home-court advantage throughout the Western Conference playoffs.

Given how we got locked out of the game in Dallas, Wahab and I had our radars on for the night's game. We didn't want a repeat performance. Craigslist offered no shortage of season ticketholders willing to dump their final home game before the playoffs for far less than the box office. With the Spurs offering full season-tickets at deals for a shade under $10 a seat in the upper bowl, it's no surprise that they were going cheap online, often with parking passes thrown in.

We found a pair near the center of the upper bowl for $10 each through a guy named Gary, and we arranged to meet at a Tex-Mex shack called Tito's. It was a ten-minute walk from the Alamo, Texas's most famous landmark, celebrating the defense of San Antonio by an overwhelmed Texan army, which lost all but two of its members at a critical point in the Battle of Texas in 1836.

After some photo ops at the Alamo, we found Tito's, but Gary was nowhere in sight. He was not answering his phone either...this was not looking good. We settled on a Mexican beer and margarita to bide our time, hoping Gary was still on his way, but it wasn't looking promising. People looking to sell things online are notoriously flakey, so it was not a shock that Gary was looking like a no-show. We asked the restaurant to call us a cab and resigned ourselves to hitting the game ticketless and going through the entire shit show we'd seen at Dallas all over again.

And just as our cab slid its brakes to the door of Tito's to pick us up, someone on a twelve-speed bike came racing toward us. Huffing and puffing, it was Gary with tickets in hand. The timing was impeccable; I had completely written him off. He seemed like a genuinely good guy who just got a bit sidetracked, and the bike explained why he couldn't pick up his cell.

Perhaps out of guilt for keeping us waiting, he knocked the price down even further off the $26 face value, asking for only $5 from each of us. It was a steal, and one that had been a long time coming for me. Even though the seats were pretty much nosebleeds, paying 80 percent off the face value to watch the best team in the West on its home court was a great deal.

During the cab ride we passed by the Alamodome, a mammoth structure that was built in 1993 to host an NFL team but never did. Instead, it was inherited by the Spurs, who soon became sick of playing in half of a football stadium sectioned off by a curtain. They went on to build their own stadium ten years later, leaving the Alamodome as a wasteland that hosts rodeos, conventions, and arena football.

The Spurs' AT&T Center, on the other hand, is bustling. For an NBA arena it's massive on the outside, and due to the favorable weather down south, it even boasts a bar that spills out onto an outside patio.

Wahab and I rocked up to the arena armed with our tickets but looking to trade up for better deals if there were any to be had.

The problem was we couldn't find anyone selling tickets. This may have been because of some modest police presence, though that hadn't stopped any scalper I'd seen before. Besides, Dallas is only a few hours' drive away, and that street trade was as busy as anywhere else.

We did a lap around the arena and approached the only people we saw idling. One was a black man in his fifties who clearly was not a scalper, but he tried to help by saying he'd just seen someone offering to sell her ticket. It was evident that even offloading was difficult without the customary middlemen.

The others were two heavily tattooed Latino guys in Spurs jerseys. Wahab asked them if they had any tickets, and the one shaped like an offensive lineman simply scowled back. It was probably his way of signaling that he felt he was getting racially profiled. The truth is the guys were standing about twenty feet from the gate while everyone else was rolling in. Normally, that kind of positioning is reserved for either the scalpers or me. So it was an innocent mistake, and one done out of desperation.

That appeared as good a sign as any for us to forget about trading up and just go in. On entry, my ragbag was searched and came up beeping (triggered by a gaudy but awesome Texas-shaped belt buckle I picked up from a gift shop at the Alamo). Emptying it only unleashed a flood of snack food I bought at a convenience store to avoid arena prices. Roasted cashews, smoked almonds, and dried and peppered sunflower seeds were unveiled like contraband floating down the Amazon. I was told that I couldn't bring them in, eliciting a giant "Aww, c'mon, man," from me. The Latino security guy took pity on my oral fixation (I need snacks to consume beer; it's important) and gave me a very generous "Shhh, just go in and don't tell anyone." It was a nice gesture. I was getting to like San Antonio, and since it's the rival city to Dallas, I like it even more.

The AT&T Center is a colossal arena. It's in danger of being too big and grey for fans to feel any kind of intimacy in there, but it manages to just pull it off. What warmed me up to the place even more were the outrageously cheap (for NBA standards) beer prices. Eight bucks for a twenty-four-ounce Bud Light or Amber bock with a Spurs souvenir cup is a good deal in my book. I've paid the same for about a third of that quantity in other arenas. Bottled water was still priced at four bucks, however, so it's not exactly philanthropy either.

It's a way above-average arena though, saddled with bars, gift shops, and food on offer. Naturally, much of the food, aside from the ubiquitous Texan Whataburger chain, was Tex or Tex-Mex themed. It's not easy to avoid in Texas, and you have to try hard not to eat Mexican. Not that that's a bad thing.

Of course, much of San Antonio and the Spurs fan base are of Mexican descent. As Wahab mentioned when we walked through Market Square to check out the Fiesta festivities, San Antonio is about as close as you can get to feeling like you're in Mexico without actually being there.

Maybe the Latino flavor adds to the intensity of the Spurs fans' cheering, which is probably closer to the soccer culture than it is in other cities. Or maybe it's just that the Spurs looked so damn impressive. I won a bet with Wahab that they'd be up by twenty before the half, and they finished the game nearly forty points over their competitors while giving the starters lots of rest.

In the interim, the usual medley of shenanigans went on. All kinds of things were being parachuted and fired into the crowd, though the beach balls were really what got Wahab going apeshit.

Up in the stands, a 104-year-old Spurs fan named Theresa Sanchez was in attendance. I love that sort of thing. There's an eighty-two-year-old woman who sits behind me at the Arsenal games. She doesn't miss a single game,[91] and that sort of passion always puts a smile on my

---

91 Except when her son died in the middle of last season. We lost her for a few games and feared the worst. But she came roaring back, bless her.

face. I'm sure Theresa Sanchez had her seat comped that night. San Antonio runs a quality franchise, and I see why its players and coaches stick around for so long. Their core big-three nucleus of Tim Duncan (the NBA's most boring, but most effective player), Tony Parker (a half-French point guard who was rumored to have cheated on Eva Longoria with an unnamed teammate's wife), and Manu Ginobili (an Argentinean with a spreading bald spot and a penchant for soccer diving theatrics) have been together for ten seasons and three championships, which is unheard of in today's NBA. At this rate they're almost certainly going to eclipse the Big Three of Boston: Larry Bird, Robert Parish, and Kevin McHale, who stayed together for twelve seasons and also won three Larry O'Brien Trophies.

Even their DJ impressed Wahab, who remarked that the tunes spinning were far groovier than the ones at Denver's Pepsi Arena. And then there were their cheerleaders, who added a Texan charm to the evening. For fan-appreciation night those boob-alishious hotties signed autographs and posed with fans, which was a sweet touch.

After the game we retreated to Pat O'Brien's off the River Walk. The New Orleans spinoff proved just as popular in Texas, with goofy conventioneers dancing to cover songs and awkwardly bumping and grinding. Naturally, sloppy make-out sessions developed as the night got messier.

There's nothing messy about the Spurs, however, and their efficiency should lead them far into the playoffs.[92]

On to Oakland to watch Golden State take on New Orleans.

FACE: $26
PAID: $5
DISCOUNT: 81%

---

[92] After taking a 2–0 lead against Oklahoma City in the second round, the Spurs' old legs got wobbly, and they lost four games in a row, crashing out of the playoffs.

OAKLAND: APRIL 25, 2012

Moneyball may win games, but it doesn't fill stadiums.

```
HORNETS 83
WARRIORS 81
ATTENDANCE: 17,598 (as usual, this
was a hugely inflated number).
CAPACITY: 19,596
```

```
A's 5
WHITE SOX 4
ATTENDANCE: 11,184
CAPACITY: 35,067
```

There are not too many places in the world where you can watch an NBA basketball game and a Major League Baseball game on the same night. Oakland is one of them. For a total of $14, I was able to split my time between two neighboring venues, which were so sparsely populated you may as well have been in Siberia. All this works great if you're a budding frugal fan. You pay the minimum and then sit pretty much anywhere you like, as long as you're not taking someone's courtside seat or sitting behind home plate.

And so it happened that as I drove into the parking lot at the Oracle,[93] I noticed the floodlights were on at the Coliseum, and the next batter was being announced with a booming echo. Intrigued, I parked and walked toward both venues (without a ticket to either game, natch). On the way I noticed a group of six or seven guys drinking beer and getting stoned. I asked them if they had any spares for the Warriors game, and one guy laughed and yelled out, "Sure, $5!"

So by a giant stroke of good fortune I bagged a deal with just the second group I approached. I handed one of them $5 while he opened his SUV door and pulled out a wad of tickets in a rubber band. "I don't even know where this seat is," I said, glancing at the section number.

"Me neither," came the reply.

And that was enough for me. Five bucks bought me a $12 ticket and what I correctly assumed was a free pass to sit anywhere in the upper level. It probably would have been fine to waltz into the lower level too, had I been so inclined. But I had another game to watch next door: the A's versus White Sox baseball game that I had purchased a ticket

---

93   Upon entry to the parking area I asked the parking lot attendant if there were any cheaper options than the $17 charge. When he saw I was ready to back out and drive elsewhere he suggested I slip him $10 and drive in through a side entrance; it worked beautifully.

for at a face value of $9 from the box office. Nowhere around either venue did I see any scalpers. It's oddly counterintuitive; you'd think they'd take on the action and double up on two events happening side by side.

Strangely, after going all around the country seeing scalpers doing their thing, I came up empty looking for street sellers at two different cities in a row. If it weren't for the guys in the parking lot, I'd have paid face value for the Warriors game too, which would have been unfortunate.

Though competitive, this could have been a developmental-league game given the talent on the floor. Aside from aging veteran Richard Jefferson of the Warriors, I couldn't name a single other active player on either team. The Warriors were benching their top guys, like David Lee and Stephen Curry, with questionable injuries in order to preserve their chances of getting a worse record, and thus more Ping-Pong balls in the NBA draft lottery system.[94]

So without their top players, the Warriors played zero defense. Same went with the Hornets, who traded away Chris Paul at the start of the season and never had a serious chance of contending after that. Every player on the court was looking at the game as a tryout to stay in the league the next season. No one wanted to pass, opting on taking ridiculous shots while teammates were left wide open. I felt like I was watching a British Basketball League game, and trust me, that ain't a good thing.

Before settling into my seat at the bottom center of the 200s section, I grabbed a freshly poured draft of my favorite beer in the world, Sierra Nevada Pale Ale. At $11 it was steep, more than each of my tickets that night, in fact, but it went down like a treat.

By the end of the first quarter, the Oracle was 40 percent full at best. What the place lacked in numbers it made up for in enthusiasm,

---

94 The system rewards teams with awful records, but not too much so as not to encourage deliberate losing. As a result, teams try very little anyway (as they have nothing to, um, lose in the process), and the worst teams end up generally staying crappy for a while.

though. Fans were vocal and even on their feet at points in the game. An Asian woman sitting in front of me was all alone, eating her packed dinner of rice and vegetables with her accompanied sauces and chili powder. She'd get up and bark, "De-fense" every once in a while and whine about how Golden State missed some easy layups. It was very cool to watch that kind of enthusiasm from such an unlikely fan.[95]

It helps that the place is the coziest NBA arena I've come across so far. It was built in 1966, so that would explain it, though after creative refurbishments over the years, it's come to hold nearly twenty thousand seats. Limiting the number of luxury boxes allows it to pack in that many people and still feel tiny by NBA standards (those layers of boxes gobble up a lot of room). It's also no-frills when it comes to concourse stands. I didn't see any real sports bars or cool places to hang out, like in most other arenas. It was just the bare-bones, boring concession stands and gift shops.

There was nothing boring about the Warrior Girls, however, who were far more impressive than the team's players. Maybe it was the camouflage outfits they were sporting, but they got my attention, which was a challenge that night.

All throughout the first half, I had my iPhone updating the score at the A's game, trying to figure out when a good time to bolt across the street would be. The baseball game was flying by at a very rapid pace, coming in at 0–0 in the top of the sixth inning. There was another time constraint going on, in that I knew baseball games stop serving beer at the end of the seventh inning, so I had a fire under my ass to make it in time to grab my second beer of the night.

By halftime, I felt enough pressure to bolt to the Coliseum. If I thought the Oracle was old and empty, I hadn't seen anything yet. The Coliseum felt nearly as old as its predecessor in Rome. I hadn't seen

95   There's a sizeable Chinatown in Oakland, about a ten-minute drive from the arena, which contributes to the team's popularity among Asian Americans. Jeremy Lin was first a Warrior before getting cut, which would have been a marketing bonanza in the Bay Area had he stayed. Someone should have been fired for missing that.

anything this concrete and rickety since visiting Loftus Road to watch Arsenal play at QPR Rangers.[96] The stadium was also built in 1966, and it shares its time between hosting the Oakland A's and the Oakland Raiders football team. I find it hard to believe the Raiders play in such an outdated facility, but that was why Al Davis moved them to LA back in the 1980s before bringing them back a decade later.

The official attendance of 11,184, or 32 percent of capacity, was pretty generous. It felt like a ghost town. The A's even make creative use of green tarp to cover the unused third tier of seating by plastering retired numbers across the canvas in each section.

After rushing through a dark and eerily empty concourse, I quickly bought my $8.50 Coors Light and settled into a perfect seat on the second tier, exactly between third base and home plate. No one batted an eyelid, which was nice since I didn't even consider checking my ticket to see where I was really supposed to be sitting. I watched the A's score two runs in the bottom of the eighth inning, then retire the side in the ninth and win the game. A's fans—the few who showed up—went nuts. Eleven thousand spectators making that much noise in an open-air venue was pretty impressive.

On the way out I passed through the Warriors gift shop at the Oracle and watched the end of the game on a plasma while buying a grey Warriors cap for $22 plus tax. The game was tied with the last few seconds dwindling, when Marco Belinelli of the Hornets raced to the basket, heaving up a layup, only for it to get goaltended by Chris Wright of the Warriors. It was a bone-headed play, gifting the game to the

---

96 Loftus Road Stadium was built in 1904 and has a capacity of just eighteen thousand, making it the smallest stadium in the Premiership by a wide margin. From the visitor's section (a soccer tradition that makes great sense), it feels like you're practically standing on top of the pitch. Sadly, QPR's billionaire owner (are there any non-billionaire owners left in pro sports?), Tony Fernandez, is seeking options for moving his team to a bigger venue.

Hornets, but that's exactly what Golden State management wants… another Ping-Pong ball and a shot at Kentucky's Anthony Davis.[97]

Walking back to my car, I heard a Warriors fan exclaim, "We fucking suck! Can't we just get a good big guy?"

It's a valid question. On to Sacramento.

```
FACE: $12
PAID: $5
DISCOUNT: 58%
```

97   They ended up getting the seventh pick, which they used on Harrison Barnes, a six-foot eight-inch small forward out of North Carolina. Ironically, Davis went to the New Orleans Hornets, the victors on that night.

SACRAMENTO: APRIL 26, 2012

```
KINGS 113
LAKERS 96
ATTENDANCE: 16,281
CAPACITY: 17,317
```

Power. Balance.

Power balance.

Power Balance Pavilion.

No matter how you slice it, the words "power" and "balance" put together sound like the name of a yoga studio, or at best a martial arts center. Chuck in the word "pavilion," and it sounds like some kind of Sunday afternoon fair for a youth karate group (think, *The Foot First Way*).

Instead, it's the name of Sacramento's NBA arena that replaced the longstanding Arco Arena. I don't really understand why companies pay so much to have their names tagged onto an arena. I don't think Staples sells more staplers because its name is plastered on the home of the Lakers. I don't think AT&T sells more long-distance plans because its name is associated with the Spurs, or that Toyota sells more cars because it's stuck on the board of the Rockets' arena.

In fact, all three of those businesses have had their fair share of crappy times in the past few years, and sponsoring arenas didn't help them one iota. It only serves as an embarrassment to both the sponsors and teams when the companies either go bust or can no longer afford to pay for the rights when renewals come up. The ever-rotating name changes in US sports venues and arenas are becoming boring, and sadly Europe has caught on. Nearly every soccer stadium in the United Kingdom is now sponsored, save for a few legendary venues like Old Trafford in Manchester and Liverpool's Anfield.

And so, after twenty-five years of sponsoring the Sacramento Kings, Arco, a chain of gas stations owned by BP, pulled the plug on its relationship worth about $1 million a year to the Kings (just a fifth of the average NBA player's salary).

In all likelihood, the decision not to renew the contract probably had to do with the massive BP oil spill, which took place from April to July 2010. Spending on arena-naming rights rather than cleaning up the Gulf of Mexico would have looked even worse for BP. But that still left the Kings' owners, the Maloofs, in a bind, and the best taker they could find was a company that makes those scam gimmicky rubber bands that supposedly help your body balance itself. Yep, Power Balance, baby.

You'd think the Kings would have screened their new partners a little bit better, because less than a year after their agreement, Power Balance filed for bankruptcy protection. A court ruling that they had to refund $30, plus shipping, to every single customer who was suckered into buying one of their trinkets did them in.

Why do teams bother to sell naming rights for only $1 million or $2 million a year when it has the potential to make them look like such a Mickey Mouse organization? Not that a team like the Kings—who are desperate to move to Anaheim—really care; I'm sure the search for a new partner is underway as I type.[98]

Searching online, I found that tickets were looking exceptionally high, starting at $35 for the upper bowl and climbing from there. True, the Lakers always command a premium as a visiting team, but this was a Lakers team resting all its starters. Maybe it being the last game of the season also factored in. Or maybe the online market was a reflection that face values for the general public were out of reach to begin with, starting at $71.50, including fees, for the worst seat in the house.

With my recent experience of witnessing scant scalpers on the premises in both San Antonio and Oakland, and knowing that Sacramento's arena is in a remote area away from downtown, I decided not to chance it, and I hit "buy" on a StubHub offer for a ticket on the baseline in the high uppers for $35 plus fees, making it a $44.95 purchase (the season ticket price was $36.50). There would always be the potential to trade up at the door if the opportunity presented itself.

To put this into perspective, for exactly four and a half times my purchase price for both recent games put together, I bought an equally distant seat to watch a lottery team play in a meaningless game. Despite the fact that the Kings boast no star power and are constantly on alert to move to a new city, demand is evidently strong.

How else can they take pricing so high? Remarkably—and I really do mean remarkably—the Kings were pawning off the same seat on Ticketmaster for $92.50, including fees. Sacramento is not New York, LA, or Miami, yet they price on par with those affluent cities.

Normally this kind of high pricing would spur a thriving street trade, but it doesn't here because Power Balance Pavilion sits six miles from downtown Sacramento and is moated by a ginormous parking lot. The situation also leaves little choice but to use the official arena parking unless you want to bus it to the game.

---

98   In October, 2012 the facility was renamed Sleep Train Arena, after the local mattress company. It's hard to believe they found a sponsor with a name even worse than Power Balance.

After paying the parking fee of $10, I took a call on my cell right as I was taxiing into a spot. The call was just enough of a distraction for me to forget to make a mental note of exactly where I parked. This, of course, did not come to mind until two hours later when the sun was down, and thousands of people were streaming out of Power Balance Pavilion. A heart-stopping fifteen-minute hunt around the Saturn rings of parked cars had me joining dozens of others clicking on their remote alarms.[99] I did find my rental in the end, but I was sweating bullets thinking about how long it would potentially take to wait for all the cars to filter out before finding mine.

At any rate I did encounter one scalper on the way in from the parking lot, a pudgy black man in his thirties who was offering a ticket in the center uppers for $120 and one in the lowers for $240. When I commented that these were pretty lofty prices, he rightly pointed out that the Kings' box office, just fifty feet in front of us, was charging even more. The possibility of trading up was clearly not on the table. I offered $20 over my purchased ticket and got an "Ohhhhhh," together with a gut-punch grimace in return.

Moving on toward the entrance, another scalper quickly approached me. This time it was in the form of a blonde woman in her forties. She quoted me $75 for an upper "by the Kings' bench" (likely in my section) and $55 for one "by the Lakers' bench." I told her what I'd paid online, and we concurred that I got a decent deal. It's always good to be reassured by a scalper that you know what you're doing. Well, unless they're selling you a fake ticket.

Anyway, Power Balance Pavilion from the inside is neither powerful nor balanced nor much of a pavilion either. It was built twenty-four years ago, which is understandably why the Vegas casino-operating Maloof brothers have been angling for the city to pony up for a new

99   Until that moment, I had never understood why car remotes feature a trigger for the alarm. All of a sudden the alarm remote became the best idea ever invented. Picture hundreds of buzzed Kings fans walking around an arena parking lot with clickers in their hands and calls of "Yes!" every thirty seconds. Very few things in life create that much instant gratification.

arena or wave bye-bye to its one and only professional sports franchise. Thickening the plot is the small matter that Sac-town's mayor is none other than former NBA All-Star Kevin Johnson, someone who knows a thing or two about NBA economics.[100]

The arena's main downfall is that it only has one concourse. Every level is accessed by the same ground-floor entrance, making it impossibly crowded during any breaks. It's almost a fire-hazard situation, and God forbid you should need to go to the bathroom at halftime, because waiting outside its entrance is a shove-or-get-shoved situation. I was bitched out by a guy in front of me for muttering, "C'mon, guys, let's move," under my breath on the way out of the men's room (back to my old Tourette's habit).

"Yeah, you go, buddy! Run! Run through the crowd!" the guy bellowed.

And so I did, grabbing a pot of Chinese chicken and veggies with extra jalapeño on the way. On the two-hour drive to Sacramento from the Bay Area I was hitting a wall and seriously contemplating staying the night in a motel before heading back. In the middle of my dinner, though, I bit into a particularly angry slice of jalapeño. Just writing about it has my head trickling out tiny beads of cold sweat.

That tiny slice of chili was up there with the hottest thing I've ever eaten in my life, alongside a lethal red pepper that my friend Amer's uncle brought with him from Pakistan. I was so on fire that my legs were kicking up and down while sitting up in row P. Drinking water is useless in this situation; in fact, it probably just makes matters worse because you're swirling that chili around to all your taste buds. I tried eating some plain white rice, but that was infused with even more pepper so it backfired. The only solace was biting into the melting ice cubes of the large Diet Coke I had drunk earlier.

---

100   As of January, 2013, the Maloofs accepted an offer from a group moving the team to Seattle. Johnson is desperately putting together a pitch from local fans pooling money to keep the team in town, but it's likely too little too late.

The upshot was I was hella-awake for the ride home after that fiasco. I watched the remnants of the game the Kings were breezing through courtesy of LA resting Kobe Bryant, Pau Gasol, and the rest of its starters.[101] Instead, DeMarcus Cousins showed why he could be a low-post force in the NBA for years to come. Cousins looks like a younger Zach Randolph, only in slightly better shape. I have no doubt he'll be out of Sacramento as soon as his rookie contract expires in another season, and with any luck, a contender will scoop him up. Guys with good low-post moves are hard to find in the league, and Cousins is a throwback to the 1980s, when the likes of Bernard King, Terry Cummings, Buck Williams, and Adrian Dantley were dominating down low.[102]

Another young King in action was rookie Jimmer Fredette, one of the deadliest shooters in recent college basketball history. In person, his shot looks like falling snow. His form is that perfect, which again is a nice throwback. Heck, Sacramento should just stick to throwback tight uniforms, complete with short shorts and armpit-thrusting tanks if only to expose the retroness of those two young guns.

In reality, the night resembled a rookie all-star game. No defense and a ton of highlight plays, capped by an out-of-your-seat dunk by Terrence Williams of Sacramento. I guess it was fair enough since they were charging All-Star Game prices for the night.

Sacramento fans were equally old school, doing some strange jumping ritual before tipoff, which somehow came off as very cool. Still, it was not surprising that the Lakers got at least half the cheers in the

---

101   Ron Artest, or Metta World Peace, as he now calls himself, had been recently suspended for a vicious elbow on Oklahoma's James Harden. So much for world peace.

102   Cousins is also an old-school head case, having been suspended for a game by the Kings in December 2012 following a profanity-laced shouting match with coach Keith Smart. It was his third disciplinary action of the season, after confronting Spurs broadcaster Sean Elliot about his televised comments, and kicking Mavs' guard OJ Mayo in the groin.

house. They're like the Dallas Cowboys, another "America's Team," but with a lot more recent success.

At one point, the spotlight focused on Blues Traveler singer John Popper in the crowd. His band was playing the next night, with tickets starting at $30. I love Blues Traveler! And at $30, their performance would provide infinitely more entertainment and value than an $80 ticket to see a bunch of bench players showcasing themselves to get picked up next season. Like in Oakland, it was another British Basketball League game masquerading as an NBA game.

And while I'm comparing British and American sports leagues, a third-quarter announcement shined a light on just how different the two cultures are when it comes to fan behavior at sporting events. The PA announcer referred to the period as the "thirst quarter," advising fans to order beers and drink up fast before the onerous NBA rule of not selling alcohol past the end of the third quarter kicked in.

In Britain, fans are banned from drinking in their seats; they need to down 'em fast before games or during halftime. Curiously, betting is encouraged though, with sports bookies setting up stalls inside stadium concourses. Drinking and betting—two strong taboos, both with sound reasoning behind them, that got shuffled somewhere across the Atlantic.

Americans don't like sports and betting to mix (unless it's in Las Vegas, where no pro sports teams reside), because of its potential to affect the course of play by illicit means. Brits don't like their fans engaging in drinking during games because of their history of violence and crowd-control tragedies in the 1980s. The Heysel Stadium disaster of 1985, which took place in Brussels, was English football's low point. Liverpool fans were blamed for the deaths of thirty-three Juventus fans and six of their own Liverpool fans. The resulting five-year ban on English teams playing in European tournaments gave way to sweeping changes in soccer spectatorship, namely the ban on standing terraces and the consumption of alcohol during games.

Another key difference between the two sporting cultures is that European soccer leagues would crown their champion on the final day of the season, dismissing subsequent knockout tournaments as lower titles to hold. The real value is in winning the trophy given to the regular-season leader.

In this case, the 2012 title would require a tie-breaker between the Chicago Bulls and the San Antonio Spurs. But that's not how it works in the United States, and for good reason. The playoffs are another ballgame altogether. That's when the real fun starts, what many refer to as the only time to watch NBA basketball.

And with that, I'm moving on to Los Angeles to celebrate playoff basketball.

PAID: $44.95

SINGLE-GAME FACE VALUE: $92.50
DISCOUNT TO SINGLE-GAME PRICE: 51%

SEASON-TICKET FACE: $36.5
PREMIUM TO SEASON-TICKET: 23%

LOS ANGELES: MAY 1, 2012

The only thing separating me from a big splat is that thin film of fiberglass.

```
LAKERS 104
NUGGETS 100
ATTENDANCE: 18,997 (sellout)
```

The dawn of the NBA playoffs spells decision time for me. Do I go to Indiana to watch the Pacers (who ranked twenty-ninth out of thirty in league attendance) take on Orlando, which recently lost star center Dwight Howard for the playoffs? Or do I drive down the 101 to Los Angeles to watch the Lakers take on the upstart Denver Nuggets in what could be a very competitive series?

Yeah, I did what you would do too. But before I hopped in the Hertz 'Stang toward the City of Angels, I decided to buy a playoff ticket for game two of the Pacers-Magic series and see whether I could turn it around online for a potential profit closer to game time. The theory is that demand will spike as the buzz of the game will awaken the current dormant interest.

So after plunking down just $12 plus StubHub fees (another $9.95) to get a center upper-bowl seat in the thirteenth row, I waited and bided the four days 'till game time. Two things were conspiring against this plan, however. The first is that the good people of Indianapolis stopped going to Pacers games in 2012. The second is that the team was apparently using StubHub to dump its entire inventory! To be fair, they did lower their own face values for the playoffs to those they deemed reasonable on the online secondary market. Sadly, there was so much stock out there that prices continued to plummet.

Recovering my $21.95 on the ticket was proving impossible, as seats in the same section were going for $5. Ultimately, I had to swallow my cost for the sake of the experiment.[103]

What does that say about the demand for Pacers tickets? It says the drive down to LA, with a stop at Zoro's Café & Cantina near Pismo Beach (highly recommended), was the no-brainer option.

LA maintained its home-field advantage by winning the series opener against the inexperienced Nuggets handily, though game two was sure to be a tighter competition.

I thought back to last year's Lakers-Clippers matchup and the fiasco that ensued outside the Staples Center, where I ended up missing the entire first quarter and still paid over the odds: $160 just to get through the door.

---

103   Indiana did get past the demoralized Magic fairly easily, and it stretched the Miami Heat to six games in the next series. I read this revealing tweet from @primetimeBU13 moments after the deciding game six in Indiana:

"Hah damn Pacers fans are wack. can't even sell out their home arena for Game 6 vs the Heat. #ticketsare9dollarsonstubhub #joke"

And that was a regular-season game. Now it's the playoffs, and the circus outside the Staples was bound to be even worse. The stomach-turning feeling of going through the motions was enough to make me consider the worst, the evil last resort: Ticketmaster.

And wouldn't you know it, Ticketmaster actually came through. I bagged a pair of seats in the very front row of the 300s section, on a corner, for $162.15, including fees. I'd be up at the top, but with no one blocking my view and no hassle on the street. It was a tradeoff. For the first time in recent memory I had swapped convenience and peace of mind via the official NBA ticket vendor for the possibility of getting better value. But it was one that I was prepared to make toward the tail end of my grinding journey.

At this stage of the game, I'm not going to deny that I was getting weary of the whole chase, and weighing the odds of getting a deal at a Lakers playoff game in Los Angeles was enough to type in those stupid, indecipherable letters on the Ticketmaster website and confirm my purchase.

Fast forward to halftime at the game. I stroll down to a lower-con-course lounge, where my old buddy RJ is waiting for me with a vodka on the rocks in hand. Over a year has gone by since our encounter at the Lakers-Clippers game, and I kept his number stored. We exchanged man hugs and pleasantries, and then, naturally, I had to ask how much he paid for his lower-corner seat.

RJ's deal: Face value was $175 plus fees. He paid $100.

I'm not worthy. I tipped my hat to RJ. With all my experience, even I found that impressive. I was getting a quote of $60 to $80 from a scalper just to walk in the door (funny, this is about half the price of the Lakers-Clippers game from last season; my demand assessment was definitely off).

As we caught up, half the Staples Center staff seemed to come up and give him soul handshakes or outrageously flirt with him, as was the case with one female usher. He was clearly in his element.

"So how'd you do it, man?" I asked.

"I just stroll in a bit late. When they quote me their prices, I just give them the 'C'mon, man,' until they come down to what I think is reasonable," he says and shrugs.

I'm sure it helps that he's there every week, and he sees the same crew at the same corner. As a Sikh, he must also stand out a bit from the crowd, so his face is memorable, another advantage. It's practically like he's got a membership card going with those guys.

Incidentally, the cops this time around made all the scalpers move away from the ESPN Zone facing the Staples and go across South Figueroa Street to plow their trade. I'm wondering, why? What difference does it make if they're another street corner away from the arena? Perhaps the reasoning is that it's slightly more sanitized for the youngsters, but who knows?

Halftime at the Staples also provided some entertainment in the terraced outdoor smoking section. As people filtered in and lined up for concessions, a giant waft of pot smoke filled the air. It wasn't just one or two guys; it was every other dude out there. Security stepped in and did a walk around about five minutes into it, but that didn't seem to stop anyone.

No wonder the guys from Cypress Hill are such big Lakers fans.[104]

My buddy Shamon bummed a smoke off a couple of guys who shared their own ticket stories. They're big San Diego Chargers fans (it's the closest NFL team to LA), and they conned their way into leaving Qualcomm Stadium to "do some bumps" by claiming one of them needed insulin shots for his diabetes. The other one claimed he had to accompany his buddy in case he fainted. A few bumps later, and they were back in there cheering on the Chargers.

I really don't get why people do coke to watch sporting events. Seriously, what is the point there? Weed, maybe (though I was never really able to remember much after a few bong hits in college, but every behind-the-back pass Bird or Magic threw was even more awesome

---

104 I sat behind B-Real of Cypress Hill at a Lakers-Celtics finals game in 2008, and we shared a man hug on the way out. B-Real spends $12,500 on his season ticket, according to ESPN.com.

baked), but coke? Odd. If anyone who actually does this wants to share why, please tweet it to me on @thefrugalfan. I'm dying to know of any rationale aside from "I'm just a fucking cokehead. Get over it." But back to the game at hand.

The benefit of my front-row, third-tier seat was that no one was blocking my view. The drawback was that there was nothing separating me from plunging 150 feet onto the arena floor, splatting to my death, other than a two-foot-high see-through Plexiglas barrier.

I was, frankly, scared shitless when we first sat down. It was like being at the edge of Half Dome in Yosemite. I was clutching onto the backrest of my seat for the entire first quarter. A couple of Jose Cuervo margaritas fixed all that anxiety though, and by the third quarter I was peering below, looking to spot RJ.[105]

So there you have it; the anxiety elixir is a couple of cold margaritas. Now you can't deny that this book hasn't improved your life at all. You can thank me by spotting me one at the next game you see me at.

On to New York to watch the Knicks play the Heat in the first round.

FACE: $81.08
PAID: $81.08
DISCOUNT: 0

---

105   In November 2010 a two-year-old boy named Lucas Tang fell to his death after climbing the glass barrier at a suite in the Staples Center. His parents sued the arena operator but lost the case.

The International Building Code calls for a minimum rail height of just twenty-eight inches if the railing is directly in front of a seat, as opposed to the end of a stairwell. (Paul Steinbach, "Should Building Codes Be Changed to Keep Fans from Falling out of Their Seats?," athleticbusiness. com, September, 2009).

This seems perilously low to me. Drinking margaritas while peering over a twenty-eight-inch Plexiglas barrier 150 feet above the court is a bad idea, just for you readers at home.

NEW YORK: MAY 3, 2012

Ladies and gentlemen, your Knicks City Dancers!

```
HEAT 87
KNICKS 70
ATTENDANCE: 19,763 (sellout)
```

Watching LeBron live is an awesome experience. Have I mentioned this? Someone got it wrong when Kevin Garnett got the nickname

"The Big Ticket" because that is the perfect title for LeBron. Of course, the title "King James" is not so bad either.

Lately though, King James has been more LeChoke than anything. He disappeared in 2011's playoff finals against Dallas, and the jury's out on whether he can put that miserable showing behind him in the 2012 playoffs.[106]

The first test, though, are the Knicks, who haven't won a playoff game since Bill Clinton was in office. No joke.

But I know that when it comes to the Knicks, their realistic ability to win a game makes no difference to how much a ticket costs on the open market. Put plainly, getting anything at or near face value is an achievement for a weekday playoff game against the Heat. And as mentioned earlier, face value is no giveaway to start out with.

After this season's increases, prices in the lower middles stand at $285 per game for the regular season, and jump to $385 per game in the playoffs. Those details came from Ben, the season ticketholder to my right whose seats have been in his family since 1968. And Ben's story is a common one. The Knicks generate an amazing amount of loyalty for a franchise so poorly run.[107] In good times or bad times, Knicks season tickets are like gold dust; fans just don't give them up.

---

106   The jury is not out anymore. Not even close, after James dominated the 2012 playoffs and Olympic Games two months later.

107   Shockingly, the Knicks would choose not to re-sign Jeremy Lin after the season, letting him go as a free agent to Houston. Though the team never officially commented, it was the first time in memory that the Knicks chose to be frugal about signing a player—the *one player* who singlehandedly made the Knicks cool again. For a month they were the most popular road ticket and most talked-about franchise in the league. Time Warner Cable capitulated on its blackout of the MSG channel because it got so many complaints from irate subscribers unable to watch the Knicks on their magic Lin ride into the playoffs.

Understandably, my courtside-holding friend Ganesh was livid. "It was pretty shocking," he says of their decision. "The numbers were baffling. [Knicks management has] been so quick to spend so much money on things that haven't been working [the list is endless]. Here you have a high

Season ticketholders get first dibs on playoff seats, and the ones that don't get optioned get sold back on the open market for even higher prices. Thus, Ticketmaster's prices on the night were in the $400s, if you could even get your hands on one.

For tonight's game, my friend Frankie scrolled through StubHub after being quoted over $1,000 apiece by a ticket broker. He bagged a pair at $550 each, a cool 43 percent above the season-ticket face.

Not surprisingly, a star-studded crowd was in attendance. Alongside Spike Lee sat Kanye West, Justin Tuck, and Ben Stiller in the front row, while Senator Chuck Schumer sat in front of us, with a Secret Service detail a few rows behind on the aisle.

During the middle of the first quarter I got up to make room for a ridiculously blinged-out NFL player passing through the row with his hot girlfriend. I can only assume he was an NFL player because he was built like a truck and had on a long diamond-encrusted necklace with a pendant in the shape of his initials dangling in even more diamonds. As though that weren't enough, a fully iced-out Audemars Piguet Royal Oak was clipped on his wrist.[108]

That model retails for $128,300. The whole set was just a little too loud to be wearing with a blue tracksuit at a basketball game. It screamed, "I'm an NFL player, bitch!" The determination for an athlete to call attention to himself is proportionate to his likelihood of

probability that things will work out financially off the court, with the revenue from the Chinese exposure, nationally televised games, and the Lin t-shirts." All true.

Lin wound up signing a $25 million deal with Houston where he turned into a respectable starting point guard, and the Knicks found better suited replacements for Carmelo Anthony's ball-hogging tendencies.

108   In hindsight, the player was almost certainly Shaun Rogers of the New York Giants. In March 2013 Rogers had $440,000 in jewellery stolen from the Fountainebleau Hotel in Miami after returning to his room with a woman and falling asleep at 7am. According to the police report, the items missing were diamond earrings worth $100,000, two watches worth $160,000, a gold necklace and pendant worth $50,000, gold bracelets worth $60,000, and a diamond necklace with a gold pendent worth $70,000.

getting cut. You never saw Michael Jordan wearing anything flashier than that relatively modest diamond hoop on his left ear.

A watch-dealer friend based in Miami told me that athletes often get sick of their blinged-out watches and sell them back to the dealers. The top makes, like Audemars and Patek Phillip, retain their value well, though many of the others don't. LeBron has a deal with Audemars Piguet, and Dwyane Wade with Hublot, so those guys are smart enough (and iconic enough) to get their watches sponsored. Ironically, they're also two of the guys who can afford to be rolling around in $100,000 watches in the first place. They may want to take security around with them when they do. Just ask Antoine Walker.

On to Boston.

FACE VALUE: $385 (invited)

BOSTON: MAY 4, 2012

Reggae and basketball are two of my favorite things in
life, and this man encapsulated both of them.

```
CELTICS 90
HAWKS 84 (overtime)
ATTENDANCE: 18,624 (sellout)
```

"C'mon, enough of your shit, guy."

"You've been here all night, guy."

And the kicker for the evening: "You wanna buy a fuckin' Hyundai
or a Mercedes? It's the same thing. You choose, guy."

I forgot about Boston accents. Even though I'd just seen *The Town*, and even though *The Fighter* was one of my favorite movies of the past few years, I forgot just how pronounced—and prevalent—the Boston accent is. Well, at least around the Boston Gaaaden it is. Or, if I'm being accurate, the TD BankNorth Gaaaden.

Boston is another city that brought me back to an earlier time in my life—when bong hits and books rode arm in arm on the T, checkbooks were still in use, and debit cards were considered cutting-edge technology. It's been exactly twenty years since I graduated from Boston University, and lo and behold, this is graduation weekend in Boston.

I've only been back once since those heady years, and taking in the two things that Boston revels in—campus life and sports—brought on a rush of nostalgia.

On this night the Red Sox were playing a late game against the Baltimore Orioles in Fenway Park, while the Celtics were taking on the Atlanta Hawks in the first round of the NBA Playoffs. Just another day in the life of what many consider the best sports town in America.

So here we go. The Celtics, the most hallowed team in the NBA, with seventeen rings, were playing in a tight first-round series. It's a Friday night, and the rabid C's fans are turning up in droves. I hit a cash machine and withdrew $400, hoping to find a pair of solid seats in the lower bowl for my good buddy Adam and me.

We called Adam "Chief" at BU, in honor of Celtics' legendary man in the middle Robert Parish, who himself was called Chief by his teammates due to his stoic resemblance to the character Chief in *One Flew over the Cuckoo's Nest*. It was great to reunite with the Chief on this auspicious occasion—the final stretch of my countrywide tour of madness. So I wanted to go out with a bang...or at the very least bag us some seats I wouldn't be ashamed of.

The first thing I noticed about the Boston street trade is that it was alarmingly white Irish Catholic. Every single guy hawking tickets surrounding the Garden had the same Massachusetts accent. There wasn't a single black homie among them. Even Salt Lake City had a

Latino guy. Nearly every city I'd been to on this tour had a predominantly black street trade, save for Salt Lake, Oklahoma City, and now Boston.

Boston's whiteness was largely a product of all those guys peddling tickets from their own agencies. They weren't scalpers in the traditional sense, buying low from fans with extras and flipping them for double their cost (though they were open to doing that as well). They held stacks of their own inventory.

That's one cool thing about Boston; it's changed a lot over the years, but it's still fundamentally old school. The era when ticket brokers gobbled up as many tickets as they could in full confidence that they could sell them at a huge markup has not yet been outdated in Boston. But can it last?

In all likelihood, Higs Tickets, planted across the street from the Garden, had sent out its lackeys to dump whatever remaining stock it had to last-minute hacks like me on the street.

So there's a different dynamic in Boston. There is a ton of legitimate inventory leading up to the gates of the Garden, though not at the malleable pricing arc of most other cities. These scalpers pay face value themselves, and they're not about to turn their tickets over for anything less without a fight, maybe even literally.

They have ticket-broker mindsets that don't switch off when they leave their offices for the streets, unlike brokers in other cities who simply pawn off their stock to street scalpers. Why scalpers not employed by agents don't bother to infiltrate this stranglehold I'm not sure. But walking by Fenway Park the next day, I noticed the same homogenized pack fanning stacks of their inventory. Even Jay avoids working in Boston, hearing that it's too difficult a market to penetrate.

As a result, a cabal of ticket agents controlled street pricing around the Garden on this night; the trade was rampant, but pricing was high. Upper-bowl centers were going for $150 each, and middle-lower centers were at $300 each. I shouldn't have been surprised, but just listening to those prices made me gulp hard.

Chief was pretty content sitting up in the 300 sections, but I was having none of it. Even though I bargained a guy down to $150 for a pair of 300s in the center (face value), I decided to retreat to a neighboring sports bar, down a Sam Adams Light, and reevaluate the situation. With five minutes to go until game time, we mentally replenished and came back.

The problem was that some guys grew weary of dealing with me because, well, because I'm the Frugal Fan, and they don't like guys who are frugal and choosy, and who scan the seating chart on their decrepit BlackBerrys. They want guys in suits and moms with their kids. Not guys like me. Which is why I got the "You've been here all night, guy," comment.

I even approached one female fan who wanted $400 for her pair of lower corners, which naturally I laughed at. It's one thing to get crazy quotes from ticket brokers, but from another fan it's just downright disrespectful.

Still, I found one kid who would give me the time of day. He looked a bit like (and talked a lot like) Christian Bale's character from *The Fighter*, Dicky Eklund. There was a lot of "How much you wanna spend?" going on, and I finally put a limit on the whole charade, saying $350 was my absolute maximum for two lowers in the center, after he stalled at $400. No matter, he went to go look for the tickets in loge 11 while Chief and I waited.

After what seemed like an eternity, he came back, claiming those section 11s got sold for $250 each. Instead he had a pair of lower corners in loge 4, row 11. It's not what I wanted, and yet he still wanted his $350. That wasn't happening. So I offered $250 for the pair.

"Oh no way, man—c'mon, guy, enough of your shit." And he was about to walk. The lower centers were all gone with at least one of the crews, and perhaps both. Tipoff was minutes away. I had to raise my offer or I'd lose these seats and perhaps pay more for crappier options. I was at the exact tipping point when inventory starts to decline and prices start to trickle up again for the latecomers who choose from the scrap heap.

He stuck to his guns at $300, and I held out $270 in cash. "Ok, just give me $280," he said, exasperated but angry.

I waited until he counted the stack, swapped a $10 bill for a $20 bill, and we were on our way in.

It turned out our seats were gems.

They were two right on the aisle, in the near corner off the baseline, where the Hawks' bench was. In fact, acclaimed Boston sportswriter Jackie MacMullan was sitting slightly to our left with her family, only two rows ahead of us.

The revamped Garden is a far cry from the old Garden, where Chief and I would buy restricted-view tickets for $12, then go and stand on a narrow concourse to watch the likes of Michael Jordan's Bulls take on Larry Bird and the C's. That fan base, like the scalpers outside, was predominately made up of white males.

Today, the Garden is much more diverse. It's not LA or San Antonio, but it has a fair share of African American representation, along with a sea of women (many somewhat scantily clad, I might add). It also has cheerleaders, something Celtic granddaddy Red Auerbach banned in the old Garden, but finally acquiesced to for the new structure while practically on his death bed.

And if LA and New York are all about the celebs in the audience, Boston is definitely about its crazy fans, dressed up in all kinds of zany Celtic gear. More than any arena I've seen, the Garden hosts more fanatics in the true sense of the word.

On the way in, Chief and I rode the escalator with a Rasta dressed in a lime-green fitted Celtics suit and oversized green specs. Out of nowhere, he rhapsodized on the genius of Bob Marley and the Wailers. "You know what made them so great? Practice. Every day they were in rehearsal. Every day, man."

Naturally, I asked him whether he smoked victory blunts instead of victory cigars, but he was already on cloud nine. And he was not alone.

There were a good twenty to thirty clowns in top hats, crazy wigs, and the like. There was even a 102-year-old woman in the stands, forced to dance to the music as her much younger relatives waved her arms for her. It was like a female version of *Weekend at Bernie's*.

In fact there were quite a few senior citizens in the audience. And young trendies. Again, this was a far cry from the Garden of yesteryear.

One thing that hasn't changed, though, is Massachusetts's onerous laws on purchasing alcohol. You need an in-state license or a passport, prompting me to drag Chief out of his seat to buy two margaritas and a bag of nuts for me ($22.50). I wasn't even allowed to hold my drink in the concourse.

During a break, I embarked on a mad scramble around the concourse looking for a Kevin Garnett jersey for a friend. At nearly thirty-six, KG still commands a cult following as one of the most intense players in the league, even if his crazy-eye stare-downs drum up less fear in the hearts of opposing players. I found a green shamrock version for $30, and I grabbed a Celtics' salt-and-pepper set along with it for another $20 before rushing back to my seat in time for the fourth quarter.

The game was very tight, with Atlanta and Boston trading leads, but Rajon Rondo, who had just come off a one-game suspension for chest bumping a ref, was stellar. He had a triple-double on the night, and he was the Celtics' lynchpin from the start. When the game went into overtime, he scored the team's first five points and nearly iced the game with a layup that went astray, only for KG to slam it home. The Garden went crazy in celebration, exuding Celtic pride all the way down the Mass Turnpike.

After a three-hour marathon of a game, fans streamed out chanting, just tasting that eighteenth championship around the corner…

FACE: $125
PAID: $140
PREMIUM: 12%

NEW YORK: MAY 6, 2012

```
KNICKS 89
HEAT 87
ATTENDANCE: 19,763 (sellout)
```

"Caveat emptor" means, "buyer beware" in Latin. Those words kept ringing in my head, over and over, as I took the C train up to Thirty-fourth Street just after tipoff for game four of the Knicks-Heat first-round matchup.

Once and for all I wanted to retest the New York scalper trade after everything I've seen and heard over the years. My experiences encompass nailing a great discount to a Knicks-Warriors game back in 2000, and having someone try to pass off a candy bar wrapper coiled in his pocket as a ticket back in 1992 before the infamous Charles Smith game. There was also the Jordan-led Wizards-Knicks battle in 2003, when I was offered a pile of fake tickets that were so bad, the cheap ink was sticking together.

So New York's been a mixed bag as far as ticket deals are concerned, but there have been no grab and runs or fake tickets that I have personally been suckered into. I can't say the same for friends and friends of friends, though. I've heard every story in the book, from fake tickets, to putting a thumb on the date of a ticket, to buying tickets to the opera instead of WrestleMania (yeah, no joke).

So I lapped the streets around MSG with extreme caution on the afternoon of Sunday, May 6, 2012. New York's Garden has one of the strangest entrances of any arena in America. The venue was actually built above Penn Station and, somehow, a concert theater known as The Theater at Madison Square Garden. Let me say that again, New York's busiest train station sits underneath Madison Square Garden. Because of its complex layout, to get into MSG you have to walk a platform and cross over from one side of the city block to the other, taking a full five to ten minutes of shuffling through the crowd to get to the turnstiles. After that you're still facing an array of escalators to get up to the main concourse.

It means two things: Scalpers are nowhere near the turnstiles when they're selling, and you're not going to go back and look for them afterward if something goes wrong. Well, you're probably not going to do that anyway.

MSG does not support a thriving scalper's market either. It's definitely not Boston, Dallas, Orlando, LA, or virtually any other major NBA market, save Chicago. There are only a half dozen regulars who congregate on the corner of Seventh Avenue and Thirty-third Street, hovering between there and the nook between MSG and One Penn Plaza, a giant office building occupying the block next door.

As I exited the subway station, I walked up the stairs leading to that nook and slid by the group of scalpers. "Tickets?" one asked.

"Yeah, I'm looking," I said. I offered $60 to $80 just to get in the door (i.e., sit in the worst seat in the house, with full knowledge that the worst seat in the house was priced at $160 at the box office before they sold out).

Understandably, my quote back was $150. I balked, electing to take a lap around the block. I went up Thirty-third Street and turned the corner to the left on Eighth Avenue. There wasn't much action going on, just a bunch of travelers coming out of Penn Station looking for cabs. Since it's situated above the biggest rail hub on the East Coast, rather than a remote gated destination like in Philly or San Antonio, there's a completely different dynamic between MSG and every other NBA arena. You get businessmen and tourists mixing with Knicks and Rangers fans on the sidewalk, as well as concertgoers from all genres.

A left turn pulled me closer to Thirty-second Street and Eighth Avenue, toward a number of black people hanging out on the corner. With any luck, someone would have a ticket for me. I got a "Tickets?" mumble from a guy with glossy red eyes, and I replied that I was looking for one.

He said he had a ticket in section 218 with a face value of $255. The usual "How much you looking to spend?" question came into play, and I responded that I wasn't looking to spend more than $60 or $80.

"I can't go under $150 for these," he countered. I was pretty skeptical. A full-blown crackhead woman walked by this guy and muttered something to him, which he acknowledged. It didn't matter what she said, but the fact that he knew her made me wonder why a scalper dealing in assets worth hundreds of dollars is associating with crackheads. I wouldn't. But then again I don't work the streets of New York.

Grandmaster Melle Mel said it best in "The Message": *It's like a jungle sometimes, it makes me wonder how I keep from going under.*

So crackheads notwithstanding, we agreed I'd go across the street and down a beer while he tried to unload his stock. If he had anything left in ten minutes we'd revisit the situation closer to my strike price of $120.

Ten minutes later I was back. He told me he'd sold one of them and had the other, which was the perfect scenario. He wanted the agreed-upon $120, though by now the first quarter had ended, and I lowered my offer to $100. He grudgingly agreed.

One hundred dollars for a $255 ticket to a Knicks-Heat playoff game in New York, sitting in the middle of the second level. I must have been dreaming. The same ticket would have gone for at least $350 on StubHub earlier in the day.

We walked in toward the back entrance of Penn Station, and he pulled out the ticket. If it wasn't New York I wouldn't think twice about it, but I grabbed it, felt it up and down, and checked everything possible for a flaw.

Its flipside was a bit rough. It had a Chase Manhattan Bank Logo on the front, and the time and date of the game, along with the price, but the back of the ticket's frayed feeling had me worried, even though it had a retail coupon on it.

So I gave it back.

"Man, that is not a fake," he insisted. He didn't plead that hard, though. He just walked into the station and carried on.

This was the equivalent of passing on the stock of a company flirting with bankruptcy. The upside was $255, and the downside equated to losing my entire $100 investment. Even the most naive investor knows better than to buy a stock like that. Ninety percent of the time you're going to get burned.

So I kept circling the arena, eventually landing back at the first scalper hangout. They had since moved to the Seventh Avenue entrance, in full view of what scant cops were around.

Along the way a guy quoted me $100 for a nosebleed. I reasoned that there were a lot of fakes out there and left it at that. But then something revealing unfolded in front of me. I saw two guys buying tickets off the small mob of traders on Seventh Avenue. The two tickets had that same cut, font, and Chase Manhattan logo on them. They were almost certainly from the same stack I had been offered. Could the ticket I passed up have been real?

I hovered around to see what was happening. A deal was struck. One guy was to go in first to make sure they were legit, and once his ticket was scanned, the other guy would pay the scalper and go in himself. This was the same ploy Jay had suggested in case tickets are in doubt. It made perfect sense.

I hovered and waited to see when that phone call would come, and eventually it did. The second guy nodded and smiled. They were in, and the tickets were real. In all likelihood so was that section 218 ticket I had just passed on. I probably just blew a chance to get a hell of a deal for a huge game.

Instead, I walked over to Stout NYC, my favorite New York sports bar, on Thirty-third between Sixth and Seventh. I ordered a pint of Bud Light and a plate of sweet potato fries for $15 and watched the game.

And what a game it was. Stout was going ballistic. Per square inch, it was probably even louder than the Garden. The Knicks and Heat were trading punches, the likes MSG had not seen since the Ali-Frazier bouts of the 1970s.

One thing about settling into a sports bar is you get to hear commentary and watch close-ups. Coaches are miked-up, injuries—like Baron Davis's horrific knee buckle in the third quarter that tore his patella—are replayed from every angle.

And so are internal squabbles. With only a minute to go and the game tied, Carmelo Anthony launched an audacious three with a hand in his face. Nothing but net. The bar went ballistic, and the Knicks were up by three with fifty-four seconds left.

Watching the instant replay, I could see the other person vying for "most selfish player in the world" on the Knicks, J. R. Smith, spotting up for an open three to Melo's left. Just as the ball swishes through the net and the Garden crowd goes bananas, Smith rushes to Melo and harangues him for not passing the ball.

It was not the time for bitchiness, but hey, that's the Knicks. I definitely wouldn't have caught that nuance at the game, and watching it moments after real time added a lot of color to the experience. There's something to be said for the sports bar atmosphere too.

We were even given orange Knicks towels to wave around. And the food at Stout is better than at MSG. And cheaper.

But it ain't the Garden.

There's a saying: If a deal looks too good to be true, then it probably is.

The thing is that's not really the case with sports tickets, especially if you're buying them off the street. Sometimes a deal looks too good to be true, but it is true.

Which is what makes the whole experience so worthwhile. It's a transparent marketplace. There's a buyer, a seller, and a product. Each of the two parties values the product separately, throws out his or her gambits, and the meeting of the supply-demand curve takes place right then and there. There is no purer, quicker pricing of any asset in the world than tickets bought and sold on the street.

Use the system to your advantage. Just be cautious out there.

PART NINE

THE BRAINS

At thirty-one, Barry Kahn is singlehandedly changing the way teams price tickets. Kahn's six-year-old dynamic-pricing software company, Qcue, has already signed up over forty clients, including half of Major League Baseball, and franchises across the NBA, the National Hockey League, Major League Soccer, and NASCAR tracks.

In 2007 Kahn, who has a PhD in economics from the University of Texas, and his partner, Jiten Dalvi, won start-up business competitions and raised $327,000 along with time at the Austin Technology Incubator. Since then they've proven that even basic versions of dynamic pricing will give teams a lift of $900,000 a season on average. His software costs teams up to $200,000 a year, though a basic model can run as low as $25,000 and provide a sizeable return on investment..

In September 2012, Kahn and I engaged in a fascinating conversation on the future of sports ticketing. Here's how it went:

Me: How has the pickup been with your business?

It's turned exponential, if you will. Teams are really embracing this. It started early on for us with the San Francisco Giants; we gathered a customer or two, and it took a little bit for teams to see what we're doing and the value we've provided, but it's really picked up. In the next two to three years, you'll see it in every team across major sports leagues in the United States.

So is it a foregone conclusion that every pro team will use some form of dynamic pricing?

Yes, although you hit the nail on the head when you say, "some form of dynamic pricing." There is really a big range amongst what teams are doing that would classify as dynamic pricing.

There are a lot of teams out there that believe what they're doing is dynamic pricing, [but] really what they have are their four pricing tiers, and maybe if the game turns hot, they'll switch the tiers or every once in a while make an adjustment in price. But there really is a big difference between that and what I would really consider true dynamic pricing, where teams are setting prices at the beginning of the year and then moving prices in a clear and consistent fashion with a set of objectives.

I think teams are starting to realize that the true form of dynamic pricing drives a lot more value than the more haphazard one-off method. It takes a little bit for teams to understand that there is a difference, because dynamic pricing has really become a buzzword in the industry. I think people are very excited to say that they do it, and actually they may or may not be.

What are the nuances in modeling between different teams in different sports?

One of the big things is the amount of inventory. I'll give you a big example: [Major League] baseball, on average, has twice as many seats in the venue as an NBA team. It has twice as many games. And [MLB] teams will typically sell about half of their tickets as season tickets, whereas an NBA team will sell closer to 90 to 95 percent of their tickets as season tickets.[109]

What do you think of pushing inventory through Groupon? Does it run counter to your model?

I'm probably going to give you an answer that you won't expect. I am a huge proponent of third-party distribution channels. We're not talking Groupon yet, but overall I think third-party distribution channels are fantastic. A large part of the reason that the secondary market has picked up market share against the primary market is not necessarily [due to] price. Price obviously plays a role, but [it mainly] has been marketing.

StubHub spends ungodly amounts of money on marketing. The value of these distribution channels is they go out to reach customers. So in a lot of ways the teams are losing the battle of the secondary market. We're past the day when teams can say, "Everyone wants to go to my games, so they're going to have to come find me wherever I put my ticket." I think the value of Groupon, though, is that you can just ping one hundred thousand people, or ten million people, whatever that number is, who aren't in the team database.

To that extent, Groupon is fantastic. To the extent that it is a one-off type offer with heavy discounting on a product that encourages people to wait and will likely bring in people who are never willing to pay full price, I don't think it provides the right value. I'm all for distribution channels. I'm just not a big believer in the [one-off] fan. You can't do ten Groupon offers during the year, so it's a one-shot pickup from sales strategy.

---

109 Doing the math, MLB teams on average have ten times the number of single-game seats available per event than NBA teams, which makes dynamic pricing far more valuable to pro baseball.

Do you think teams are discreetly using StubHub to clear their inventory? I am convinced of it.

If they're not, they should be, and they shouldn't be discreet about it. StubHub is a great distribution channel. There are a percentage of people who will use StubHub before they use Ticketmaster. And if that's where your customers are going to buy tickets, then why shouldn't you be offering your product there?

Anything the teams can do to leverage their inventory and make sure it's in front of their fans, they should do. Distribution is just as big of a problem as pricing.

I agree, however, I think there is a legal issue for teams that signed with Ticketmaster to list their tickets elsewhere.

There is, and part of the problem in the industry is the way ticketing contracts are structured. Ticketing contracts are set up so that the ticketing system [i.e., Ticketmaster] is the exclusive ticketing channel of individual tickets, which was fantastic back twenty years ago before the internet was what it is today. [Back then] teams leveraged the ticketing system because they didn't want their fans to have to come directly to the box office. So they gave them outlets in the back of strip malls, and the grocery store, and wherever else it was, to reach out to the customer wherever the customer was.

And now that is no longer the distribution channel. [The new system is] now forcing people to a website. But yes, [rerouting inventory is] a complete violation of every Ticketmaster contract. Those contracts will have to get rewritten.

When are they expiring?

It varies by team. Teams typically sign about five-year deals; it's very staggered.

Some are coming up this year, some more are gonna come up next year, and it's gonna be year after year. What you are seeing is teams are—really under the table—using these distribution channels. Teams are starting to push back a bit and say, "You can't restrict me from sell-ing my inventory when you're not able to sell it."

Why do they even need Ticketmaster? Each league could easily have its own site.

Part of the issue is the way the ticket deals are structured. Essential-ly, the teams all operate on their own. Typically, the ticketing system [company] pays the team upfront. So they are buying the right to be the exclusive distribution channel of the inventory. They don't buy the inventory.

So if you're Ticketmaster and you sign a deal with the Knicks, you say "I want to be the exclusive distribution channel for your tickets, and I want to charge a service fee of "X" on a ticket. And in exchange for this I'm going to give you the software for managing your ticket stock. I'm going to install the barcode scanners or whatever else you need at [Madison Square Garden], and I'll front you $500,000." That's what a lot of these deals look like; so depending on the cash situation of the team, it's easier or harder to walk away from that.

You actually have to have a team with a little more foresight to say, "No, we're actually going to pass on this upfront money." Financially for the team, it would be better off passing. Over the course of that five-year deal they actually would do better if they paid for the soft-ware on some sort of licensing terms and, in exchange, didn't have to give those service fees to the ticketing system.

Have you suggested this to the teams?

There are a handful of teams that have started doing things differ-ently. The teams…(sigh). I think most people at the teams understand this, but there is an issue of cash today, and nobody ever gets fired for doing the status quo.

Right now there's not a great alternative to a ticketing system. I think there will be, but right now, yeah, there isn't the version of what you see like with theaters in London, where they sell tickets on every ticketing system they can find. They are going wide on distribution; that doesn't exist in the United States right now.

Let's drill down on your algorithm. Is it completely automated like the stock market, or more mechanical, like the way the stock market was run fifty years ago?

It's a very different situation from a stock market. The stock price is moving with buyers and sellers, and they are adjusting their bid and ask price. So this looks a lot closer to airline pricing or hotel pricing. We will be at a point, probably by the end of 2012, where we have our first clients going fully automated.[110] The way it works right now is that they have an interface that they can log into. We sort of automate the process of what new prices should be, but there's a manual confirmation step where once they approve that, then it gets pushed through.

Is there a risk that if it's fully automated that the guy in row J will pay three times more than the guy sitting in front of him?

You could do that manually too. There is a risk of that. It happens on flights. I've been on my share of flights where I've paid three times what the guy next to me paid. I can actually think of one where I paid ten times.

Yes, that's possible, but it depends on what the club is trying to achieve with dynamic pricing. And if that is pushing up pricing on scarce inventory in high-demand situations, you can see something like that happening. [But] a lot of time the goal [is more about] moving people around the venue.

My number-one sign of mispricing is when you can visually determine where the pricing breaks are when you look at the venue. I'm sure you've seen it thousands of times. You go in there, and by a certain area there is just a line where nobody is sitting in the better seats, and all of a sudden there is a big clustering of people because that seat

110   In a March 2013 update Kahn said Qcue's functionality for full automation was nearly ready, and that it was "highly likely" one of his clients in baseball would adopt it by the summer.

one row over is a price break. Or my personal real pet peeve is when you go to a partially empty stadium where people are lined at the top row of the upper deck.

A lot of what we're trying to work on has really been a big shift in terms of dynamic pricing. [We aim] to move prices around the venue to not have that.

It doesn't make sense to have fifty price points on something that is not really selling, because the purpose of differentiation, of having seats at a higher price, is to save them for someone who is willing to come in and pay a higher price. But if that person isn't going to come, why aren't we taking the fan who's purchased tickets farther back and moving him up?

There's an opportunity through pricing to provide better seats and a better experience for the fans and at the same time generate more revenue for the club, because a lot of time what the fan says is, "I don't see the difference between these two areas so I'm going to sit in the cheaper seats," or "The only thing that matters is just getting into the stadium." That's why you see this person sitting in the top row of the upper deck. [Whereas] if you put them in a better seat they're going to have a better experience and come back more frequently.

And perhaps buy more beer or baseball caps or whatever because they think they got a freebie, and they say, "Hey, you know what? I saved twenty bucks, and I may as well spend it."

Exactly, and you know the thing is, there's nothing that makes you feel less cared about than when you're being pushed in that top row and there are seats twenty rows below you that are empty.

I think you have to have a bit of a screw loose to just sit up there, why don't you just walk down a few rows?

Well, that's another problem that teams have. How do you prevent someone from doing that, when people at your venue know that they can [move down a number of rows]? Maybe they can't get into that section right behind the players' bench because there is some security there, and they don't have the tickets to get into that area, but they can clearly move into the best seat within their section.

Which begs the question, then, of how teams should price the unsold season tickets to those empty seats? There's a strong argument that unless teams are selling out those sections, they shouldn't sell season tickets in them.

Instead of guaranteeing that they won't undersell their few season ticketholders in the upper deck, they can then price them as low as they want whenever they want.

There is an argument to be made for that. But it also comes back to how [teams] sell season tickets in [certain] areas if fans know they can go to a game basically for free in other sections? [Teams have] got to be careful that they don't do it in such a way that their season ticketholders decide not to become season ticketholders.

You know, it's a tough one. For instance, there were loads of Nets games with tickets for sale at one penny on StubHub [when they played in Newark in 2012].

So let me give you how that turns into your counterpoint, though. Those tickets didn't sell. Think about that for a second. Those tickets were listed for a penny on StubHub, and people still weren't buying them. That tells me that price isn't the issue.

[Maybe it's] the time commitment to going there, [or that] it's a great experience on TV, [or it's] the cost of parking; it's [ultimately] still not worth going. Maybe what we should be doing now is focusing on the fans who are actually there, and what you have to say is that in some situations there's nothing I can do to get that extra person through the door.

So teams with very low attendance shouldn't give away their tickets to get people through the door and make their revenue on ancillary sales?

No. If you can't get people in for a penny, you're not getting them in for free. That's a huge issue that teams have. There are actually questions on how you comp a ticket. I've had this discussion with teams.

Because when you give someone something for free, and they don't have to give you anything for it, the odds of them showing up is so low. You can't just walk down the street and give away tickets.

So comping the ticket doesn't really solve the problem.

The question is, how do you actually get people in there? The other thing it does is demean the value of the product. By putting that zero price tag on it, what does that say to your season ticketholders or the people who did pay full price on it? You have to be very careful if you're going to do that.

It's a delicate balance.

It's a very delicate balance. It's not quite like a diamond ring, where the value of the ring essentially is what you paid for it, or at least that's how it's going to be judged. But there is some element of, you put a higher price tag on it and people are going to value it more.

The same comped ticket, if someone handed me a ticket that says $500, you would view it very differently from a ticket that says $5. I'd probably make sure I would go to that game, and if someone handed me a comped ticket, I probably would not go. It could be the same exact seat.

[Instead of focusing on comping tickets, teams should be asking,] "Is there something we can do to better set relative prices across the venue to at least have people sitting where we want them to sit?"

The example I'll give you started with a baseball team that averages 50 percent or under in attendance. I asked them, "Why do you open your upper deck? Half those seats are upstairs. How would you feel if you only put ten thousand people in the park, and they all sat downstairs?"

They said, "Actually, we had that once, and it was a great feeling because you can't even see the upper deck, and downstairs it feels like the park's full; it's a great atmosphere."

And then I said, "Well, why are you setting prices to incentivize people to sit upstairs? What if we adjusted prices in such a way that we tried to push everyone downstairs?"

Two things are going to happen: They're going to make more money, because now people are not going to choose the downgrade option and take the $5 seat upstairs, but you're now also going to create a better vibe, and it's going to feel like a full park. That has to be the focus.

And did they take you up on it?

(Pause) We're working on it.

It's an industry of baby steps. You take small steps. You've got to realize it really is a very public-facing industry. There is a lot to be said for how [changing ticket prices] looks and how it impacts the public. There's probably a bigger incentive, just based on ownership structures and everything like that, to not mess up, as opposed to drive revenue and do the right thing. You see some teams that operate like a very well-run business that take risks and do cutting-edge things that really change the paradigm, and then you have some teams that are content to do the status quo.

And you probably have that in every industry; entertainment is just a little different.

Well, airlines seem to be very flexible; they pull inventory very quickly, they shift seating around, and they do lots of things. But then they're constantly going bankrupt too.

But that's why they have to do it; they are constantly going bankrupt so they need to be running it like a business. But here's the thing: If you run an airline, the reason you're doing it is to make money. If you run a sports team, owners are willing to lose money. Owners are much less concerned about the annual winning or losing of money. They are much more concerned about whether they get to stand on that court with the trophy at the end of the season than they are about what their bottom line looks like that year.

A lot of teams have fairly undersized front offices for the size of that business. There is a lot more devotion to the player-development side of things than the operational side. Not all teams, not even by a stretch, but there is clearly this divide where it's not whether you make or lose money as a whole in the year. It doesn't matter that much. In some ways, people—I don't want to say, "Blame it on the performance"—but there is an element of thought that, "Hey, if the team does well, we'll make money and sell a lot of tickets, and if they don't, we won't." There isn't this notion that [making profits at the gate] has to happen independently of that.

Let's chat about the future of the season ticket. Based on my experiences, if 70 percent of the time fans can get tickets for under face value, why on Earth would they splash out for forty-one tickets in advance?

Umm…that's a very very tough question.

Unfortunately, this has been partly the effect of the secondary market. You used to buy a season ticket for those events that you couldn't even get a ticket for, not just for those events that you couldn't get a ticket below face for. Before StubHub if you wanted to go to Yankees-Red Sox games, you couldn't go. It just wasn't possible.

If your team made a run to the NBA Finals, the only way you could get tickets was to be a season ticketholder.

You could have gone through a ticket agent. You'd pay over the odds though.

You used to pay completely exorbitant amounts, as those people provided a service. Now with how prevalent the secondary market has become, everything has come down in price on a resale market, and everything is affordable, and you're right; if you do the math, it doesn't make sense. So [from a team's standpoint, their] problem, to be fair, is that in the past they marketed the secondary market to their season ticketholders, saying, "Sure, you're not going to go to forty-one games, but you can sell these other tickets to StubHub or ticket exchange or whatever it is, and get your money back."

And that worked for a few years, and now what you're starting to see is that season ticketholders are looking at it as, "Wait a second, if I can just buy whatever I want on the secondary market, why do I need the season ticket? In fact, previously I was buying forty-one games to resell thirty and go to eleven. [Now] I can save and just go to eleven games." There are a lot fewer transactions, it's a lot easier, and so you're definitely seeing that shift.

Two things are going to have to happen. One is teams are going to have to start focusing—and a lot of teams are—on the non-monetary benefits of the season ticket. There are plenty of people who like their season tickets because they're sitting with the same set of people, day after day; there's a community aspect to it. A lot of [teams] do things like season-ticketholder events, which maybe people find valuable, maybe they don't. There's going to have to be some sort of a different [added] product because people don't go to every game.[111]

Here's something else you're going to see, and I'm confident of this: Prices are going to go up as a whole on the secondary market over the next few years, because there's not going to be as many season ticketholders, which is going to reduce the amount of inventory. I think the speculators in the market who got in here and thought, "This is an easy way to make a profit," [are waning]. That might have been, but now with the number of season ticketholders out there, that market is just flooded on StubHub and the other secondary-market exchanges.

---

111   In September 2012, the Boston Red Sox—enduring their worst season in years—announced they would gift their season ticketholders a chance to take batting practice at hallowed Fenway Park.

So as you reduced the number of season ticketholders, and therefore you reduced the volume on the secondary market, you'll now start seeing prices take off.

The higher the prices on the secondary market, the more your point [on season tickets being obsolete] goes away.

Let me ask you something. I know your thesis out of the gate on this is tickets are mispriced, which I obviously agree with strongly, but what brought you to that conclusion?

Experience, plain and simple. Over the years I've been able to rock up to the venue—not all the time, mind you—but very often if I play my cards right and follow a certain set of rules, I can wait it out and get a pretty good deal. Then once sites like StubHub and Craigslist started becoming more viable alternatives, I thought the genie was completely out of the bottle.

I did some fishing around where I'd go on Ticketmaster and find a seat, then see one on StubHub in the exact same row at a third of the price. My reaction was, "This is just an insult to my intelligence that they're trying to sell me these tickets and tack a fee onto them." So I said, "Screw this, I'm going to try to hit every NBA town I can and see what kind of deals I can get, and then share my experiences with the public."

I think there are a couple of things I would point out just based on that. In some ways, yes, there's that discrepancy on the price of the ticket being sold on the resale market versus what's going on with the price the team is selling it for. That said, any ticket you find on the street, or on StubHub or on Craigslist, was sold in the first place.

Indeed.

So that means the team didn't do badly on that ticket. So maybe there's an issue here related to [pricing] too big a discount to season ticketholders, and there's an incentive to buy that season ticket and be a broker.[112]

Have you used scalpers in the past?

Of course. And I don't want to say it's a good experience every time, but you know what you're going to get. And whether that's buying it online, something like a StubHub, or whether it's just walking to the event and getting something on the way to the gate, you know something's going to be there. If you're willing to take the risk that maybe you're going to be priced out and will have to leave, it's a great way to do it.

112   This point was made in an in-depth study by Bill King of the *Sports Business Journal*. King looked at the secondary pricing of fifteen Major League Baseball games on August 5, 2011. The teams with the largest gaps between season-ticket prices and single-game prices saw between 25 percent to 53 percent of their secondary-market seats sold at the sweet spot above the season-ticket price, but below the team's single-seat price for that game.

PART
TEN

In October 2012 I traveled to Los Angeles to sniff out some real estate opportunities, only to realize that the Lakers would be playing in Portland's home opener of the 2012-2013 season later that week. Naturally, I wound up hopping on a plane going north.

PORTLAND: OCT 31, 2012

Blazermania baby!

TRAIL BLAZERS 116
LAKERS 106
ATTENDANCE: 20,401 (including standing room)
CAPACITY: 19,980

Free Lakers Floor Seat for Lucky Lady—$1 (Portland)

Date: 2012-10-30, 12:00AM

Good Looking guy that just had a last minute break-up and now has an extra floor seat to the Laker game. Need a hot date! If you are single, hot and like the Lakers and want a great seat, please reply to this message with a picture (only emails with picture will be responded to)
- *Location: Portland*
- *It's NOT ok to contact this poster with services or other commercial interests*

Hello, Portland! And thank you, Craigslist, for the most entertaining classified ad since the *Village Voice* nixed its "Anything Goes" section. Well, that's one way to bag a date, or make an ex-girlfriend jealous as hell: Give away her floor seat to the lucky winner. Bonus points if you manage to get on the kiss-cam!

My first impression of Portland was of a wet city surrounded by forest, full of hemp-wearing hipsters who don't believe in razors—like an updated version of Seattle in the 1990s. But it's a hell of a sports city too, with Blazermania in full force on Halloween night. Checking into the Hotel Lucia on Broadway, I wasted little time firing up the laptop and scouting the ticket market online.

This time, however, I relied on SeatGeek, a recent discovery, as my barometer for what good deals were out there. For someone who's been searching high and low for ticket deals for years, seatgeek.com makes things almost too easy by aggregating nearly all the online secondary-ticket sellers, organizing their inventory and ranking the deals from "amazing" to "awful" on a corresponding seating chart. Where's this site been my entire life?

So I loaded up the game's entry page and kept refreshing every ten minutes or so. As it got closer to tipoff, deals were continually climbing up the score sheet until finally the holy grail of rankings, an "Amazing Deal," flashed up with a score of 94/100.

The niggling issue was that, though it was considered an amazing deal, it was stuck up in the 300-level seats, and seeing as how this would be my first opportunity to witness the new-look Lakers in person (featuring Dwight Howard and Steve Nash), I wanted a shot at getting up close.

With about one hundred minutes to go until game time, I was forced into a decision: Jump on a cheap 300-level center seat going for a fraction of face value ($9 versus the season-ticket price of $28), pay for a lower-level corner seat going for $145, or revert to the street game.

I hedged my bet before the deals got pulled offline, and I bought one of the "Amazing Deals" going on StubHub: $9 for the ticket plus a $4.95 "delivery fee" plus a $5 "service fee" to sit in the second-to-last row at the Rose Garden. Suspiciously, twenty-one other tickets in section 332 were dumped onto StubHub only hours before tipoff, while Craigslist offered an entire row's worth of seats in the same section, "cheap at $20 each."

Who carries an entire row of inventory, aside from the originator of the tickets? I'm not saying, I'm just saying…you know what I mean?

Portland is one of only six NBA teams to circumvent Ticketmaster as their official distributor. Instead they, along with Philly, rely on a company called Paciolan for their ticketing software. The Blazers have also employed their own tiered (but inflexible) ticketing scheme, which for this game lists the same tickets in section 332 for a whopping $79 plus a $5 "order charge fee."

Clearly the Trail Blazers are way behind the dynamic pricing curve, despite being owned by Paul Allen, a co-founder of Microsoft and a man the world owes a great deal of technological debt to. What kind of moron would pay $84 for a nosebleed seat two hours before game time when he can find the same seat for less than $20 through a liquid secondary market? Or a better question is what kind of moron is trying to sell that ticket for $84?

I'll go out on a limb here and say it's the same moron I bought my ticket from on StubHub: the Trail Blazers themselves. It's like the Blazers are caught in a dysfunctional marriage with their ticketing partner that they can't get out of. So instead, they're having a raving affair with StubHub, all the while pretending like they're selling out the Rose Garden. And like all spouses having affairs, they're leaving trails everywhere and lying through their teeth.

The Blazers claim to have sold out an ongoing streak of 193 home games in a row. Having been on the Blazers' website watching how many seats were available on game day, and then seeing those same seats dumped online two hours before tipoff, and finally sitting in that section with a number of empty seats around me that night, I'd bet my apartment that they're fudging the numbers (proving this definitively without a whistleblower is perhaps impossible, though).[113]

And so, armed with my amazing deal, I had exactly seventy-five minutes to scarf down some bar food and make it to the Rose Garden in time for intros. My concierge steered me toward Henry's Tavern, which was an excellent recommendation. They had over one hundred beers on tap, and I settled on a light local brew fantastically named Amnesia Dusty Trail Pale Ale, which I used to wash down some tasty California rolls and calamari.

From there I had a very wet walk rushing to a Max Light Rail, which took me straight to the Blazer's arena for only $2.50, quite a bonus when you're used to forking out for parking or cabs. In fact, the Rose Quarter (which houses two arenas, a theater, and a convention center) is the one stop in town that every single Max line has to cross. Thousands of freaks streamed out of the metro in costume that night, including my two favorites: a guy with a red beard who was a dead ringer for Bill Walton, and his friend dressed as Kurt Rambis, tape between the glasses and all.

Portland is one of those towns with a thriving scalper trade; there were pockets of them loitering beside the Rose Garden armed with

113   The streak would officially come to an end three home games later against the Atlanta Hawks. The sanctity of the streak was dubious to begin with, as the Blazers exclude standing-room-only tickets in their capacity, yet include them in attendance figures.

seating charts. They also carried a ton of printout tickets, which didn't seem to bother any of their clientele. A young woman I saw paid $80 for two printout 300-level seats, doubling my price per ticket on StubHub.

I asked around, but there were no singles in the lower-bowl available and very few in the second level. A pair of lower-bowl seats toward the baseline were going for $150 each, and another on the corner for over $100. Nothing was tempting enough for me to ditch my purchase (more so when I realized it had no trade-in value) so I headed for the entrance.

And I was very pleasantly surprised. The Rose Garden is not one of those mammoth arenas where the upper-level seats are in the clouds. Rather, there's only a modest break between the lower and upper levels for the single level of box seats and a squeezed 200 club section. With my mild prescription lenses on, I could see the action perfectly well enough to zone in.

Just as intros were being called out, I took advantage of some empty seats, moving a few rows down and closer to center court. Though Blazers management may lie about attendance figures, Blazers fans rock the house. They were loud and passionate, and the Blazers themselves responded by entering the court through various sections in the lower bowl, high-fiving and hugging fans along the way. I'd never seen that before, and it's a terrific idea, one bestowing a down-to-earth town like Portland. I can't see that happening in New York somehow.

Once the action started, I formed two quick observations: The Lakers were nowhere close to a cohesive unit, and the Blazers had a future star on their hands at point guard. Rookie Damian Lillard zipped all over the floor, wearing number zero and looking a lot like Derrick Rose. In his first official outing as a pro he finished with twenty-three points and eleven assists to go along with a bundle of turnovers (six), that rookies are prone to. The fact that the Blazers found their future franchise point guard from little-known Weber State University suggests they may have finally shaken off the draft curse that's plagued them for so many years.[114]

Portland ended up winning by ten, though the Lakers kept it exciting until the last three minutes. In fact, it was a night of ample entertainment. Aside from seeing half the fans dressed in wacky Halloween costumes, I was treated to seeing a future All-Star in Lillard, a gob-smacking dunk from Portland forward Nicolas Batum, and the Lakers' All-Star quartet of Kobe, Pau, Dwight Howard, and Steve Nash (who left the game in the second half with an ankle sprain).

All this for $18.95. That 94/100 value rating on SeatGeek was perfectly accurate. For the section I was in at the Rose Garden, on opening night for one of the league's most popular home teams, against a team in the top echelon of star power in the league, purchasing the ticket was a no-brainer. And assessing whether I was getting a good deal or not was never made easier.

So how exactly does SeatGeek know this stuff? Moreover, how does its business model work? The questions were burning in my mind. And so, as you would expect, I flew to New York and paid a visit to their nifty headquarters on East Eleventh Street.

SeatGeek is the brainchild of business partners Jack Groetzinger and Russ D'Souza, who started the business model a couple of years out of Dartmouth College while working the graveyard shifts at private equity firms in Boston.

Leave it to the twentysomethings to pave the way for innovation.

"It's a burdensome process to comparison shop across websites, be it StubHub or Craigslist or eBay," Will Flaherty, SeatGeek's director of communications explains while showing me around their cozy loft space. "You don't really know where prices are going, you don't have

114   Most famously, Portland bypassed drafting Michael Jordan in 1984 for the rights to Sam Bowie, a seven-foot injury-prone center. Twenty-three years later they did the same thing with Kevin Durant (today's most fluid scorer) and drafted Greg Oden, a seven-foot injury-prone center, ahead of him. Oden is already out of the league.

much intelligence as a consumer, and you don't know when and where to buy from."

Flaherty elaborates on SeatGeek's secret sauce, its Deal Score rating. "The algorithm takes into account a number of factors: The historical prices for a given stadium and team, the number of tickets [in the venue], and where the seats are in the section. The score is [also] anchored across all events of that given type in the building."

Practically speaking, this means the deal I got in Portland with a score of ninety-four was one of the best deals in the past few seasons for all Trail Blazers home games. That said, I wanted to know how long an amazing deal with a score of ninety-four would ordinarily last on the market.

"Not very long, a matter of minutes sometimes," he explained. "And you'll have random stuff happen; these ticket brokers are manually inputting prices, so sometimes a fat finger error will get in there." I never thought about it, but it made sense. Sometimes human error does lead to amazing deals.

On the SeatGeek side of the fence, they're up to their necks in data that the twenty-person team closely (and silently) monitors in the warehouse. "The process of ingesting information on all the upcoming events every day is incredibly complex. We have 150,000 events on SeatGeek at any given time, everything from NBA games to rodeo competitions to off-off-off-Broadway shows," Flaherty explains.

And, armed with three years of SeatGeek back data, I was dying to know one thing in particular: When is the best time to buy a ticket off the online secondary market?

"Looking at it now, it's pretty clear that getting closer to the event, in nearly every circumstance the ticket prices almost always fall. Whether it's a football game, baseball game, Broadway show, whatever. If you wait till twenty-four to forty-eight hours [before game time], that is the sweet spot when you're going to find the best deals."

It's an interesting bit of advice, considering I've been waiting until game day at nearly every city to test the online market. Perhaps I'd been biding my time for a bit too long and allowing the inventory to shrink. At the same time, Flaherty's advice is based on people looking for a pair to "just get through the door." He advises purchasing seats more than three days in advance if you're aiming to get, say, six seats together in the lower bowl.

Flaherty also concedes that SeatGeek entirely ignores the classified ad market, which offers a plethora of cheaper deals that cannot be verified for authenticity. The decision was made because Craigslist discourages relisting its merchandise, but chiefly because it doesn't offer fraud protection—something all SeatGeek affiliates must provide.

But—fraud protection be damned—in the very next breath Flaherty confided he'd been to a concert at the Brooklyn Bowl the night before by finding a seller through Craigslist.

SeatGeek's an awesome tool, but my advice is to keep all options open at all times. Besides, those Craigslist classifieds can be pretty amusing.

PAID: $18.95

SINGLE-GAME TICKET FACE VALUE: $79
DISCOUNT TO SINGLE-GAME TICKET: 76%

SEASON-TICKET FACE VALUE: $28
DISCOUNT TO SEASON TICKET: 32%

EPILOGUE

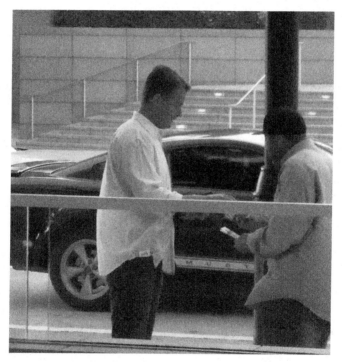

Scalper? Did you call me a scalper? Listen gentlemen, I perform a service here, and the service costs money. Now do you want the tickets or don't you?
—Mike Damone, *Fast Times at Ridgemont High*

Been around the world and I, I, I, we've been playa hated...I don't know when, and I don't know why, why they want us faded...I don't know why they hate us. Is it our ladies? Or the drop Mercedes?
—P. Diddy, featuring the Notorious B. I. G and Mase

Ok, so I haven't exactly been around the world on this excursion, and I've never driven a drop Merc. But I did rent a ragtop Mustang from Long Beach Airport. And I've definitely been all around the United States. And I dropped into Toronto for a night. And amazingly, I even witnessed the first regular-season NBA game in my hometown of London.

The flights were too frequent to count. The car rides were too long, and the train rides were too bumpy. But all that arduous travel, even the airport stopovers with the dodgy Filipino food (in Utah no less[115]), was in an effort to show my fellow sports fans that there's a way around the rip-offs put in front of us by sports teams. Tickets very often can be had for cheaper than the exorbitant face values—dynamically priced or not—if we play our cards right.

So the next time you want to watch your home team play the Knicks or the Heat or the Lakers (or especially the Raptors), don't be discouraged; the numbers do not lie.

On this journey that spanned 2011 and 2012, I purchased tickets on the open market for twenty-five games. In sixteen of those games I walked into the arena paying less than what the season ticketholder paid, and in nearly every instance I paid less than the box office's single-game price.[116]

Non-season ticketholders looking to purchase single-game tickets to the Trailblazers, Clippers, or Jazz through the official team channels

---

115   At the UFood Grill. Avoid the chicken tinga in adobo sauce with tinga salsa.

116   Nearly all of my tickets were originally purchased by a season ticketholder at the start of the chain. In my calculations I counted the face value shown on the ticket; I backed up the data by checking the season-ticket pricing charts on the team's website. Same goes for tickets purchased on StubHub.

would pay up to triple the face values that I've listed, never mind what I actually spent. In total, I paid $1,629.30 for access to twenty-six games. The results ranged from floor seats in Washington and Brooklyn up to nosebleeds in Utah and Sacramento, not to mention duds like the Indianapolis ticket experiment.[117]

Let me be clear about something: I paid just about what those tickets were worth in every instance, even the one time I used Ticketmaster to see a Lakers playoff game. But what the initial purchasers of those tickets actually paid for them —collectively $2,865.01—is something else entirely.

See the difference? It's $1,235.71 to be exact.

Let's take the data crunching just a tad further. If I exclude the most extreme points of data in my range—the $900 courtside seat in Washington and the free ticket from the bartender in Milwaukee, along with the mix-up in Chicago and the wasted Indiana playoff ticket—and average my discount or premium to each game, it worked out to a savings of 25 percent every time I passed a turnstile.

And that sounds pretty accurate. For all the talk of dynamic-pricing models being used in professional sports today, there's still a cushion where informed fans can talk their way down to paying about 75 percent of the face value that the season ticketholder pays, on average.

When bargaining on the street, I tend to grab a ticket out of a scalper's hand (not too forcefully, mind you), examine the face value, and immediately blurt out half the figure on the ticket. They will wince and curse and sometimes let out a high-pitched, sarcastic laugh, but ordinarily that scalper will meet you somewhere between face value and 50 percent. If the ticket costs $100, look to pay $70 to $75, and be happy if you get there.

---

117   This worked out perfectly for me, as I ended up selling my pair of Arsenal seats to five separate matches over those two seasons, netting me the equivalent of $1,666, or $37 more than I paid for twenty-six NBA games. I now wish I had been a little less frugal in some of those cities…especially Dallas.

The median points of my range (i.e., the prices where exactly half the numbers are above and half below) came out to a face value of $68 and a purchase price of $50. So on an average night, in a generic NBA town (and there are a few out there), with $50 in your pocket, you can and should get a good view to watch an NBA game.

My sample size on this cross-continental excursion is admittedly small, but I have all the confidence in the world that you can do just as well as me, if not better. I know this because friends of mine have done exactly that. They've picked up on my style and gone even farther.

In August 2012, my friend Cesc came out to London to follow the Spanish basketball team in its quest for the gold medal. For the championship game featuring the United States versus Spain—without a doubt, the hottest ticket at the London 2012 Olympics—he managed to bag two seats for under face value.

Despite all the talk about how every event to the Olympics was sold out, there was still a way around the mad scramble on the dysfunctional London 2012 official ticket website.[118] Amusingly, more and more of those unused corporate seats found their way to Craigslist. By the end of the fortnight Craigslist was a full-on thriving market, listing tickets to all the events, from judo to the closing ceremony.

And what do you do on an open market with efficient pricing? You can try to wait it out until the demand drops to where your target price meets the equilibrium point.

---

118   The ticketing sham during London 2012 warrants an investigation. Nearly every event had swaths of empty rows, while the paying general public was desperate for access, and the reasons were never explained. Meanwhile, the prices of the actual tickets sold were jacked up to exorbitant fees (an early-round day of athletics at the Olympic Stadium with no big names competing—aside from murderous blade-runner Oscar Pistorius--went for £150). I met a guy at a pub who flew in from LA with his wife and couldn't find a single ticket. Instead he drowned himself in a whiskey glass with his Jordan Team USA jersey on, moaning, "This sucks!"

Hopefully, Brazil will learn from this and curb the sponsorship ticket allocation to Rio 2016, making tickets more plentiful and affordable to the masses.

In Cesc's case he bagged two prime seats with a face value of £425 ($675) each for £350 ($555) each. He bumped into Tyrese and Ludacris on the way in and took cell phone pics with Vin Diesel.

How? The guy he bought the tickets from very likely got them as freebies (he was a nervous wreck throughout the whole transaction). For that guy, any price he got was pure upside. And for Cesc, the price he paid saved him hundreds had he gone through the official channels...like I did. Unfortunately for me, I ignored my own advice, went through the official ticket seller a month in advance, panicked (because I saw it as my only window), and bought a ticket in a VIP suite for £1,200 ($1,900).[119]

I met guys across the country, like RJ in LA and Joe in Oklahoma City, who have defaulted to the street trade as their method of choice for procuring tickets. It's low on commitment and high on exhilaration, and what man can resist that combination? It's like driving to a date with Lindsay Lohan in a rental Corvette from Hertz. In fact, if you're at the Staples Center you're likely to see both Lilo and a yellow Hertz Corvette on any given night.

One thing is certain, though, and that is the future of ticketing will be about teams trying to get more of our money more efficiently. Much of that has to do with cutting out the middlemen and repricing upward as often as possible without completely alienating fans.

The more teams pay attention to the action being had by the likes of eBay and StubHub, the more they're turning to the likes of Barry Kahn's Qcue to arm themselves with the ability to shift values when they see demand rising. When prices balloon, everyone gets desperate for a piece of that action. That includes Ticketmaster, whose hand has been forced by StubHub to integrate a secondary-ticket platform alongside its primary market.

Without a doubt, the ticket market will become increasingly digitized. Tickets on cell phones will come into play sooner or later ("We

---

119   I later averaged this cost down by buying a ticket in the uppers for £300 and sneaking my girlfriend into the box.

are absolutely headed in that direction," says Nathan Hubbard of Ticketmaster), making the easy transfer of paper tickets between fans that much rarer.

Where does that leave the currently thriving online secondary market? With true proliferation only as recent as 2005, it is a relatively new phenomenon. But more players are entering the market, and sophistication with smartphone apps is making the service omnipresent (I've personally found the StubHub app on my iPhone very useful). Meanwhile, secondary-market aggregators like SeatGeek, are empowering fans with more useful data than ever before.

Even social networking helps. There's no easier way to find or sell a spare ticket now than putting up a post on your Facebook status. Sometimes you need look no further than your own network and a great deal will emerge.

Lastly, there's always the scalper, whose time dates back to when Romans were selling premium seats at the Coliseum to watch lions eat prisoners. In the United States, scalpers have been helping fans get into games since the Yankees' World Series runs after World War I. Since then, they've been as etched into the American way of life as McDonald's, Starbucks, and SUVs.

And they're not fading away anytime soon.

Somehow, someway, twenty years from now in a frosty Midwestern town, on a dimly lit side street an hour before tipoff, the haggard scalper will still be there. Wrapped under a wool hat, his eyes come alive when a fan in a replica jersey approaches.

Cold mist seeping from his mouth, the scalper utters the magic words, "Are you selling?"

"No, but I'm looking," the fan fires back.

"How many you need?"

Another pure marketplace is born. It's a beautiful thing.

OVERTIME

REFLECTIONS: THE BEST, THE WORST, AND THE WEIRD

That's pretty hardcore

Best Arena Ambiance: This award has to go to **Chicago's United Center**. The Madhouse on Madison boasts the most electric atmosphere in the NBA, with its crowded vertical layers of seating resembling a Chinese pagoda. The six championship banners along with His Airness's retired number hanging from the rafters add mystique and—for opposing teams—at least some level of intimidation.

An honorable mention goes out to the **Staples Center,** when it hosts Lakers games, and **Madison Square Garden**, which is consistently packed and loud, no matter how poorly the Knicks are faring. **The Barclays Center** in Brooklyn is sleek, loud, and hip. Now all it needs is a team that can contend for a title.

Worst Arena Ambiance: Though it boasts the coolest-looking arena in the NBA, with its black chairs and kop-style seating on one side of the court (i.e., a smooth ride all the way up the aisles with no luxury boxes in between), **Phillips Arena in Atlanta** is nearly always empty. The few fans who do show up seem happier at the arena's sports bar than inside watching their team.

Honorable mention to **Washington's Verizon Center;** though D.C. is the only city other than Chicago to land Michael Jordan, the franchise has nothing to cheer about for the ten seasons since his retirement. Of course, this lack of fan enthusiasm also allowed me to bag the best deal of my entire trip.

Best Arena Facility: Charlotte's Time Warner Center is a feast for the eyes, with luxury seating, terrific bars and restaurants in the concourses, and the best score box in the league. Sadly, the team is so pathetic that it will be years before the arena realizes its potential as an NBA landmark. In the interim, hosting the 2012 Democratic National Convention will have to make do as its proudest moment.

An honorable mention goes out again to the **Staples Center**, which is a gorgeous piece of arena architecture that singlehandedly revived downtown Los Angeles. Over a frantic four-day stretch in May, 2012, the busy facility played host to six playoff games featuring the Lakers, Clippers, and hockey's LA Kings. It also showcases the Grammy Awards every year.

Worst Arena Facility: This award goes hands down to **Sacramento's Sleep Train Arena (formerly Power Balance Pavilion)**. It's old, the name sucks, and because everything rotates around only one concourse, it's horribly cramped. Its days are firmly numbered.

Utah's Energy Solutions Arena, with its endless flight of stairs to the upper bowl, is a distant second.

Best Arena Food: The samplings at **Philadelphia's Wells Fargo Center** were simply scrumptious. An endless variety of subs and sausages were on offer, while that braised short rib sandwich still lingers in my mouth. Mmmm.

Best Bar in an Arena: This is a tough one. Every arena comes armed with multiple bars that take away from the action when the game is slow, or when you're just looking to get sauced. Some are terrific, and some are hilariously lousy (like the upper-deck bar/disco in Sacramento). I avoided these watering holes, except to dash in and out for a drink, but the sports bars in **Atlanta's Phillips Arena, including the Gentleman Jack Bar,** and the open-plan upper-deck bar in **San Antonio's AT&T Center** (where you are able to see the court) stood out as top quality. **The Staples Center**, unsurprisingly, boasts a full-on club with bottle service. **The Hyde Lounge** lets you watch the game, order $13 cocktails, and mix with the trashy and trendy for a $25 cover (no jerseys and sneakers). I can't say I had the urge to check it out, though.

Best Sports Bar near an Arena: As mentioned, I'm a big fan of **Stout NYC in New York,** just a block away from Madison Square Garden. It's not the biggest, and it doesn't have the greatest food, but the place is just the right size and shape and has just enough flat screens to make it work. It's the place to be in New York on game days, and they show European soccer games to boot.

On equal footing, though much bigger and way trendier, is **Real Sports Bar & Grill** by Toronto's Air Canada Center. Terrific food, an amazing jumbo HD screen, and babes galore. Can't beat that.

Most Rabid Fans: Boston Celtics fans are probably the most enthusiastic in the league. They turn up in all kinds of getups ready to rock the Garden, and they stay positive throughout games. While calling a

January 2013 game against the Knicks, Marv Albert alleged the Celtics pump in crowd noise over the loudspeakers. The team vehemently denied it, and I tend to believe them. Their diehards don't need artificial propping—in contrast to Knicks fans, the second most rabid group, who could have used a cheer machine to drown out the boos during the recent bleak years. Honorable mention to **Lakers fans** and **Portland Trail Blazer fans,** who are proud and loud and own the record for consecutive NBA sellouts at 814 over the course of eighteen seasons.

Hottest Cheerleaders: I'll be honest; most cheerleading squads look alike. The women are all medium sized to petite and boast dancers' bodies with long, flowing hair of various colors (there's an auburn one in every city) and, likely, extensions. In this day and age, there's also a good racial mix in every group.

But the **Honeybees,** the dancers of the New Orleans Hornets, do throw down the most salacious routine out there. For a second I felt like I was back at the Maiden Voyage on Bourbon Street, with girls stripping down to (what appeared to be) G-strings and skimpy tops. I was slightly taken aback, since the game started out with a sermon from a preacher. Gotta love the South!

Most Thriving Scalper Trade: Orlando, Philadelphia, and Toronto.

Most Barren Scalper Trade: Sacramento, San Antonio, Chicago, and Golden State.

Most Unexpectedly Fun Downtown: Some cities like New Orleans and Miami are obvious party destinations, but **San Antonio** and **Orlando** sneaked up on me. Both boast rows of bars and restaurants, many with great cover bands throwing down some live music.

Players Most Worth the Price of Admission: A chance to see **LeBron James** live is a must, and behind him are burgeoning stars

Blake Griffin, **Ricky Rubio**, **Derrick Rose**, and **Rajon Rondo**. **Kobe Bryant** can still turn it on full throttle at times, but it's not a given that he'll put on a show at this stage of his career (recovering from an Achilles tear won't help).

One to watch is Timberwolves rookie **Alexey Shved**, a six-foot, six-inch Russian guard who lit up the Olympic Games. He's quick and very creative, making him a dream pair-up with Rubio. Neither is adept at playing defense, though. **Damian Lillard** of Portland zips around the court and has the ability to start and finish an alley-oop. Although he can be sloppy with the ball, **Jeremy Lin** is always on the verge of his next breakout game, and his motor only knows one speed: full throttle.

Most Selfish Players: Growing up playing JV and varsity basketball, I had teamwork and passing instilled in me at a young age. The high school coaches of **Carmelo Anthony**, **J. R. Smith**,[120] and **Nate Robinson** were probably more of the "get them the ball and get out of the way" variety. Robinson, who is only five-foot, nine-inches, is probably the most egregious of the bunch. Watching him call out his own number time and again coming up the floor is enough to make fans go nuts, not to mention his coaches over the years. In 2012 he signed with the Bulls to back up Derrick Rose. Stay healthy, Derrick, for the sake of everyone who appreciates team basketball.

Biggest Surprise Tourist Attraction: Elvis's grave, Memphis. I'd always heard of Graceland. I know a thing or two about Elvis Presley. I absolutely had to swing by on the way out of town, but what was there alongside the pool stopped me dead in my tracks. Four graves

---

120   Smith – who once took 18 three-pointers and scored 60 in a Chinese League game -- had his best season in 2012-2013, winning the Sixth Man Award. Knicks coach Mike Woodson's tactic of playing Smith off the bench limited his overlap with Carmelo to just half of every game. Carmelo also had his best season, winning the NBA scoring title. Mike Woodson is a genius. He could possibly be the solution to the Palestinian – Israeli crisis.

lying side by side, the final resting places for Elvis, his parents, and grandmother. I had no idea he was buried right there in his backyard, so it was an unexpected honor to be standing so close to the King.

Everything about Graceland is smaller than you'd think it is. The house and the pool were nice, but nothing you'd be raving about if you were in the fourth grade and just found out your best friend lived there. I wasn't able to go inside the mansion, as it was closed on Tuesdays, but just walking around the estate (for free) was a real treat.

This easily could have been a book about beer and airports as well as basketball, so with that...

Best Airport: A few interesting things about **Oklahoma City's Will Rogers World Airport.** First, it's the only airport anywhere to have "world" in its name though it hosts no international flights. Even stranger, it's named after someone who died in a plane crash, local comedian and cowboy Will Rogers.

As mentioned in the OKC section, I loved its design, best described by its Wikipedia entry: "The architecture of the building uses native stone along with loft-ceilings, plate glass, and brushed metal. Compared to the old concourses, the improvements provided a more open feel to the terminal waiting areas, similar to larger-hub airports without being quite so large in scale."

Worst Airport: Hartsfield-Jackson Atlanta International Airport is as huge and cumbersome as its ridiculous name. It's also the busiest airport in the world, in terms of flights (nearly 1 million a year) and passengers (240,000 per day). Yet it squeezes all this into only two terminals and six concourses.

If you have a connection here, good luck. I missed my flight to New Orleans because it was impossible to tell which gate I was supposed to be at (three flights were leaving to NO at nearly the same time, all full and with crowds on standby). I was happy to see the back of that place.

Best Beer: Fat Tire Amber Ale and **Dale's Pale Ale** (6.5 percent and canned!) from Colorado, **Gluek Red** (5.8 percent) from Minnesota, **Sierra Nevada Pale Ale** from Chico, California, **Abita Amber** from New Orleans, and finally Hop Trip and Chasin' Freshies IPA, two fine winter brews from the **Deschutes Brewery & Public House** in Portland.

Best Mascot: I watched a lot of mascots on this trip. They dance, they get the crowd up, they shoot t-shirts into the stands, and they show crazy acrobatic skills dunking off trampolines. But by far the coolest thing I saw was **Clutch of the Houston Rockets** slamming a giant cake in the face of a 76ers fan. It was easily the most entertaining thing about that game and had me in stitches. Clutch performs this shtick at every game, so it's likely that opposing fans come dressed knowing this will be their fate

And finally…The most commonly heard phrase after describing my trip:
"You're doing a tour of basketball cities? I've heard of a guy/ two guys who did that for baseball. Never basketball, though. Have you heard about those baseball guys?"
Yes, yes, I heard.

ACKNOWLEDGMENTS

An undertaking of this magnitude could not have been possible without the support of a number of close friends and people whom I admire.

From the tipoff two years ago, Stacey McNutt was as supportive as ever, offering her thoughts as an experienced book scout and editor. Stacey also allowed me to ask, "What would Jan think?" offering insight into her late, great husband Jan Hartman's mind.

I also owe a debt of gratitude to Jan himself, for fostering me as a writer back in 2000. To come clean, I only joined his class because I had a crush on a girl who was "in love with his mind," and not only was I praying to run into her at the class, but I hoped he'd brush some of that mind of his that she was so in love with onto me. Jan, I hope I did you proud, and I miss you.

Rebecca Abou-Chedid offered me her support as an NBA fan, vented her frustration and LeBron love/hate feelings as a Cavs fan, and loaned her editing skills and apartment as a true friend. Most importantly, the pregame ritual of calling her for good luck worked wonders. And the few times I forgot to, namely in Chicago and Dallas, proved that it's unwise to mess with a good thing. Becks, thanks for being a good-luck charm.

Wahab Al-Qatami, my varsity basketball team roommate and great friend, has also been a big supporter of my project; he and his wonderful mom generously put me up in their house on the Denver leg. Thanks for the airport rides and that legendary drive back from the Pepsi Can. Thanks also for doing the driving on that rollicking road trip through Texas, and for bearing with me in Dallas when I could swear a better deal was just a few minutes away (same to you, Samer Keilani).

Thanks to my cousin, Big Mo Al-Mazidi, an awesome rapper and fellow Arsenal Gooner, for putting me up in his place in Chapel Hill, and driving all the way to Charlotte. May we have more adventures to come, my man.

Thanks to Shawna and Htut Zaw for allowing me to use the loft in San Francisco as my home base for a week. You guys are special, and I promise to hustle up the best deal I can for a Giants ballgame next time.

Thanks to Natasha Alibhai for your awesome spirit and know-how, and for very kindly showing me around Toronto.

Thanks to Sami Kamhawi for being the best host in Chicago, and showing me what's what at the United Center.

Big up to my homeboy from Stuyvesant Town and buddy since kindergarten, Sully, for your awesome insight and generosity. Go Nets.

Thanks to Ganesh for all your help and kindness in New York. I had a blast and am looking forward to more good times down the road.

Thank you, Johara Fahad, for graciously lending your superb photo-editing skills, and to Sian Tichar and Damon Mills for your time and thoughtful suggestions.

A big warm thanks goes to Salwa Karam for always having a comfortable sofa bed and some home-cooked food in New York when I needed them the most.

And finally, thanks to all of my super friends who motivated me with encouragement, as well as all the fantastic characters I met along the way who shared their experiences that made this crazy journey worthwhile.

Joe, it's time to leave the dance floor.

See you all on the next adventure.

REFERENCES

Prologue

Amount Americans spent on attending sporting events according to a 2009 figure cited by the Huffington Post.

Part 1

Chris Granger quote from Darren Rovell, "New NBA Site Sells Fans' Tickets Too," (ESPN.com), August 20, 2012.

NBA revenue figures from "Stern Estimates NBA Revenue up 20 Percent to $5b," (AP), November 13, 2012.

NBA season-ticket renewal figures from John Lombardo, "NBA Season-ticket Sales Heat up Box Office," (Sports Business Journal), October 22, 2012.

Detroit's median household income figure is according to the US Census Bureau.

Pistons ticket-pricing data from the *Team Marketing Report.*

Bill Schlough quote from Joel Schectman, "San Francisco Giants CIO Says Dynamic Ticket Pricing Helped Pack the Stadium," (WSJ.com), April 6, 2012.

Mark Cuban quote from Don Walker, "Box-Office Smash, How Dynamic Pricing Will Change the Game," (Consumerdigest.com), July 2009.

The 2012 *Team Marketing Report* cites a tweet from a StubHub employee quoting that figure.

Chris Tsakalakis analysis from, "Why Reselling Tickets Is Good," (The Huffington Post), July 12, 2010.

Part 3

Ari Emmanuel ticket figures from Andy Fixmer, "Not Even $20,000 Makes Norman Pattiz Part With Lakers, Celtics," (Bloomberg), June 10, 2008.

Knicks season ticketholder quote from Marc Berman, "Knicks Ticket Hike Prices out Some Fans," (*New York Post*), March 16, 2011.

Part 4

Statistic on players going broke from a 2009 *Sports Illustrated* study.

Walker's mom's insight from Shira Springer, "For Walker, Financial Fouls Mount," (*Boston Globe*), October 25, 2009.

Shaquille O'Neal's monthly spending from documents related to his divorce in 2008, as reported by the *Palm Beach Post*.

Part 7

White scalper insight from E. James Beale, "The Way of the Scalper," (archives.citypaper.net), September 30, 2008.

Mona Halem insight from Denise Balkissoon, "Mona Halem Runs the Party Line to the NBA," (thestar.com), March 13, 2010.

DeMar DeRozan story on his drinking age from Hanna Karp, "Why Pro Athletes Love Toronto," (WSJ.com), March 19, 2010.

Epilogue

Lyrics to "Been Around the World" by Puff Daddy featuring The Notorious B. I. G and Mase written by Lisa Stansfield, Ian Devaney,

Andy Morris, Sean Combs, Mason Betha, Romn Lawrence, Deric An-gelettie, and Christopher Wallace. That's quite a mouthful.

Nathan Hubbard quote from The B.S. Report podcast (ESPN.com), October 20, 2011.

ABOUT THE AUTHOR

When Motez Bishara is not racing to attend another music gig or sporting event, he spends his time in London managing an institutional stock portfolio and freelancing as a journalist. On the side, he tries to revive the Notting Hill hippie movement through Ashtanga yoga and an acoustic guitar. This is his first book.

CPSIA information can be obtained
at www.ICGtesting.com
Printed in the USA
LVOW04s1435220216

476187LV00019B/413/P